Creativity and *The Paris Review* Interviews

Creativity and *The Paris Review* Interviews

A Discourse Analysis of Famous Writers' Composing Practices

Ronda Leathers Dively

ANTHEM PRESS

Anthem Press
An imprint of Wimbledon Publishing Company
www.anthempress.com

This edition first published in UK and USA 2024
by ANTHEM PRESS
75–76 Blackfriars Road, London SE1 8HA, UK
or PO Box 9779, London SW19 7ZG, UK
and
244 Madison Ave #116, New York, NY 10016, USA

First published in the UK and USA by Anthem Press in 2022

Copyright © Ronda Leathers Dively 2024
Copyright © by *The Paris Review*, used by permission of The Wylie Agency LLC.

The author asserts the moral right to be identified as the author of this work.

All rights reserved. Without limiting the rights under copyright reserved above,
no part of this publication may be reproduced, stored or introduced into
a retrieval system, or transmitted, in any form or by any means
(electronic, mechanical, photocopying, recording or otherwise),
without the prior written permission of both the copyright
owner and the above publisher of this book.

British Library Cataloguing-in-Publication Data
A catalogue record for this book is available from the British Library.

Library of Congress Control Number: 2024934309

ISBN-13: 978-1-83999-262-9 (Pbk)
ISBN-10: 1-83999-262-X (Pbk)

Cover credit: Creative pencil design illustration concept for creative process - Hand Drawn Sketch Vector illustration, By Redshinestudio / Shutterstock.com

This title is also available as an e-book.

CONTENTS

List of Illustrations   vii

Preface   ix

Acknowledgments   xi

1. Impetus, Contexts and Methods   1
2. Composition through the Lens of Creativity Theory   19
3. First Insight, or the Glimmer of Possibility   35
4. Preparation, or Research Broadly Conceived   51
5. Incubation, or Breaks from Conscious Attention   73
6. Insight, or the Eureka Experience   89
7. Verification, or Evaluation   103
8. Emergent Patterns   123
9. Implications for Writing Instruction   149

Appendix A: Coding Table   169

Appendix B: List of Cited Paris Review *Interviewees*   175

Appendix C: Diagram of Analytical Categories, Subcategories and Themes   177

References   181

Index   189

ILLUSTRATIONS

1. The Creative Process Model and Composing Process Model Juxtaposed   31
2. Coding table   169
3. List of cited *Paris Review* interviewees   175
4. Diagram of analytical categories, subcategories and themes   177

PREFACE

I started (and finished) my undergraduate career as an English major. In those days, at my university, English major meant literature major, and I was pleased with that focus. In fact, I loved that program so much that I stayed on to earn a master's degree. But at some point during those two years of graduate study, a shift occurred in the way I approached literature. Gradually, I could feel my attention turning from questions about the "whats" of the product to focusing increasingly on the "hows" of the processes that generated the poetry and prose I was reading.

I believe this shift had to do, in part, with the fact that I was also preparing to be a teacher. Having pursued teacher certification at the undergraduate level, I had already completed 16 weeks of student teaching at an area high school, and, as a master's student, I was tutoring several hours weekly in my university's writing center. The challenge of mentoring students who struggled with writing, trying to offer them strategies for composing that could make a difference in the quality of their work as well as in their attitude toward it, altered my focus. I became consumed with trying to understand why, on one end of the spectrum, some individuals suffered under the strain of a given writing task while, on the opposite end, others took it in stride and achieved success relatively easily.

Observing this shift in my attention, one of my professors suggested that I pursue doctoral work in rhetoric and composition, a more eclectic, interdisciplinary field that would welcome such inquiry and allow a broad latitude in approaches to addressing the questions that now motivated me. I took his advice, and, to fast-forward a few decades, I have spent the better part of my career observing, reading and writing about composing processes. Though at different stages of inquiry I've applied different lenses, the most compelling to me is creativity theory, a subfield of psychology that explores the cognitive and affective phenomena involved in problem-solving.[1]

---

1. Viewing expository writing as problem-solving is an established approach in the discipline of rhetoric and composition. Moreover, the discipline has sustained a healthy

Within this subfield exists a corpus of scholarship that illuminates questions at the heart of my professional agenda[2] and that will captivate readers who are concerned with invention in any discipline—that is, research examining retrospective accounts of famous creators' visions and realizations of their greatest accomplishments. I have published other books and articles that integrate retrospective discourse to illustrate certain claims about writing, and, while I was working on those projects, I began discerning patterns across authors' representations of their writing practices. My subsequent, more comprehensive reading of writerly retrospection confirmed the existence of these patterns, convincing me to pursue a more systematic study of them, the study detailed in the nine chapters constituting this book.

In these nine chapters, readers will encounter arguments for viewing all writing as creative and for studying and reflecting on writing processes (albeit with qualifications) when learning to write and/or teaching writing. Readers also will be introduced to a preeminent repository of author commentary on writing processes, *The Paris Review* interview series, and to the methodology informing my systematic investigation of patterns in composing practices as represented in a large sample of retrospective accounts from that venue. Colorful and enlightening excerpts from these accounts will provide concrete illustration of these patterns for those inclined to apply them to their own writing or to help those whom they may be teaching. Ultimately, that is the goal of this project: to identify tendencies or themes in reports on process from some of the most famous writers in modern history with the intent of entertaining their instructive potential. Indeed, I've employed lessons from other authors' reflections on their writing practices to great benefit with regard to my own writing life, as well as to the benefit of my students, or so they say. My hope is that readers of this book will enjoy the same outcomes.

---

interest in the question of what problem-solving in expository writing and in fiction and poetry writing (more traditionally regarded as "creative") might have in common.

2. My scholarship joins that of other rhetoric and composition researchers who have applied creativity theory to overtly link expository writing with scientific and artistic problem-solving. Their work is cited throughout this book as it supports or clarifies aspects of my study.

ACKNOWLEDGMENTS

My family has always inspired and encouraged my writing. Relevant to this study, in particular, I want to highlight the contributions of my husband, John A. Dively Jr. (EdD, JD), who provided valuable feedback in response to my research methodology and participated in data analysis as a check on my own findings. His observations and ideas challenged me in ways that significantly elevated this project's final iteration, and his enthusiasm for the subject matter kept me energized. I am grateful for his support.

Chapter 1

IMPETUS, CONTEXTS AND METHODS

How can I improve my writing?
Why is writing so difficult?
How can I make it easier?

Most readers poised to engage this study have asked themselves these questions, even those who have enjoyed authorial success; moreover, those who mentor developing writers are bound to have faced such questions from their charges in one form or another. Responses to these questions are abundant and disparate regardless of genre or composing context, and they arise from a diversity of research lenses. One historically prolific lens is the study of writing processes—namely, reflecting on one's own processes and analyzing the processes of others. Pertinent to *expository* genres and composing contexts, the ultimate focus of this monograph, process considerations have long occupied the discipline of rhetoric and composition, early on in attempts to describe writers' processes and identify patterns in their approaches to given writing acts and, later, in post-process warnings about the dangers of promoting a single set of steps that fits all individuals in all rhetorical situations.[1] With due attention to post-process concerns, over time the discipline has come to take for granted that writers are most successful when they are cognizant of their own default composing practices (the effective and the ineffective) and when

---

1. The notion that it's futile to impose a given process on writers (or even across writing tasks for a single individual) is a widely accepted truism in rhetoric and composition scholarship. Treatments of the disciplinary evolution from a penchant for rigidly applied rules about THE writing process to a greater focus on the fluctuating influences of social context and genre that impact writing *processes* can be found in most any history of rhetoric and composition, as well as in most of its post-process scholarship. A foundational collection on post-process theoretical concerns is *Post-Process Theory: Beyond the Writing-Process Paradigm*, ed. Thomas Kent (Carbondale: Southern Illinois University Press, 1999).

they have resources and opportunity to fuel experimentation with alternative strategies.[2]

Working from this theoretical vantage point and with special concern for expository writing, the research informing this book poses possible answers to the questions asked at the outset of this chapter, but it pursues this aim through perhaps unexpected means—that is, analyzing established literary figures' retrospective accounts of their own writing processes. While this perennially intriguing but insufficiently vetted resource of composing advice is applicable to creative writing in obvious ways, its relevance for expository discourse is, at best, underexplored. This seems unfortunate given the widely entertained assertion and central premise of this study that all writing, including expository writing, is creative,[3] and that, therefore, famous authors' commentary on what does and doesn't work when they are writing is potentially applicable in all composing situations.

Anecdotes about composing processes appear liberally in authors' memoirs and in biographies they've inspired, and they are scattered through literary histories and composition scholarship. However, empirical treatments of such reflective discourse across authors—particularly, large subject pools of established authors—are sparse. The project described herein contributes in addressing that oversight with a large-scale discourse analysis of retrospective

---

2. Early process research in composition is typically associated with cognitive theory, which was later challenged by social constructivist and post-process perspectives. Although cognitive theory never outrightly ignored social and contextual influences on acts of composing, those latter theoretical perspectives helped heighten interest in and broaden understanding of such influences. Nevertheless, early cognitive research left enduring marks on the discipline relevant to empirically studying (i.e., via protocol analysis) and taxonomizing (i.e., via model building) composing processes. More recent trends in cognitive research foreground metacognition, knowledge transfer and neurobiology. Metacognition (thinking about thinking relevant to writing) and knowledge transfer (applying similar skills and strategies across genres of writing) are inherent to the study presented in this monograph as will become apparent in subsequent chapters. There exist vast bodies of scholarship on both phenomena, but those interested in succinct overviews of such scholarship, as well as earlier focuses of cognitive studies relevant to composing, will wish to consult the following collection: *Contemporary Perspectives on Cognition and Writing*, ed. Patricia Portanova, Michael Rifenburg and Duane Roen (Boulder: University Press of Colorado, 2017).
3. In other words, all writing is a form of creativity. A voice of specificity on this point is Jan Morris, one of the authors whose reflections on composing provide data for this study. Morris insists that her genre of choice—travel writing, which is typically labeled as a brand of creative nonfiction—can be every bit as literary as novels and short stories and employs the same processes and techniques. See Jan Morris, interview by Leo Lerman, in *The Paris Review Interviews*, vol. 3, ed. Philip Gourevitch (New York: Picador, 2006), 308, 323.

commentary on writing processes as presented in *The Paris Review* (*PR*) interview series, an expansive and esteemed collection of authorial retrospection. Patterns or tendencies drawn from this analysis promise to help writers and teachers of writing expand their repertoire of writing strategies and/or those of their students with the collective backing of revered and prolific literary figures. What's more, knowledge about writing gleaned from this research resides in stories told by exceptional wordsmiths who have lived fascinating writing lives and who convey lessons about composing in an especially engaging and accessible manner.

Retrospection and Creativity

Retrospective accounts of famous creators' ways of working surface in various genres, including research reports, biographies, autobiographies, memoirs, reflective essays, letters, journals and interviews. Unfortunately, some of these genres aren't inviting or readily available to the general public, but certain scholars have sought to popularize reflective discourse on creativity[4] beyond academic circles. One example publication that satisfies this objective is Howard Gardner's *Creating Minds*, which summarizes personal experiences and creative methods informing the professional accomplishments of individuals as diverse as theoretical physicist Albert Einstein, modern dance aficionado Martha Graham and political activist Mahatma Gandhi. In the pages of this book, Gardner interweaves historical data with his subjects' own words, as he fashions detailed, multifaceted portraits of their creative selves.[5] Of course, this brand of engaging and readable biography relies less on retrospection than do anthologized collections of primary sources, such as interviews, journal entries and personal essays. Examples of this type of publication include editors Frank Barron, Alfonso Montouri and Anthea Barron's *Creators on Creating* or Brewster Ghiselin's *The Creative Process*, both of which by their very nature provide more direct lines to artists' and scientists' perspectives on creative output.[6]

---

4. The definition of creativity adopted for the purposes of this study is termed "interdisciplinary" by creativity expert R. Keith Sawyer, in *Explaining Creativity*, 2nd ed. (Oxford: Oxford University Press, 2012), 4. Sawyer characterizes the phenomenon as involving matters of cognition, personality and sociocultural environment.
5. Howard Gardner, *Creating Minds: An Anatomy of Creativity as Seen through the Lives of Freud, Einstein, Picasso, Stravinsky, Eliot, Graham and Gandhi* (New York: Basic Books, 1993).
6. *Creators on Creating: Awakening and Cultivating the Imaginative Mind*, ed. Frank Barron, Alfonso Montouri and Anthea Barron (New York: Jeremy P. Tarcher/Putnam, 1997); *The Creative Process: Reflection on Invention in the Arts and Sciences*, ed. Brewster Ghiselin (Berkeley: University of California Press, 1985). For the sake of efficiency, the current

Both of the anthologies mentioned above include the musings of accomplished writers. In the discipline of English studies, works of this nature pose special interest for aspiring poets and fiction writers, as well as for those who study literature in support of pedagogy or criticism. From Wordsworth's "Preface to Lyrical Ballads" to Stephen King's *On Writing*,[7] these works illuminate the theory and practice of a craft that draws many, confounds many others and, in the minds of most, carries an undeniable mystique and prestige. But insights and advice about composing processes are only part of the appeal in the retrospective accounts of famous writers. Like those of their counterparts in other disciplines, these reflections allow scintillating glimpses into the lives of creative souls who, in many instances, have become bona fide celebrities. Typically, and often related to craft, they recall colorful family backgrounds, attitudes toward formal education and religion, heart-wrenching tragedies, awe-inspiring triumphs, bouts with drugs and alcohol, love affairs, devoted partnerships (both personal and professional) and even brushes with other celebrities. In other words, they contain the stuff of great storytelling in and of themselves, and writers, in particular, are well equipped to render such creation stories in gripping and detailed fashion.

Appeal of *The PR* Interviews

Behind-the-scenes snapshots of authors' personal lives and observations about craft are signature ingredients of one of the most prominent, prolific and enduring sources of writerly retrospection in existence: *The PR* interviews. First published in 1953, *The PR* was a revolutionary magazine (at least, by some accounts) established by three Americans living in Paris on the heels of the so-called Lost Generation.[8] Irked by the critical bent of most literary journalism of the day,[9] these three men, Peter Matthiessen, Harold L. Humes

---

study employs the phrase "arts and sciences" broadly conceived to encompass the scope of human inquiry and activity.

7. Some other notable titles that showcase authors commenting on their own writing processes include *Ernest Hemingway on Writing*, ed. Larry W. Phillips (New York: Scribner, 1984); *Writers Dreaming: Twenty-Six Writers Talk about Their Dreams and the Creative Process*, ed. Naomi Epel (New York: Vintage, 1993); *Why We Write*, ed. Meredith Maran (New York: Plume, 2013); *Light the Dark: Writers on Creativity, Inspiration, and the Artistic Process*, ed. Joe Fassler (New York: Penguin, 2017).
8. Rachel Donadio, "*The Paris Review* Faces Its Future, Finds New Editor," *The New York Observer*, January 5, 2004, https://observer.com/2004/01/the-paris-review-faces-its-future-finds-new-editor/.
9. Robert Strauss, "Still in the Game; At Times It Was a Struggle but George Plimpton's *Paris Review* Has Made It to Its 50th Anniversary," *Los Angeles Times*, June 14, 2003, https://www.latimes.com/archives/la-xpm-2003-jun-14-et-strauss14-story.html.

and George Plimpton, pledged to produce a publication that would—as described by sometime editor William Styron in the preface to the first issue of the journal—"give predominant space to the fiction and poetry of both established and new writers, rather than to people who use[d] words like Zeitgeist."[10] Because the weight of such "learned chatter" was perceived to be "smothering" the literature itself,[11] the move away from critical speculation and pigeon-holing was predicted to be a welcome turn for purposes of attracting poetry and fiction lovers, and it seems the purity of this approach did provide traction in establishing *The PR* as a reputable source of literary news and exposure. Nevertheless, it turned out that an equally (if not more) enticing feature of this venture was the interview with a famous novelist or poet attending each issue.[12] In these interviews, subjects shared wisdom about writing and life experiences in conversation with interviewers typically enlisted for their extensive knowledge of the authors[13] or for their personal relationships with them.[14]

The sources of interest associated with retrospective accounts as discussed earlier in this chapter are on full display in the collection of *PR* interviews accumulated since the mid-twentieth century, when E. M. Forster agreed to initiate the series. Although the early interviews profiled fiction writers and poets, *PR* editors eventually cast a wider net, encompassing renowned nonfiction

---

10. William Styron, "Letter to an Editor," *The Paris Review*, Spring 1953, https://www.theparisreview.org/letters-essays/5220/letter-to-an-editor-william-styron.
11. Ibid.
12. Usha Wilbers, "The Author Resurrected: *The Paris Review*'s Answer to the Age of Criticism," *American Periodicals* 18, no. 2 (2008): 195, 198; Andrew Calcutt, "Reconstructing the Public Sphere: From *The Paris Review* to Intelligent Life," *Reconstruction: Studies in Contemporary Culture* 8, no. 1 (2008), http://reconstruction.eserver.org/Issues/081/calcutt.shtml; Peter Carlson, "Post-Plimpton *Paris Review* Is Thriving," *Chicago Tribune*, October 19, 2006, https://www.chicagotribune.com/news/ct-xpm-2006-10-19-0610190010-story.html; Margaret Manning, "Writers Talk about Writing and Other Writers," *Boston Globe*, August 26, 1984, https://search-proquest-com.proxy.lib.siu.edu/docview/294200496?accountid=13864; Stephen Phelan, "Unravelling the DNA of Literature," *Sunday Herald*, January 21, 2007, https://search-proquest-com.proxy.lib.siu.edu/docview/331277165?accountid=13864; "*The Paris Review* Reviewed," *University Times*, January 20, 2010, http://www.universitytimes.ie/2010/01/the-paris-review-reviewed/#; James Linville, Jeanne McCulloch and George Plimpton, "*The Paris Review* at Forty," *Publishing Research Quarterly* (Winter 1993–94): 62; Christopher Bains, "Critics Abroad: The Early Years of *The Paris Review* (1953–65)," in *The Oxford Critical and Cultural History of Modernist Magazines*, ed. Peter Brooker and Andrew Thacker (Oxford: Oxford University Press, 2012), 761, 765, 772.
13. Wilbers, "The Author Resurrected," 196.
14. Malcolm Cowley, "Introduction," in *The Paris Review Interviews: Writers at Work*, ed. Malcolm Cowley, 1st Series (New York: Penguin, 1977), 6.

writers, critics and even publishers. Today, the entire collection—this "DNA of Literature"[15]—totals 320+ interviews, and many have been anthologized in different combinations. In 2004, thanks to a grant from the National Endowment for the Arts,[16] *PR* staff began the Herculean project of transferring the interviews in unedited form to an online database (https://www.theparisreview.org/interviews), finally catching up to all previously published issues in 2010. This ambitious initiative is a testament to the interviews' wide appeal, and it fuels the potential for increased research on this impressive repository of writerly reflection and advice.

As for the treatment of *The PR* interviews in published research, references to them commonly appear in histories of literary works and biographies of famous authors. Scholarship focused on the magazine or the interview series as objects of inquiry is less abundant, limited to a smattering of articles and dissertations.[17] Collectively, such scholarship offers a detailed account of *The PR*'s history and of the dedication attributed to its intrepid long-term editor, George Plimpton. Some of that work explores the lasting allure and influence of the interviews themselves, as well as the processes for securing, conducting and editing them. Especially intriguing with regard to the interviews are the editorial prefaces to the interview anthologies mentioned in the preceding paragraph.[18]

Value of *The PR* Interviews for Aspiring Creative Writers

Commentaries on *The PR* interviews that characterize them as valued sources of advice and encouragement for aspiring creative writers are plentiful. Nevertheless, some who study writing and/or write for a living may be primed to question their value, maintaining that isolated stories of individuals' successes and failures at crafting prose or poetry are of limited instructional benefit. Indeed, many fiction writers and poets accept this premise based on practice alone, and some are rather outspoken on the matter. But, at the risk of "throwing out the baby with the bathwater," it's crucial to note that to

---

15. George Plimpton, quoted in Phelan, "Unravelling."
16. Mark Hazlin, "*Paris Review* Digs into Literary History," *USA Today*, November 10, 2004, http://usatoday30.usatoday.com/life/books/news/2004-11-10-paris-review_x.htm.
17. Of particular note are Usha Wilbers's "Enterprise in the Service of Art: A Critical History of *The Paris Review*, 1953–1973" (PhD diss., Radboud University, 2006) and Kelley Penfield Lewis's "Interviews at Work: Reading *The Paris Review* Interviews 1953–1978" (PhD diss., Dalhousie University, 2009).
18. While the focus here is on academic publications, readers should note that there exists an abundance of journalistic commentary on *The PR* and its interviews. The bibliography for the current study contains numerous examples.

debunk the notion of some one-size-fits-all writing process is by no means a call to disregard any and all advice about composing processes from individual practitioners, a sentiment succinctly summarized by author David Joy in a brief article that touts *The PR* interviews' instructional impact. Reflecting on early fears that he wouldn't make it as a writer because his writing processes did not mimic those of a key mentor, Joy recalls the following:

> One day I was looking through old interviews in the *Paris Review*'s "Art of Fiction" series, and I stumbled onto an interview with Raymond Carver in which he discussed his own process. He said that when he wasn't writing it felt "as if I've never written a word." Then the time would come when the words would surround him and he'd write and write, "one day dovetailing into the next." When I read that I thought, "That's me. That's exactly how I am." And that's all it took for me to suddenly realize that I didn't need to have the same process as a writer like Ron [Rash].[19]

Joy continues by observing that "all writers need that justification early on and one of the places we find it is through other writers, writers we love and respect."[20] But Joy clearly draws more from the interviews than mere justification for pursuing his own inclinations regarding process, as he ends his article with ten writing "tips" he's latched onto through his own encounters with *The PR* interviews. As Joy's reminiscence makes clear, to discredit the notion of a universal writing process is *not* to say that studying the composing processes of other writers yields no fruit.

In fact, there is no shortage of published praise from accomplished creative writers focused specifically on the assistance they received from other creative writers, whether in the context of personal relationships, writing groups, formal educational settings or rumination on what others have to say about the craft (these themes are explored more fully in Chapters 3 through 8 of this book). Given that *The PR* interviews have solicited advice about craft from many of the most revered writers in history, it seems inevitable that those exchanges would prove especially attractive. Again, no writer who has thought seriously about the nature of the craft would expect to unearth some failproof formula for effective writing, or even some nugget of specialized knowledge that would serve at all times, in all situations. In the context of a single interview, different readers will seize on different messages as their needs dictate. In

---

19. David Joy, "10 Tips from *The Paris Review*'s Art of Fiction," *The Strand,* March 10, 2017, https://strandmag.com/10-tips-from-the-paris-reviews-art-of-fiction/. Reproduced with permission of David Joy.
20. Ibid.

the end, for writers, the value of *The PR* interviews (and other such works) lies in their capacity for stimulating productive individualized reflection on composing activity and in fostering individualized experimentation with the array of perspectives and strategies that they bring to light, the end result being to expand one's repertoire of possibilities for working through the diverse challenges associated with writing—from generating ideas to capturing those ideas on page or screen, to overcoming blocks, to interacting with editors.

In illustration of this potentiality, consider the following observation from Turkish writer Orhan Pamuk (a *PR* interviewee himself) about the benefits he derived from reading *PR* interviews while struggling with his first novel. His words are worth quoting at length for the specificity he offers regarding that reading experience.

> In the beginning I read these interviews because I loved these writers' books, because I wished to learn their secrets, to understand how they created their fictive worlds. [...] These were writers who were already established and world famous, and in these interviews they talked about their writing habits, the secrets of their trade, their ways of writing, their fragile moments, and the ways in which they overcame the difficulties they encountered. I needed to learn from their experience as quickly as I could. [...] [Through the interviews] I discovered that there were many others who shared my passion, that the distance between what I desired and what I achieved was normal, that my loathing for normal, everyday life was not a sign of sickness but of intelligence, and that I should embrace most of the little eccentric habits that fired my imagination and helped me write. I feel as if I learned a great deal about the craft of writing novels—how the first germ formed in the writer's mind, how lovingly it was grown and how carefully plotted, or not plotted at all. Sometimes it was by reacting with fury against a certain idea of the novel suggested in these interviews that I developed my own ideas on the novel as well.[21]—Excerpt from "Driven by Demons" by Orhan Pamuk, originally published in *The Guardian*. Copyright © 2007 Orhan Pamuk, used by permission of The Wylie Agency LLC.

As Pamuk's words attest, whether to draw courage, become reinvigorated toward the craft or extract strategies for pulling oneself out of a rut in thought or practice, reading *PR* interviews can be a powerful facilitative force for creative writers who take time to consult them. As for expository writers, the

---

21. Orhan Pamuk, "Driven by Demons," *The Guardian*, October 26, 2007, https://www.theguardian.com/books/2007/oct/27/fiction.orhanpamuk.

relevance of famous authors' reflections on their craft is less well documented. Yet, to be convinced that expository writers, as well as creative writers, might profit from engagement with the interviews, one need only consult the array of scholarship establishing significant overlap between all modes of writing.[22] (This proposition is foundational to the current study and, as such, consumes the entirety of Chapter 2.)

Of course, whether for creative or expository writers, casual consumption of *The PR* interviews reveals their usefulness in piecemeal fashion, with readers pulling out isolated jewels of wisdom here and there. But what might be the advantage of mining jewels with an eye toward clustering those of similar size, color and clarity in a fashion that would magnify their relative quantity? Surely, the impact would be more stunning than that of a single stone. Such would presumably be the case with the myriad instances of composing advice embedded in *The PR* interviews; that is, the impact of an isolated piece of wisdom backed or supported by others of its kind becomes more stunning in the sense that—because more than one brilliant individual has noted it—its relative veracity is intensified.

This assumption drives the research methodology informing the project discussed in this book, its primary purpose being to identify and specifically represent, across a sizable sample of *PR* interviews, pieces of advice that ostensibly fall into clusters given their thematic similarity. While it is presumed that creative writers reading about these patterns can easily adapt them relevant to their own fiction and poetry, routes for transferring those findings to expository composition and composition instruction may not be as apparent. Thus, they ultimately will be translated into concrete strategies for facilitating expository writing processes, strategies that might become the focus of the kinds of repertoire-expanding experimentation advocated earlier in this introductory chapter. In service of that prospect, the features, contributions and limitations of the research methodology are discussed in the following sections.

---

22. W. Ross Winterowd, "Creativity and the Comp Class," *Freshman English News* 7, no. 2 (1978): 1–16; Linda Flower and Linda J. Carey, *Foundations for Creativity in the Writing Process: Rhetorical Representations of Ill-Defined Problems* (Washington, DC: Office for Educational Research and Improvement, 1989); Wendy Bishop, "Crossing the Lines: On Creative Composition and Composing Creative Writing," *Writing on the Edge* 4, no. 2 (1993): 117–33; George T. Karnezis, "Reclaiming Creativity for Composition," in *Teaching Writing Creatively*, ed. David Starkey (Portsmouth: Boynton/Cook, 1998), 29–42; Ronda Leathers Dively, *Preludes to Insight: Creativity, Incubation and Expository Writing* (Cresskill, NJ: Hampton Press, 2006); Douglas Hesse, "The Place of Creative Writing in Composition Studies," *College Composition and Communication* 62, no. 1 (2010): 31–52; Patrick Sullivan, "The UnEssay: Making Room for Creativity in the Composition Class," *College Composition and Communication* 67, no. 1 (2015): 6–34.

Objectives and Methods for This Study

In light of the theoretical premises reviewed earlier in this chapter regarding the benefits for aspiring writers of studying other writers' composing experiences and advice, this study set out to determine whether or not a respectable sample of *PR* interviews would reveal trends in the ways the interview subjects represented their craft, not only the intricacies of their processes but also the conditions that facilitated them. The research methodology employed to investigate this potentiality is a brand of discourse analysis most accurately labeled "thematic textual." Rhetoric and composition research specialists Ann Blakeslee and Cathy Fleischer define "thematic textual analysis"[23] in contrast to linguistic and rhetorical analysis, clarifying that—instead of focusing on grammatical structures or rhetorical elements characterizing the artifacts in question—the former focuses more broadly on content. Doing so enables the researcher to determine if "a particular idea or subject recurs in the writing or if there are particular places where contradictions arise."[24] Searching out themes across a large corpus of documents is an exercise involving some interpretation; therefore, although thematic analysis may involve counting instances of themes, it is considered a qualitative, as opposed to a quantitative, methodology. Rather than seeking definitive conclusions, qualitative methodologies acknowledge and embrace the tentative nature of their findings, with the intention of sparking further thought and scholarship about the research constructs. In addition, because qualitative research is by definition a flexible, open-ended enterprise, it invites treatment of emergent patterns (i.e., those not necessarily anticipated as part of an analytical or coding scheme) as germane to the overall findings. Such is the case with the study described herein. Procedures used to illuminate anticipated and emergent patterns in this thematic discourse analysis of *PR* interviews are detailed below.

Data analysis

The coding scheme employed to analyze the interviews sampled for this study is the paradigmatic creative process model based on the work of Graham Wallas and George F. Kneller.[25] This model consists of five elements:

---

23. The terms "textual analysis" and "discourse analysis" are widely treated as synonymous. I prefer the latter because it more readily connotes an empirical approach in contrast to literary criticism, for example.
24. Ann Blakeslee and Cathy Fleischer, *Becoming a Writing Researcher* (Mahwah, NJ: Lawrence Erlbaum Associates, 2007), 124.
25. Graham Wallas, *The Art of Thought* (New York: Harcourt Brace, 1926); George F. Kneller, *The Art and Science of Creativity* (New York: Holt, Rinehart and Winston, 1965).

- first insight, or the initial glimmer of possibility;
- preparation, or research broadly conceived;
- incubation, or breaks from conscious attention to a creative challenge;
- insight, or the Eureka moment when a solution to the challenge is discerned;
- verification, or evaluation of an insight.

Given that, in the end, this research seeks to provide composing advice for expository writers, in particular, it might have seemed fitting to apply a coding scheme drawn from the paradigmatic composing process model: invention, drafting, revision and editing.[26] Nevertheless, the creative process model makes more sense in this context given that (1) this study posits all writing as creative; (2) the sample transcripts concentrate almost entirely on fiction and poetry—that is, traditionally, "creative writing"[27]; and (3) the creative process model subsumes, yet builds productively on, the composing process model. Elements of the creative and composing process models, as well as the manner in which they overlap, are more specifically characterized in Chapter 2 and revisited relevant to findings in Chapters 3 through 8.

Through the lens of the coding scheme described above, select interview transcripts (which totaled over two thousand pages) were subject to multiple readings—initially, four by the author and one by an education professor well versed in qualitative research methods.[28] As often happens in thematic discourse analysis, the initial five-category coding scheme became more precisely developed with each reading. To elaborate, the first reading of each transcript consisted of identifying statements that seemed to fit definitions of the five elements constituting the coding scheme. These statements were marked in the margins of the text with abbreviations for the element portrayed by the passages in question (e.g., FI = first insight; Inc = incubation).[29] Upon

---

26. As already established, in this post-process era of rhetoric and composition, the idea of a model as a formula for writing is outdated and reductive. Readers should understand that models in this study are used merely for their capacity to efficiently categorize different types of composing activity. Moreover, despite their linear arrangement, readers should understand that the activities these models represent are recursive.
27. Though not based on systematic discourse analysis, Malcolm Cowley's introduction to the first installment of *The Paris Review's Writers at Work* series (see note 14) reveals that the interviewees' retrospective accounts of their composing practices commonly speak to elements of the creative process model.
28. The second reader is John A. Dively (my spouse), who is an EdD (in educational administration), as well as a retired professor of qualitative research methods and an accomplished writer in his field.
29. Although passages were routinely coded in accordance with their most dominant theme, double coding did occur. For example, a passage may have been assigned as representing two different patterns if it featured balanced reflection on both. In

subsequent readings, the five initial coding categories, or creative process model elements, were divided into subcategories to reflect patterns that began to materialize. Moreover, several patterns came to light that didn't seem to fit the five-element scheme but that were, nonetheless, intriguing ancillaries to the creative process model (i.e., the emergent patterns noted earlier). Once the initial five passes through the interviews were finished, all marked statements were coded by anthology volume and page number into a table that began with five cells representing elements of the creative process model and, then, gradually expanded to account for subcategories and ancillary themes elucidating the five elements. With the growing precision of the coding scheme and the finer analysis it provoked, certain statements were recoded or moved to subcategories or themes that seemed more appropriate, and a few subcategories and themes actually collapsed as their populations decreased. Such reconfiguring (a common occurrence in qualitative discourse analysis) continued in the context of drafting the book manuscript as the content and location of cited *PR* interview passages were verified.

As is the case with most projects that rely on discourse analysis, the coding experience presented some challenges. The most vexing centered around the somewhat fluid boundaries between the initial five categories and subsequent decisions relevant to what should count as distinct sub- or ancillary categories. As mentioned earlier, thematic discourse analysis is highly interpretive. In this study, assigning the marked passages to anticipated and emergent patterns was complicated by the fact that, because the interviews were not standardized and the interviewers concentrated on their own special interests, they did not necessarily follow up on questions that elicited commentary on elements of the creative process model. Therefore, in contrast to each other, interviewees' references to elements of the creative process model were never assured of being leveled with the same degree of detail.

Despite the reality that coding of interpretive or amorphous concepts defies exactness, it seems reasonable to assert that the number of reading cycles (with one performed by a reader other than the author), the cumulative weight of the statements assigned to each category (no theme survived with fewer than 18 members, while the strongest had over 160) and the care devoted to categorization lend credence to the identified patterns and suggest that characterizations of each are viable. Appendix A of this study presents the finalized coding table recording all categories, subcategories and themes discerned through the multilayered discourse analysis, as well as the number

---

addition, if two separately coded passages occurred in the same volume and on the same page of the interview anthology, that identifier (volume and page number) exists in both of the pertinent cells in the coding table.

and location of interview passages coded to each. While the numbers of coded units per cell carry significance in establishing the presence of the constructs and suggesting the relative dominance of certain patterns, readers should avoid assigning those numbers too much import given the interpretive issues previously discussed.

Text selection

Earlier this introduction noted that there are well over three hundred *PR* interviews in existence and that they are now accessible through an online database. The sheer number of interviews and the time required for multiple close readings in the interest of credible coding pointed to the wisdom of working with a sample as opposed to the entire corpus of interviews. That sample is the 2006–9 four-volume anthology edited by Philip Gourevitch, editor of *The PR* from 2005 to 2009.[30] Certainly, this collection would be considered a "convenience sample" in the respect that it was preexisting and nonrandomized,[31] but its usefulness extends well beyond ease of access. First, as Gourevitch contends, this anthology compiles some of the best interviews that the series has ever produced.[32] Those interviews capture the thoughts and experiences of "some of the finest writers in the English-speaking world," as Laurie Hertzel calls them in her review of the Gourevitch collection.[33] This sentiment is echoed in a number of other reviews,[34] despite some reservations that, all together, the interviewees are a bit too "conventional" or "mainstream."[35] Second, in contrast to the previously published *PR* interview anthologies, the Gourevitch collection is more representative across time, gender and nationality. To that point, the collection spans 64 interviews occurring from 1953 to 2008, it includes interviews from several women and it includes authors from

---

30. Philip Gourevitch, ed., *The Paris Review Interviews*, 4 vols. (New York: Picador, 2006–9).
31. Nonrandomized sampling techniques are employed regularly in qualitative research. While potentially biased in some ways, they are often preferable in the context of qualitative inquiry for ensuring a substantial occurrence of the constructs under investigation (i.e., ensuring that the sample will capture the focal construct).
32. Philip Gourevitch, "Introduction," in *The Paris Review Interviews* (New York: Picador, 2006), 1: x.
33. Laurie Hertzel, "Great Writers Make Their Work an Open Book for *Paris Review*," *Star Tribune*, December 5, 2009, http://www.startribune.com/great-writers-make-their-work-an-open-book-for-paris-review/78475222/.
34. "*Paris Review* Reviewed"; Scott Sherman, "Talking On against Time," *The Nation*, June 7, 2010, 41, 43; "Declarations of Genius," *The Scotsman*, December 14, 2007, http://www.scotsman.com/lifestyle/declarations-of-genius-1703847#ixzz3z7f87zmt.
35. Sherman, "Talking On," 44.

16 different countries. (See Appendix B for a complete list of the interviewees cited in this study.)

The Nature of Interviewing and *The PR* Interviews

Considering that the objects of analysis for the study delineated in this book are interviews and that interviews as methodological tools are subject to some controversy (at least from the perspective of positivistic research ideology), it would be remiss to end this introduction without attention to the challenges and benefits of interviewing as a research tool. Beginning with the challenges, as with other modes of self-reporting, the interview breeds skepticism with respect to its capacity for eliciting trustworthy information. More specifically, naysayers will point out that reflective insights gleaned from an interview are filtered through the interviewee's subjectivity and can't be regarded as factual data. Skepticism grows if the interview addresses matters that occurred in the distant past, given the presumption that memories inevitably become cloudier with time. In fact, those who study self-reporting methodologies (particularly retrospective self-reporting) leave little doubt that the passing of time can skew recollections as they fade or morph to fit coherent narratives of experience.[36] *The PR* interviews are particularly suspect from this vantage point in that most of them were attained in the late stages of an author's career.

These claims about the nature of interview methodology breed little debate. Presumably, nobody would be apt to deny based on personal experience alone that memories are affected by intersecting threads of human subjectivity and the passage of time. But more to the point of the theoretical assumptions informing this study, such criticisms presume that the goal of interviewing is to unearth facts or "the truth." Putting aside the question of whether or not pure objectivity is even attainable (a philosophical discussion beyond the scope of this monograph), most researchers who employ interviews[37] would not purport any such outcome or even worry about its being possible. On the contrary, they fully recognize the limitations of their approach (in the eyes of positivistic research paradigms, that is) and even celebrate it as the unavoidable, defining status of the human condition. Often, that very complexity (the multifaceted nature of the psyche and its perceptions of the self) is what

---

36. Stuart Greene and Lorraine Higgins, "'Once Upon a Time': The Use of Retrospective Accounts in Building Theory in Composition," in *Speaking about Writing: Reflections on Research Methodology*, ed. Peter Smagorinsky (Thousand Oaks: Sage, 1994), 119.
37. Quantitative researchers may subject interview data to statistical analysis, but, of course, even their studies can be considered objective only to the extent that the interview responses can.

they've set out to investigate and preserve so as to fully represent it, even if it is created to some extent by the interviewee. Beyond the benefits of capturing that complexity, there is simply no other method than interviewing to gather certain types of information, particularly information about the self that requires reflection and that profits from additional probing through immediate follow-up questioning.

In addition, some researchers appreciate the spontaneity of the method, the idea that the interviewer is catching the interviewee in an unadulterated state. This potentiality points to a unique line of interrogation leveled at *The PR* interviews by those who have looked to them for a sense of famous authors' lives and creative abilities: that is, the interview transcripts were heavily edited after the fact by the interviewees themselves. More specifically, upon reading the transcript, each interviewee was given the option (and very few refused) to revise his or her initial responses. Some interviewees even revised the interview questions and/or concocted some themselves. Thus, so the argument goes, they were able to mold their respective transcripts to accommodate the images they hoped to project[38] as opposed to their actual selves.

This interviewing practice receives an unapologetic and eloquent defense from the editor of the four-volume anthology containing the current study's sample of artifacts:

> Although the writers who reveal themselves in these pages […] had the opportunity to clarify, correct, retract, and amplify their remarks, they never used that opportunity to hide themselves better—but rather, whether knowingly or inadvertently, the deeper they got into rendering their accounts the more they tended to unmask themselves.[39]—Copyright © by *The Paris Review*, used by permission of The Wylie Agency LLC.

Relevant to the current study, the polished, revisionary nature of the interviews is of little concern. In fact, one might argue that a more concentrated level of reflection is desirable given its tendency to yield greater depth of response.[40] Again, as discussed above, all interviews deal in perception. Extended periods of time to think through and even rethink answers to interview questions doesn't necessarily skew them toward inaccuracy. Conversely, if an author is inclined to fabricate responses to questions, he or she likely will do so regardless of the amount of response time provided. Moreover, it is possible that accuracy in relaying perceptions could be increased in the context

---

38. Wilbers, "The Author Resurrected," 209; Bains, "Critics Abroad," 766.
39. Gourevitch, "Introduction," 1: x.
40. Phelan, "Unravelling."

of extended, lone reflection time when contrasted with the more compressed and more stress-filled context of an oral exchange.

On this point, consider the words of Joyce Carol Oates who, in her introduction to volume eight of *The PR* interviews' *Writers at Work* series, attests that "we are likely to be most faithful to our convictions when we have had time to contemplate them."[41] *New York Times* book reviewer Richard Eder seemingly backs Oates's claim when—while praising one of the many *PR* interview anthologies—he notes that in order "to produce a portrait that actually succeeds [...] you need sufficient time and space, since too brief a chase reveals more about the aims of the pursuer than about the character of the pursued."[42] In the end, there can be no guarantee with respect to any form of self-reporting that the subject is being wholly honest. But Malcolm Cowley, in his introduction to the initial *Writers at Work* anthology, shares a persuasive defense of *The PR* interviews on this front, namely that the interviewees were highly devoted to the profession and to the responsibility of trying to help aspiring writers who were struggling, as they once did.[43] It seems reasonable, then, to believe that the majority of *PR* interviewees (though, granted, some were reportedly a bit cantankerous) strove to portray memories of their pasts and the conditions that produced their greatest works with integrity.

A Glimpse Ahead

One compelling impetus for a study like the one described in the chapters to follow is that it demonstrates patterns in the environments, personalities and cognitive moves of some of the most fascinating and prolific creative minds to ever live. This sort of intellectual history may hold interest for many disciplines, not the least of which would include literary studies and psychology. From the perspective of rhetoric and composition (as well as creative writing), the impact of the aforementioned patterns on acts of composing is paramount. Indeed, the theoretical assumption that there is value in analyzing others' creative processes for the breakthroughs they can activate by means of personal experimentation is foundational to this study of *PR* interviews. Again, the purpose of this project is not to suggest that aspiring writers can find within its pages surefire solutions to all their writing problems or some

---

41. Joyce Carol Oates, "Introduction," in *Writers at Work: The Paris Review Interviews* (New York: Penguin, 1988), xii.
42. Richard Eder, "Pursuing Writers, but Letting Them Lead the Chase," *The New York Times*, January 6, 2007, http://www.nytimes.com/2007/01/06eder.html?emc=etal&_r=0.
43. Cowley, "Introduction," 6.

formula for succeeding on the writing challenges they engage. Rather, the purpose is to open up possibilities for working through those challenges, to offer diverse ways of thinking about composing and of applying that information to cultivate potentially more productive dispositions and a more complex repertoire of composing strategies.

Systematic pursuit of that goal unfolds in the chapters to follow with relevant information distributed in the following manner. Chapter 2 delves more deeply into the relationships between creative and composing processes, with the intention of further justifying the transfer of writing advice across genres and selection of the coding scheme employed for analyzing the data. Chapters 3 through 7, respectively, report findings for each element of the paradigmatic creative process model: Chapter 3—first insight; Chapter 4—preparation; Chapter 5—incubation; Chapter 6—insight; Chapter 7—verification. Additionally, these chapters illustrate the nature of all identified subcategories and themes with excerpts from the sampled *PR* interviews. Chapter 8 echoes this approach, but with a focus on emergent patterns. Finally, Chapter 9 will offer concluding thoughts about the value of the findings for expository writing teachers and their students.

Chapter 2

COMPOSITION THROUGH THE LENS OF CREATIVITY THEORY

As established in Chapter 1, the ultimate goal of this study is to mine a collection of *The Paris Review* (*PR*) interviews for advice that expository writers might employ to negotiate writing challenges and facilitate their composing processes. Chapter 2 lays theoretical groundwork for such cross-genre application since some readers—though accepting that wisdom drawn from the interviews could be helpful to fiction writers and poets—might be skeptical of the notion that this same wisdom could benefit writers of news articles, academic papers, blog posts and other expository texts. Perhaps such skepticism is to be expected given that, historically, writing curricula have maintained rather sharp divisions between expository composition and creative writing. Painting an especially bleak picture of this situation, compositionist George T. Karnezis differentiates between what he terms the "Creative Writing Oasis," where students enjoy the fun and imaginative work of fashioning stories and poems, and the "curricular Wasteland" of "other school-taught 'writing'" courses, where students are subjected to the drudgeries of preparing for subsequent coursework and careers.[1] This educational architecture is displayed in overtly labeled "creative writing assignments" that celebrate freedom, risk-taking and inventiveness in contrast to expository assignments that impose rigid formulas and regurgitation of others' ideas, often in strict adherence to standardized assessment initiatives.[2]

---

1. George Karnezis, "Reclaiming Creativity for Composition," in *Teaching Writing Creatively*, ed. David Starkey (Portsmouth: Boynton/Cook, 1998), 30.
2. One prominent embodiment of this attitude toward expository writing is the five-paragraph theme (introduction that presages three points to be made; three paragraphs, with one on each of those points; a conclusion that repeats those points). This essay format dominated composition instruction for decades and, despite intense critique, still survives as a vehicle for prepackaging essays in high-stakes evaluation or testing environments. Despite its function as a crutch for quickly organizing content, its formulaic essence typically stifles critical thought about subject matter and relationships between ideas.

Troubled by these disciplinary divisions between composition and creative writing and the damage they can do, especially in the eyes of students, several rhetoric and composition teacher/scholars in line with Karnezis have questioned the practice of so radically distinguishing the two fields. A pioneering voice in this conversation, Wendy Bishop argued years ago that language curricula "need to be crossing the line between composition and creative writing far more often than [they] do" and that, perhaps, they need "to eliminate the line entirely."[3] In support of her contention, Bishop relates stories of confusing school-imposed distinctions between creative and expository genres, as she depicts former students who struggled with defining and/or satisfying expectations relevant to appropriate subject matter, presumed target audiences and required truth value of claims or observations.[4] To combat such confusion, Bishop recommends including fiction and poetry in first-year writing courses; sharing various forms of writing research in all writing classrooms; studying the "best, most exciting, most creative texts in all genres"; and viewing teachers and students, first and foremost, as writers.[5]

Bishop's prescient concerns and calls to action are recently echoed in articles published by *College Composition and Communication* (*CCC*), the preeminent journal in rhetoric and composition. In one of these articles, Douglas Hesse (past chair of the Conference on College Composition and Communication, as well as past president of the National Council of Teachers of English and the Council of Writing Program Administrators) portrays the historical separation between creative writing and composition as one of mutual "disdain" rooted in different research traditions and perceived usefulness ascribed to their respective crafts.[6] While he notes benefits for both disciplines (e.g., a richer understanding of writing and the teaching of writing) in bridging what in his view are some largely artificial boundaries, Hesse's interests ultimately center on the danger posed for composition by foregrounding knowledge *about* writing (e.g., analysis of others' discourse or discursive practices) at the expense of time spent producing "different kinds of writing for wider audiences and purposes."[7] De-emphasizing the latter, he contends, can be marginalizing—especially in this digital age wherein "knowledge and belief are shaped less by special isolated rhetorical acts than by countless encounters with any manner

---

3. Wendy Bishop, "Crossing the Lines: On Creative Composition and Composing Creative Writing," *Writing on the Edge* 4, no. 2 (1993): 117.
4. Ibid., 117–19.
5. Ibid., 129–30.
6. Douglass Hesse, "The Place of Creativity in Composition Studies," *College Composition and Communication* 62, no. 1 (2010): 32–33.
7. Ibid., 35.

of texts."[8] In the end, Hesse observes that students need to develop dexterity for composing in myriad genres that collectively represent writing as a "creative, productive art," one that is practical in broader terms than disciplinary conventions have dictated and that is viewed as "a life activity with many interconnected manifestations."[9]

With praise for Hesse's work, Patrick Sullivan's *CCC* article on the composition/creative writing divide broadens the scope of concern from creative writing per se to creativity at large, encouraging the field to openly apply "this radiant and revolutionary human capacity" in the composition classroom for the purpose of mainstreaming it, of undoing its segregation in the creative writing classroom.[10] After reviewing recent key developments in creativity scholarship drawn largely from psychology, Sullivan lists a number of strategies for cultivating creativity in the composition classroom with a particular emphasis on supplementing existing assignments with what he calls (albeit vaguely) "creative activities" and inviting students to compose in a diversity of genres such as "poems, plays, songs, raps, short stories, memoirs, profiles, interviews [...] slam poems," etc.[11] While acknowledging that there are countless ways to highlight creativity in the composition classroom, he expends nearly a fourth of his article on a description of his own creativity-based composition pedagogy. In an effort to provide students with challenging academic subject matter, his approach engages students with three different knowledge domains—history, fine arts and human sciences—and a range of writing assignments, from poems to academic essays. With its overt focus on creativity, the fine arts unit grounds the course, punctuated as it is with a culminating assignment that Sullivan refers to as "the UnEssay."[12] Ending with some questions intended to guide content, the prompt for this exercise reads as follows:

> The UnEssay! I would like you to think about all that we've done in this unit and then construct an "UnEssay" that pulls together your thinking about the fine arts and creativity! But it can't be a traditional essay. It can't be a five-paragraph theme. It has to be something else and it can be whatever you want it to be. Invent a new form! Write the kind of "paper" or essay you've always wanted to write in an English class. Feel

---

8. Ibid., 48.
9. Ibid., 45.
10. Patrick Sullivan, "The UnEssay: Making Room for Creativity in the Composition Classroom," *College Composition and Communication* 67, no. 1 (2015): 6.
11. Ibid., 22.
12. Ibid., 23–24.

free to include pictures, photos, links, and multimedia if you wish. Most importantly: Have some fun with this![13]

Sullivan reports that, in response to this request, students generate a variety of multimodal compositions including websites and PowerPoint presentations, which he views as more overtly creative than the types of essays historically assigned in composition classes. Sullivan recognizes multimodal composition as "authentic and worthwhile intellectual activity" and joins Hesse in acknowledging its value for promoting twenty-first century literacies.[14]

Bishop, Hesse and Sullivan are all motivated by the same general problem: the aforementioned curricular divisions between composition and creative writing. Further, they all seem especially interested in how these divisions impact understanding of written *products*—more particularly, perceptions of who owns which genres, the extent to which they bleed into each other and the need for exposing developing writers to a diversity of texts. While I share their interest in such queries and regard them as important considerations in educating composition students, my own scholarship is more invested in understanding the processes behind these products. The genesis of my fascination with composing processes as potentially elucidated by theory about creative processes is captured in a pair of anecdotes I've published elsewhere but that are worth repeating here to illustrate the kind of aforementioned damage that a lack of interdisciplinary inquiry between creative writing/creativity studies and composition can render.

The first anecdote speaks to my struggles as a graduate student trying to achieve a reasonable level of efficiency with respect to my own writing practices in the midst of increasingly more sophisticated writing challenges.[15] As the memory goes, ordinarily when I took up my keyboard to tackle a new project, I knew exactly where I was headed in a global sense, and I could plunk out an introduction pretty easily since I had written it in my head the night before. (I still do this, for I am one of those linear minded, one-drafters[16] who

---

13. Ibid., 26.
14. Ibid., 28.
15. Ronda Leathers Dively, *Preludes to Insight: Creativity, Incubation and Expository Writing* (Cresskill: Hampton Press, 2006), 17–18.
16. Muriel Harris, "Composing Behaviors of One- and Multi-Draft Writers," *College English* 51, no. 2 (1989): 174–91. Harris makes a useful distinction that speaks to the folly of attempting to prescribe a single writing process across writers. In contrast to "one-drafters," "multi-drafters" tend to jump into drafting much earlier without a clear or detailed trajectory for the document. For multi-drafters, the drafting process itself is generative and excessively recursive. One-drafters, on the other hand, would be discombobulated without a well-defined plan prior to drafting, and they tend to engage in less large-scale revision (i.e., their drafting processes typically are less recursive).

engage in plenty of prewriting and always polish their introductions before tackling the remainder of a document.) Once I crossed into the body of a text, however, the efficiency marking my early composing processes decreased significantly as I bore the scourge of writer's block with a perverse tenacity, often sitting at my computer for hours having failed to type a single word.

Of course, the snags that inevitably disrupt complex writing tasks would lead many writers to simply divert their attention elsewhere, and I have thought plenty about why, in contrast, I used to torture myself, chaining myself to my desk chair instead of taking a break. After considerable reflection, I've pretty convincingly traced this behavior back to an image fed to me throughout my schooling that success requires discipline and that procrastination is discipline's enemy. It wasn't until I enrolled in a doctoral seminar on creativity that I realized taking breaks from conscious work on a project is recommended practice as backed by empirical scholarship. Creativity theory refers to this practice as incubation,[17] clearly distinguishing it from procrastination, which is deliberate avoidance for lack of motivation or preparation. Once I understood the difference between incubation and procrastination and began allowing myself to move away from the computer when a block occurred, my writing life changed drastically for the better. It changed not only with respect to the hours I gained in what previously would have been wasted time but also with respect to my attitude toward my craft. I came to know it didn't need to be as painful as it once had been.

The second anecdote I'll share in illustrating the benefits of interdisciplinary inquiry between creative writing and expository writing processes comments on my first stint as an instructor in a university-level academic composition course filled with students who were just starting to become immersed in their major areas of study.[18] Informed by core curriculum guidelines at the institution where I was teaching, my 16-week syllabus required six formal essays, and common practice of the seasoned teachers in the composition program at that time was to assign a different topic for each one. Of course, it probably shouldn't have surprised me that the essays I received under those conditions were largely lackluster, superficial, patched-together rehashings of what my students had read in source materials they consulted. But, at that early stage of my career, it did surprise me, and I couldn't shake the feeling that this situation was not the fault of the students but, rather, an inevitable result of the course design.

---

17. At this point, Chapter 2 begins referencing terms defined in Chapter 1.
18. Ronda Leathers Dively, "Incubating the Expert Persona: Theory and Practice for Enhancing Academic Literacy," *Writing on the Edge* 10, no. 1 (1999): 85–100.

Thankfully, in the same creativity seminar that helped me grow as a writer, I found an answer to the question of how I might help my students grow as writers through this academic writing course. The answer involved incubation, but it required more than that; it also required immersion, or what might be termed "deep preparation." Immersion, which requires time as well as breaks to reflect on what one knows and still needs to learn, is the act of dedicating oneself to a subject matter until familiarity with it is rich enough to enable insight—that is, a fresh contribution or perspective.

With these constructs in mind, I petitioned to alter what had become standard delivery of the course in ways that would allow the students to capitalize on processes that more closely emulate scholarly creativity, or the quest for academic insight. In short, I still required six major writing assignments, but, instead of asking students to write on a different topic for each, I requested that they focus all assignments on the same area of inquiry from different angles or with different purposes. Then, for project six, a research-based article on a topic within their major, they could incorporate ideas and even fully polished prose from any of their former papers. This change allowed them to properly immerse themselves in a subject matter (at least as much as is possible in a single semester), as well as to incubate their ideas—opportunities that resulted in substantially improved academic discourse as contrasted with that I received in the course's previous version.

The terms "incubation," "preparation" and "insight" invoked in the previous anecdotes are elements of the paradigmatic creative process model introduced in Chapter 1. Surprisingly, despite composition studies' fixation on writing processes in past decades, these terms have earned relatively limited cachet in the field's scholarly conversations.[19] Reasons for this relative indifference are difficult to pinpoint. Perhaps it results from the rigid disciplinary divisions mentioned earlier in this chapter, or maybe the blame should be attributed to the mystique of capital "C" creativity[20] (that associated with masterpieces of fiction and poetry) as viewed by teachers and scholars who have been trying to demystify expository composing processes. Still another potential explanation derives from the weight of the four-stage paradigmatic composing process model (invention, drafting, revision, editing), which has dominated expository writing scholarship and instruction as shorthand for representing composition's primary activities.

---

19. See Chapter 1 for a brief overview of this history.
20. The field of creativity studies has long distinguished between "big C" and "little c" creativity, the former being associated with efforts leading to "great works" of art or science that carry a significant cultural impact, the latter being associated with the productive, inventive capacity that all individuals possess.

Whatever the reason, the study described in this book takes for granted that constructs contained in the creative process model have revealed fresh routes for facilitating expository writing and have encouraged developing writers and their teachers to look beyond established composition textbooks and pedagogies for strategies that can lead to more efficient writing processes and better written products. The findings of this study will build on a notable but slim research tradition acknowledged in Hesse's historical overview of composition studies' deliberations over creative writing scholarship, a resurgence of which he hopes will spur "new interest in writing activities and processes."[21] As Hesse depicts it, the thinking that drives this research thread holds that "writing is an art whose techniques are broadly transferable from one situation to another,"[22] and it extends so far as to include processes from arts other than writing.

Investigating transfer between the arts of expository writing and creative writing in this study depends, in part, on the capacity of the paradigmatic creative process model for elucidating the paradigmatic composing process model. The value of the former is realized in its more robust characterizations of writing subprocesses as represented in the composing process model. In addition, the creative process model brings to light additional subprocesses that expository writers should consider, and it clarifies suggested points of emphasis in the effort to promote all creative acts, including expository writing. The section to follow more thoroughly defines the elements constituting both models and discusses how the creative process model, when juxtaposed with the composing process model, expands on potentially superficial interpretations of the latter.

A Closer Look at the Paradigmatic Composing Process and Creative Process Models

Though briefly referenced in this project's research methodology (see Chapter 1), a fleshing out of concepts and terms in the paradigmatic composing process and creative process models is essential to clarifying and affirming this study's assumptions about transfer between these arts, about the research methods employed to analyze creative processes as reported in *The PR* interviews and, ultimately, about the findings and conclusions of this monograph. In many, if not most, scholarly works that invoke them, these models are represented as lists indicating linearly deployed activities; nevertheless, as discussed in Chapter 1, post-process qualifications have cemented

---

21. Hesse, "The Place of Creativity," 43.
22. Ibid., 39.

understanding that the subprocesses accounted for by the models seldom, if ever, occur in lock-step fashion. Rather, they are marked by rampant recursivity, which finds creators/writers circling back, frequently and to varied extent within a given project, to previously engaged subprocesses. With that qualification in mind, this chapter now turns to more fully characterizing elements of both models, beginning with the composing process model so it may then be read through the lens of the creative process model, which expounds on the former as a creative act.

The composing process model: Invention, drafting, revision, editing

Activities associated with early efforts on a writing project are commonly referred to as *invention*. In many of today's composition classrooms, this practice is virtually synonymous with prewriting techniques (e.g., brainstorming and freewriting) or heuristics (e.g., Burke's Pentad and Tagmemics)[23] designed to stimulate critical engagement with a given topic of inquiry. Expository writing instructors regularly assign such mind-stretching exercises at the beginning of major essay units, potentially drawing on the obligatory pages devoted to invention in popular composition textbooks. Of course, prewriting techniques and heuristics are by no means confined to the classroom; professional nonfiction writers depend on them for their livelihoods, as any memoir author, for one example, would likely insist on the necessity of keeping a diary or journal. Beyond prewriting techniques and heuristics, invention also denotes memory search, conversation with others, library and internet research, close reading, as well as empirical research strategies such as observing, interviewing, surveying, conducting experiments, etc. In addition to a focus for writing, invention often leads to at least an initial vision for arranging ideas in the projected document.

Drafting per se can be defined as the moment when a writer feels ready to begin grappling with some sort of formalized response to a writing

---

23. Kenneth Burke, *A Grammar of Motives* (New York: Prentice-Hall, 1952); Richard Young, Alton Becker and Kenneth Pike, *Rhetoric, Discovery and Change* (New York: Harcourt, Brace and World, 1970). In contrast to less-structured prewriting activities such as freewriting, heuristics ordinarily run students through a number of specific questions or tasks with the goal of compelling them to consider a topic from multiple and diverse perspectives. Burke's Pentad asks students to look at a subject from five different perspectives—act, agent, agency, scene, purpose—and to analyze them in relationship to each other. Rooted in Tagmemic linguistic theory and fashioned by Young, Becker and Pike, the Tagmemics heuristic asks students to observe a subject from nine vantage points relevant to viewing it as a unit, part of a system and so on.

invitation—or at least more formalized than products generated in response to invention activities, which typically result in outlines of words and phrases or fledgling sentences and paragraphs. This is the subprocess that aspires to turn a holistic vision or general plan into a series of coherent and effectively ordered paragraphs, often in service of a central claim or thesis. Drafting conjures an image readily associated with a writer's life; that is, it brings to mind an individual locked in concentration on a text with words and sentences streaming from pen or typewriter onto paper or from keyboard onto screen. A particularly taxing aspect of the composing model, drafting involves marrying the requirements of the rhetorical scenario with the specific products of invention into a coherent, cohesive expression. The weight of that exercise frequently triggers cognitive and affective blocks.

To be sure, the challenges of drafting predict the need for *revision*, which is distinguished from editing (the final element of the model to be discussed) by the former's attention to global matters. In the throes of revising, writers may find themselves gauging audience appropriateness, refining focus, further developing certain observations, dropping entire paragraphs and/or rearranging large sections of text, all in the quest to improve the overall quality of a document. Of course, recursivity pervades the subprocesses represented in the composing process model, and many writers will arrest drafting processes to engage in revision as needed, in contrast to waiting until they have a full manuscript. Because the labor of drafting is so intense, revision is viewed by many writers (especially those who are inexperienced) with considerable dread and resistance; others embrace it as further opportunity to realize or hopefully perfect their initial vision. Regardless, revision places the back-and-forth movement associated with composing on full display as authors willfully turn a critical eye on what they have produced so far with the intention of making improvements.

Though also focused on making improvements, *editing* processes are concerned with the surface level of a text and are to some degree synonymous with proofreading. In other words, in contrast to revision, editing's critical eye adopts a narrower gaze, concentrating on issues such as syntax, word choice, spelling, punctuation and other local concerns. Certainly, standard usage as determined by the rhetorical situation draws significant attention during editing processes. As is the case with revision, some writers edit as they draft, just as they may return to inventing in the context of drafting and revising. The point is that, beyond representing a creative act that is anything but linear, editing and the other subprocesses in the model just described will progress and intermingle in myriad ways depending on the writing challenge in question and on the author's composing preferences.

The creative process model: First insight, preparation, incubation, insight, verification

Turning now to the creative process model, *first insight*, or the initial glimmer of an idea for a project, ordinarily manifests in the sense of a promising avenue of inquiry or, at least, a murky impression of a final destination. This subprocess is often portrayed as the intuition or inspiration that propels creativity and, thus, calls to mind the Muses, those goddesses of ancient Greek mythology credited with famous creators' proclivity for conceiving unique responses to creative challenges.[24] Typically, first insight's objective is not formed adequately enough to launch an immediate, comprehensive endeavor at seeing a project to fruition; rather, that glimmer of an idea demands additional scrutiny in the interest of clearing pathways for more specific investigation or sharpening the impression of its eventual culmination.

That's where *preparation* enters the equation. This subprocess encompasses all efforts the creator expends to crystallize first insight. As such, examples of preparation mirror many of those associated with invention in the composing process model, including prewriting exercises and all sorts of library and empirical research. Reflection on experience can also contribute to productive preparation. Of course, because the creative process model covers all creative acts, modes of preparation it represents are potentially more diverse than those tapped for writing alone. For example, a choreographer might deem contorting one's body in unusual positions an essential practice in formulating new moves, whereas a writer would be less inclined to do so unless, perhaps, writing about dance as a subject matter (or finding a comfortable position for writing, which is an environmental versus a cognitive concern).[25] Whatever the discipline, all preparatory activities benefit from studying methods of production, as well as sources of content.

Intermittent with or following preparation, the creator will usually take breaks from conscious attention to the project at hand. These breaks, or bouts of *incubation*, may be voluntary or forced; they may be wholly unconscious (as when dreaming) or partially conscious.[26] They may be long or very brief.

---

24. Some might be inclined to associate the Muses with insight as opposed to first insight, but doing so aligns with a Romantic vision of creativity that negates the necessity of preparation and hard work in arriving at the solution to a creative problem.
25. The findings of this study trace cognitive moves as represented in the creative process model, as well as environmental and affective issues as revealed in emergent patterns. Environmental concerns are choices writers make about their surroundings and their positions within them as distinguished from mental activity focused on the topic of the creative enterprise.
26. Robert M. Olton, "Experimental Studies of Incubation: Searching for the Elusive," *Journal of Creative Behavior* 13, no. 1 (1979): 11. While many creativity researchers

Regardless of the nature or length of breaks, scholars theorize that they enable a more relaxed or less fixated mind to act in unique ways on the material it has stored during preparation. In particular, a relaxed state of mind is theorized to be especially adept at connection-making, more likely to foster unusual associations between ideas than a fully conscious mind that is intensely focused. This unique connection-making power of a loosely focused conscious or the subconscious is widely credited with spawning solutions to creative problems, often on the heels of debilitating mental blocks.

The onset of the solution to a creative problem is referred to as *insight*, also known as the Aha! or Eureka experience. As previously mentioned, insight is distinguished from first insight in that the former emerges after a project is specifically conceived and is in the process of formal development. Whether it occurs moments after beginning to construct a projected artifact or requires years to achieve, it is marked by feelings of exhilaration. Equated with the dissolution of "cognitive dissonance,"[27] insight is a signal that first insight was viable and that preparation was adequate.[28] Still, it is possible to have a misleading or false insight—that is, a belief that the solution has been ascertained only to discover later that it is, in fact, incorrect.

Determining whether an ostensible solution is workable occurs during *verification*. This subprocess of the creative process model involves both evaluation and elaboration of the perceived solution to the task at hand. This is the point at which proposed answers to problems meet sources of assessment informed by standards of the field. Evaluation is necessarily performed by creators themselves, who apply standards for valid insights that they have internalized as members of their disciplinary communities. Upon rendering a positive evaluation of a proposed solution, they feel confident in further elaborating or developing it. Another level of verification occurs once a creative artifact has

---

locate incubation squarely in the unconscious, Olton regards what he calls "creative worrying" as a form of incubation. Creative worrying describes the familiar experience of assuming a problem has been left behind for the moment only to have it pop unwittingly back into conscious attention. Often, creative worrying manifests in a repetitive cycle.

27. Mary M. Murray, *Artwork of the Mind: An Interdisciplinary Description of Insight and the Search for It in Student Writing* (Cresskill: Hampton Press, 1995), 2, 6.
28. Romantic views of creative insight, ala Coleridge's recollections of penning his poem "Kubla Khan," suggest that viable insights can pop into the brain fully formed. While some may indeed come more quickly and in more extensively developed form than others, no credible insight will come to the unprepared mind, one that is not steeped in disciplinary knowledge and the tools of one's craft. Said another way, preparation is cumulative, and at any given moment, the missing piece to the solution of a problem might be encountered, giving the sense of a sudden, almost magical, onset.

been submitted for review to those charged with judging the value or efficacy of contributions to their respective fields. In the end, just as insights may occur at various points in the context of a creative act, so, too, can verification.

The above characterizations of subprocesses constituting the composing process model and the creative process model should provide enough general knowledge about specialized terminology employed in this study to effectively weigh the persuasiveness of its findings and conclusions. But, in addition to understanding the elements of these models, it is essential, in accepting the foundational premises of this study, to grasp how the models align. To be more specific, accepting the trajectory of this research project's central argument—that studying famous fiction writers' and poets' composing processes carries important insights for positively impacting the composing processes of expository writers—requires acknowledging expository writing for the creative process that it is. Juxtaposing the models, exploring their points of intersection, will help illustrate this assertion.

Expository Composition and Creative Production: Two Models Aligned

Those who have spent time writing in any genre, laboring to come up with something insightful to say and articulating it in a way that is comprehensible and engaging, would likely agree that it is a creative enterprise, particularly in the respect that it, like other arts, is a problem-solving activity.[29] One way of corroborating the lessons of experience, at least to some degree, is to observe the significant connections in paradigmatic representations of the processes involved in expository writing and other creative activity, including creative writing. Table 2.1 displays these connections, demonstrating that the processes as separately portrayed expose different points of emphasis but, when viewed side by side, reveal considerable overlap.[30]

---

29. Numerous foundational studies in rhetoric and composition have posited that composition, at its core, is a brand of problem-solving. These studies draw upon work in psychology that places problem-solving at the center of all creative endeavor. See, for example, James Britton et al., *The Development of Writing Ability (11–18)* (London: Macmillan Education, 1975); Linda Flower and John Hayes, "Problem-Solving Strategies and the Writing Process," *College English* 39, no. 4 (December 1977): 449–61; Linda Flower and John Hayes, "The Cognition of Discovery: Defining a Rhetorical Problem," *College Composition and Communication* 31, no. 1 (February 1980): 21–32; Janice Lauer, "Writing as Inquiry: Some Questions for Teachers," *College Composition and Communication* 33, no. 1 (1982): 89–93; Richard Young, Alton Becker and Kenneth Pike, *Rhetoric, Discovery and Change* (New York: Harcourt, Brace and World, 1970).
30. Ronda Leathers Dively, *Invention and Craft: A Guide to College Writing* (New York: McGraw-Hill, 2016), 25.

Table 2.1 The Creative Process Model and Composing Process Model Juxtaposed

Paradigmatic composing process	Paradigmatic creative process
Invention	First insight
	Preparation
	Incubation
Drafting	Insight
Revision	Verification
Editing	

With the composing process model listed on the left and the creative process model listed on the right, the horizontal lines in this table show how, and the extent to which, the subprocesses in the composing process model align with subprocesses in the creative process model. Specifically, the model reveals that invention, or the idea-generating phase of the composing model, potentially subsumes the initial four activities constituting the creative process model: first insight, a vision for the text (possibly murky at first, possibly quite detailed); preparation or research, perhaps in various forms; incubation, time away from the project to ruminate on challenges or blocks impeding the author's vision; and insight, the arrival at a solution to the creative problem. Drafting, at least when it is proceeding smoothly, depends largely on a fairly well-refined insight and a sense that the vision is being effectively translated to the page, a form of verification.

It is at this point—when writers are suspended somewhere between insight and verification, spilling words on to the page rather effortlessly, emboldened by a sense of the text's "rightness"—that writers (and creators in other disciplines) are most likely to experience "flow." Though not an element of the paradigmatic creative process model, flow is a concept frequently addressed in contemporary scholarship on creativity, thanks to the work of Mihaly Csikszentmihalyi. Having popularized the phenomenon in his bestselling book *Flow: The Psychology of Optimal Experience*[31] and revisited it several years later in *Creativity: Flow and the Psychology of Discovery and Invention*, Csikszentmihalyi

---

31. Mihaly Csikszentmihalyi, *Flow: The Psychology of Optimal Experience* (New York: HarperCollins, 1990).

describes flow as "an almost automatic, effortless, yet highly focused state of consciousness" in the midst of "painful, risky, difficult activities that stretch [personal] capacity and [involve] an element of novelty and discovery."[32] This joy-inducing state of mind is a key motivator for all creatives, including writers, agrees Susan K. Perry, who in her book *Writing in Flow* characterizes the construct specifically relevant to poetry and fiction writing:

> You know you've been in flow when time seems to have disappeared [...] you forget yourself and your surroundings. You delight in continuing to write, even if you get no reward for doing it—monetary or otherwise—and even if no one else cares whether you do it. You feel challenged, stimulated, definitely not bored. Writing in flow, you're often certain you're tapping into some creative part of yourself—or of the universe—that you don't have easy access to when you're not in this altered state. Sports figures call this desired condition being "in the zone."[33]

As in all arts, writers in this state are producing at their quickest and best potential. Drafting is proceeding smoothly, and, to the extent that they are aware that their writing is "going well" (i.e., an evaluative judgment), they are edging the boundaries of verification.

Returning to overlap of the models proper, the most explicit manifestations of *verification* are revising and editing. During both of these activities, writers apply increasingly more textured evaluative lenses to a document they consider to be near completion. Regarding the parallels illustrated in Table 2.1, readers should be reminded that all of these processes are recursive, and, thus, across individuals and exercises, they may occur in somewhat random order, may interrupt each other and may be repeated multiple times within a given task. Crucial, then, to productively applying the findings of this study is the observation that the models are most accurately construed as catalogs of tendencies in composing/creative behavior as opposed to formulas for successfully producing written documents or other creative artifacts.

Of course, there exist other models for representing composing/creative activities,[34] but those portrayed above seem most fitting for the purposes

---

32. Mihaly Csikszentmihalyi, *Creativity: Flow and the Psychology of Discovery and Invention* (New York: HarperCollins, 1996), 110.
33. Susan K. Perry, *Writing in Flow: Keys to Enhanced Creativity* (Cincinnati, OH: Writers Digest Books, 1999), 1. Reproduced with permission of Susan K. Perry.
34. For a recent overview of composing process models, see Lauri A. Sharp, "Acts of Writing: A Compilation of Six Models That Define the Processes of Writing," *International Journal of Instruction* 9, no. 2 (July 2016): 77–90. For a recent synthesis of creative process models, see Carol R. Aldous, "Modelling the Creative Process and Cycles of Feedback," *Creative Education* 8 (2017): 1860–77.

of this study given their prevalence and enduring status in the scholarship of their respective disciplines, as well as their succinct depictions of composing/creative subprocesses. In light of the arguments shared in this chapter establishing expository composition as a creative process and because the source of information about writing processes consulted for this study is a collection of interviews with creative writers, subsequent chapters will regularly employ concepts and terminology encompassed by the creative process model. Concepts and terminology encompassed by the composing process model will be relegated to emphasizing applications of findings across genres of writing.

The findings themselves, as presented in Chapters 3 through 7, are perhaps most accurately described as portraits of the elements contained in the creative process model, with each portrait depicting a number of themes or tendencies that serve to define the element in question. Chapter 8, then, constructs portraits of writing practices that are extraneous to the model but, nevertheless, help illuminate its elements and provide depth in representing the act of composing at large. All of these portraits work to illustrate and complicate understanding of the creative process elements as experienced by the featured writers. Appendix C offers diagrams providing at-a-glance depictions of relationships between subcategories and themes characterizing each of the five elements, as well as the emergent patterns. Each subcategory and theme addressed in the findings points to strategies that tend to invite success in the context of creative writing and, by extension, in the context of virtually any expository writing scenario. The next chapter advances the first of the aforementioned portraits.

Chapter 3

FIRST INSIGHT, OR THE GLIMMER OF POSSIBILITY

Arguably the most unnerving period of time in the professional life of any creative individual is the purgatory between projects, when the satisfaction of successfully responding to one artistic or scientific challenge is superseded by the call to get started on the next. The drive to answer this call can be intense, often inciting feelings of desperation as time progresses in the absence of promising, fresh concepts for new endeavors. Relief for this state of being, according to the paradigmatic creative process model, comes in the form of first insight, defined in earlier chapters as the initial glimmer of an idea that serves as a catalyst for innovation. Readers may remember from discussion of the paradigmatic creative process model in Chapter 2 that first insight and insight[1] mimic each other to the extent that both serve as breakthrough moments. However, the former is distinguished by its status as the inception of a creative act and, as follows, by its comparatively underdeveloped nature. Put another way, while insight alleviates cognitive blocks that arise once work on an already formulated project is well underway, first insight alleviates cognitive blocks impeding the birth of a project.[2]

---

1. Insight is defined in Chapter 2, and its relationships to other elements of the creative process model are clarified.
2. Admittedly, the recursive nature of creative/composing processes renders first insight and insight difficult to differentiate at times. For example, certain writers actually compose to generate first insight—that is, they begin writing before they have any sort of destination, murky or otherwise, as a means of finding some direction. In such cases, it might be argued that drafting (which is associated with insight in the alignment of the creative and composing process models in Table 2.1 of Chapter 2) preceded first insight as characterized at the beginning of this chapter. Counter to that is the understanding that drafting, as defined via the composing process model, is a purposeful pursuit of predetermined writing objectives. The sort of composing that typically occurs before a project has even been conceived is more akin to a loosening-up exercise, a stream-of-consciousness-like meandering of pen across paper or fingers across keyboard. If this were to be termed freewriting, which usually is associated with preparation (and, thus, succeeds first insight), the sort of composing that typically occurs before first insight

Instances of first insight reported by fiction writers and poets[3] in *The Paris Review* (*PR*) interviews sampled for this study depict a diversity of experiences, ranging from vague sensations that a revelation is imminent, to flashes of concrete starting points for focused reflection or investigation. The coding process for first insight ultimately yielded 125 references in accordance with the methodology outlined in Chapter 1 and the definition established in the previous paragraph. Although the aforementioned similarities between first insight and insight presented occasional difficulty in assigning textual units to one category over the other, multiple passes through the data reinforced the integrity of the coding scheme.[4] In the end, textual units classified as first insight branched into four distinct subcategories: felt sense, cognitive dissonance, preference for certain literary elements and specific images. The number of subcategories reveals that first insight adopts various guises, an observation that is illustrated in the remainder of this chapter. Discussion of these findings begins with a subcategory characterizing first insight as a highly nebulous phenomenon and then moves through the other subcategories in an order that depicts the construct as increasingly well demarcated and capable of accurately foreshadowing the essence of a final product.

Felt Sense

Many years ago, composition scholar Sondra Perl, with credit to philosopher Eugene Gendlin,[5] published an article in which she applied his concept of "felt sense" to the act of writing, emphasizing its recursive nature and bringing welcome attention to its inherent physicality.[6] Establishing that it may occur with or without a prescribed writing task, Perl explains in her article that felt sense

---

would be considered a different bird in that freewriting categorized as an invention or preparation technique points to a task-specific context, whether that be an author proceeding with at least a topic in mind (which, as Chapter 3 reveals, is regarded as a type of first insight) or, in the classroom, a student responding to a specific writing assignment.

3. Numerous *Paris Review* interviewees cited in this study are deceased, while others are still actively writing. Readers should note, however, that the data analysis to follow does not signal such distinctions.
4. Initial coding revealed significantly more than 125 units for first insight. Nevertheless, on subsequent readings (see the methodology outlined in Chapter 1), as the nature of constructs in the paradigmatic creative process model became more refined relevant to writing in particular, several of those initial units were recoded, often to the category of insight.
5. Eugene Gendlin, *Focusing* (New York: Everest House, 1978).
6. Sondra Perl, "Understanding Composing," *College Composition and Communication* 31 (December 1980): 363–69. After broaching the concept of felt sense in this article, Perl

depends on "careful attention to one's inner reflections" and is frequently signaled by "bodily sensations."[7] While felt sense can coincide with any creative or composing subprocess, Perl concentrates attention on the construct relevant to the genesis of a work, indicating that the impetus to write commonly elicits "vague fuzzy feelings" that are moored in the writer's body and asserting that such stirrings are synonymous with "what professional writers call their 'inner voice' or their feeling of 'inspiration.'"[8] Because such descriptors from Perl's research so perfectly account for a significant number of textual units coded as first insight in this study, "felt sense" seems an obvious label for one of the four subcategories exemplifying the initial element in the creative process model.

In line with Perl's research, each instance of first insight marked as felt sense in this study exhibits a pronounced physicality, typically experienced as some kind of internal impulse of enigmatic quality. Of course, all first insights are inchoate to a certain degree when considered in contrast with their polished articulations. Nevertheless, of the four types of first insight emerging from this analysis, interview passages designated as felt sense are by far the most amorphous. Perhaps not surprisingly, then, the writers inclined to speak in detail about this indicator of creative potential regularly invoke metaphor in hopes, it seems, of representing hard-to-verbalize physical sensations as tangibly as possible.

All metaphors invoked by these writers lend credence to prior research on felt sense, and they are instructive insofar that they make the ineffable at least somewhat more intelligible, portraying it, for example, as a feeling of internal fullness, a surge of momentum or a possibility lurking at the fringes of consciousness.[9] Even more successful en route to intelligibility are metaphors that rely on more acutely tactile imagery, referring to the phenomenon as "a throb," "a tingle," "a scratch on the mind."[10] Still other metaphors dabble in aural imagery as represented in the following observation by novelist Paul

---

expanded her unique take on it in book form several years later. See Sondra Perl, *Felt Sense: Writing with the Body* (New York: Heinemann, 2004).

7. Perl, "Understanding," 366.
8. Ibid., 365, 366.
9. Salman Rushdie, interview by Jack Livings, in *The Paris Review Interviews*, vol. 3, ed. Philip Gourevitch (New York: Picador, 2008), 394; E. B. White, interview by George Plimpton and Frank H. Crowther, in *The Paris Review Interviews*, vol. 4, ed. Philip Gourevitch (New York: Picador, 2009), 138; James M. Cain, interview by David L. Zinsser, in *The Paris Review Interviews*, vol. 1, ed. Philip Gourevitch (New York: Picador, 2006), 224.
10. Martin Amis, interview by Francesca Riviere, in *The Paris Review Interviews*, vol. 3, ed. Philip Gourevitch (New York: Picador, 2008), 335, 336; Isak Dinesen, interview by Eugene Walter, in *The Paris Review Interviews*, vol. 3, ed. Philip Gourevitch (New York: Picador, 2008), 60.

Auster: "Each book I've written has started off with what I'd call a buzz in the head. A certain kind of music or rhythm, a tone. Most of the effort involved in writing a novel for me is trying to remain faithful to that buzz, that rhythm."[11] In a similar vein, poet Ted Hughes recalls his efforts to contain "a kind of musical energy" in the period leading up to his first successful lyric, and he attributes later successes to "tuning in on his own transmission" while "tuning out the influences, the static and the interference."[12]

Auster and Hughes offer some of the most elaborate and specific reflections on felt sense in the interviews sampled for this study. Moreover, their examples affirm a sentiment evident in all the references to this construct: its promise is rooted in an evolved level of self-awareness regarding the paralinguistic aspects of writing. Whether presaging poetry or fiction, felt sense epitomizes, at least more so than other types of first insight, that visceral thrill that many writers associate with composing. It is a revelation on the inside, a gut-level (versus merely cerebral) reassurance that their creative juices are bubbling.

Cognitive Dissonance

Most every branch of psychology, including creativity studies, finds relevance in the concept of cognitive dissonance: "an unpleasant psychological state resulting from inconsistency between two or more elements in a cognitive system" and which is "presumed to involve a state of heightened arousal […] similar to physiological drives (e.g., hunger)." The intellectual discomfort triggered by this state of mind "creates a motivational drive" to eliminate, or at least mitigate, said dissonance.[13] Certainly, one of the most thorough explorations of cognitive dissonance as a springboard for writing is Mary M. Murray's study of insight across a variety of academic disciplines, including composition studies. Murray identifies dissonance as a prerequisite for insight, characterizing it as conscious or unconscious "incongruity" signaled by emotions including "puzzlement, wonder, curiosity, disappointment, and suspicion."[14] In other words, dissonance is the circumstance of having encountered something that needs to be worked through or set right, something that is unfinished and begs for attention. Whether relevant to insight occurring at the genesis of a project or internal to a draft in progress, cognitive dissonance, similarly to felt sense, is associated with

---

11. Paul Auster, interview by Michael Wood, in *The Paris Review Interviews*, vol. 4, ed. Philip Gourevitch (New York: Picador, 2009), 328–29.
12. Ted Hughes, interview by Drue Heinz, in *The Paris Review Interviews*, vol. 3, ed. Philip Gourevitch (New York: Picador, 2008), 296–97.
13. *American Psychological Association Dictionary of Psychology*, s.v. "Cognitive Dissonance," accessed April 9, 2020, https://dictionary.apa.org/cognitive-dissonance.
14. Mary M. Murray, *Artwork of the Mind: An Interdisciplinary Description of Insight and the Search for It in Student Writing* (Cresskill, NJ: Hampton Press, 1995), 24.

feelings. Nevertheless, beyond one's being psychologically based and the other's being physically based, they can be distinguished from each other on two additional counts. First, authors tend to experience felt sense as largely invigorating, whereas they experience cognitive dissonance as largely unsettling. Second, but perhaps not as surprising given their respective channels, authors are able to render memories of cognitive dissonance with greater precision.

Experiences of first-insight-inducing cognitive dissonance in the sample interviews elicit a striking diversity of labels asserting the construct's unsettling nature. Words and phrases used to describe it include uncertainty, uneasiness, apprehension, irritation, anomaly, tension, resistance, dread, a pull of opposites, a need to purge, a lack of direction and even craziness. These labels clearly resonate with definitions of cognitive dissonance in the scholarship cited earlier, as do the additional, most commonly coded descriptors in this study: "problem" and "question"—both of which connote a disquiet state of mind. These two labels take on special significance in the list of descriptors for cognitive dissonance in that interviewees who apply them are typically also able to pinpoint specific conundrums that directly inspired a given project, thereby offering fuller glimpses into the inner workings of their invention processes. Sometimes the problems or questions they identify are singular, and sometimes they are multiple; sometimes they are focused on content, sometimes on form. Regardless, recollections of such moments help concretize the psychological challenges and/or creative uncertainty writers often endure when heeding the call to compose.

Novelist Marilynne Robinson, for example, reflects on the role of religion in her personal and writing life, particularly the way in which it serves in establishing parameters for her craft. Raised in a devout family, she views religion as a "framing mechanism" that, through a lengthy period of history, has pervaded the "high arts."[15] Specifically, relevant to problem- or inquiry-based cognitive dissonance, she acknowledges:

> Religion [...] is a language of orientation that presents itself as a series of questions. It talks about the arc of life and the quality of experience in ways that I've found fruitful to think about. [...] We're cultural creatures and meaning doesn't simply generate itself out of thin air; it's sustained by a cultural framework.[16]—Copyright © by *The Paris Review*, used by permission of The Wylie Agency LLC and with permission of Sarah Fay.

---

15. Marilynne Robinson, interview by Sarah Fay, in *The Paris Review Interviews*, vol. 4, ed. Philip Gourevitch (New York: Picador, 2009), 444, 448.
16. Ibid., 448.

Although admittedly not as troubling as the examples to come, this instance of first insight in the form of question-fueled cognitive dissonance is worth highlighting for its allusion to constructive constraints as represented by the boundaries of a conceptual space, which creativity specialist Margaret Boden characterizes as a set of "organizing principles that unify and give structure to a given domain of thinking," a "generative system that underlies that domain and defines a certain range of possibilities: chess moves, or molecular structures, or jazz melodies." Along with this definition, Boden names English grammar as a conceptual space, using a single sentence from Dickens's *A Christmas Carol* to show how expectations of that space can be tweaked (exhibiting a novelty in expression) by effectively employing seven adjectives, as opposed to the typical few, in describing a character (Scrooge).[17] When creators explore the boundaries of a conceptual space as such, they are exhibiting a form of creativity within a given knowledge domain.

Returning to Robinson's example, it seems apparent that, for her, religion is a knowledge domain rich with conceptual spaces to be explored, and that thinking about those spaces' possibilities and limitations—particularly as they intersect with conceptual spaces in the knowledge domain of literature—stimulates an endless flood of avenues for inquiry. As exciting as that prospect can be, the strife of negotiating the boundaries between constraint and freedom relevant to conceptual spaces can spawn career-defining struggles as writers seek to maintain a level of recognizability within a domain (or intersecting domains) so they will be regarded as credible while simultaneously pushing against constraints in ways that will set them apart from crowds of other writers and mark them as original or innovative.

As a reminder of the enabling qualities attributed to exploring knowledge domains and conceptual spaces, Robinson's reflection on religion as a framework for conceiving projects is instructive as it broaches a type of ongoing, broad-based manifestation of cognitive dissonance. But, as implied earlier, more precisely articulated examples of the construct abound. Toni Morrison's interview, for instance, points to a specific series of works when discussing first insight, as well as a list of questions that drove those works. Confessing that some of her ideas are actually mundane, she insists that she turns all of them into questions that challenge her understanding, and she offers the following anecdote in illustration:

> Specifically, since I began the *Beloved* trilogy [...] I have been wondering why women who are twenty, thirty years younger than I am are no happier than women who are my age and older. What on earth is that about,

---

17. Margaret Boden, "What Is Creativity?," in *Dimensions of Creativity*, ed. Margaret Boden (Cambridge, MA: MIT Press, 1996), 79.

when there are so many more things that they can do, so many more choices? [...] Why is everybody so miserable?—Copyright © by *The Paris Review*, used by permission of The Wylie Agency LLC and with permission of Claudia Brodsky.

Morrison goes on to explain that, ultimately, the questions she ponders when starting a book reveal a core idea that yields even more questions for her to consider, thus drawing out the complexity or vulnerability of that core idea. Rather than writing out of what she, in the moment, believes the answers to the initial questions might be, she strives to regard them as open-ended so that the processes of overcoming the dissonance remain highly exploratory.[18]

Another illustration of cognitive dissonance represented in the form of questions surfaces in an interview with horror story aficionado Stephen King, whose rumination on the inception of *Cujo* reveals a mind locked in rapid-fire interrogation of a possible story line that materialized in the midst of prosaic daily activity.[19] On the heels of a visit to a motorcycle mechanic's shop where he met a huge and aggressive St. Bernard, King reportedly began reflecting on how he might turn the fear that gripped him during that encounter into a novel. Struggling to forge a conflict more captivating than a man possibly being attacked by a large dog, he suddenly wondered weeks after the encounter what would have happened if—instead of his making the trip to that shop on his motorcycle—it had been his wife in their beat-up Ford Pinto, and it had stalled. That thought, he explains, launched a series of questions pointing to a potential plot:

> Instead of the dog just being a mean dog, what if the dog was really crazy? [...] Then I thought, Maybe its rabid. That's when something really fired over in my mind. [...] Well why didn't somebody come to rescue her? People live there. It's a farmhouse. Well, you say, that's part of the story. Where are they? [...] Where is her husband? Why didn't her husband come and rescue her? I don't know, that's part of the story. What happens if she gets bitten by that dog? And that was going to be part of the story. What if she starts to get rabid?[20]—Copyright © by *The Paris Review*, used by permission of The Wylie Agency LLC and with permission of the estate of Christopher Lehmann-Haupt. Excerpts from *The Paris Review* Interviews by Stephen King. Copyright © 2006

---

18. Toni Morrison, interview by Elissa Schappell and Claudia Brodsky Lacour, in *The Paris Review Interviews*, vol. 2, ed. Philip Gourevitch (New York: Picador, 2007), 364.
19. This example also speaks to the power of connection-making, which is addressed more fully in Chapter 6 on insights achieved later in the creative act.
20. Stephen King, interview by Christopher Lehmann-Haupt and Nathaniel Rich, in *The Paris Review Interviews*, vol. 2, ed. Philip Gourevitch (New York: Picador, 2007), 467–68.

by Stephen King. All rights reserved. Used courtesy of Darhansoff & Verrill Literary Agents.

Although he later realized the inefficacy of extending the plot to account for rabies' long incubation period, this barrage of questions ushered in a set of problems that provided scaffolding for his narrative. In this recounting of *Cujo*'s genesis, King offers the most detailed portrait of question-based, dissonance-inducing first insight in all the interviews consulted for this study.

While, obviously, questions can serve to isolate problems, many of the interviewees who equate first insight with dissonance frame it as a problem per se. William Gaddis falls into this subcategory, and his interview is uniquely intriguing for its focus on methods of structuring literature as opposed to generating literary content. In response to his *PR* interviewer's query about the impetus for writing the novel *Carpenter's Gothic*, Gaddis states, "I cannot really work unless I set a problem for myself to solve." Describing that problem as setting up an "exercise in style and technique," he speaks about his desire to write "a shorter book, one that observes the unities of time and place to the point that everything, even though it expands into the world, takes place in one house, and a country house at that, with a small number of characters, in a short span of time."[21] The cognitive dissonance that initiated this work, then, had little to do with a desire to pursue a given observation about the human condition or an actual occurrence as it did, respectively, with Morrison and King. Instead, the dissonance that Gaddis describes centers on the challenge of experimenting with the margins of form in contradiction to the predictable.

Whether rooted in content or technique, cognitive dissonance as a harbinger of first insight places emphasis on problem-finding in the context of creativity. Indeed, as was established decades ago in the context of creativity scholarship, problem-finding capacity is as crucial as problem-solving capacity in determining the quality of an end product, and that conviction—having been validated in numerous empirical studies—has not changed over time.[22] That realization serves to heighten the profile of first insight in the creative process model, endorsing its addition to Wallas's initial rendering of the creative act by placing additional emphasis on the mental labor that must occur before a creative individual is able to actually prepare for and assemble an artifact.[23]

---

21. William Gaddis, interview by Zoltan Abadi-Nagy, in *The Paris Review Interviews*, vol. 2, ed. Philip Gourevitch (New York: Picador, 2007), 277–78.
22. Ahmed M. Abdulla et al., "Problem Finding and Creativity: A Meta-Analytic Review," *Psychology of Aesthetics, Creativity, and the Arts* 14, no. 1 (2020): 3–14.
23. See Chapter 2 for a discussion of the creative process model and its history.

Preference for Given Literary Elements

William Gaddis's description of first insight in the previous section privileges certain elements of fiction, particularly as they become sources of cognitive dissonance—that is, he confronts the problem of how he might deploy them in unexpected ways in a given novel. It is his emphasis on dissonance that distinguishes his portrayal of first insight from those assigned to the subcategory now under review. Although the textual units assigned to this subcategory also speak of fixations on literary elements or structure, this brand of first insight ostensibly bred little if any dissonance. Moreover, in these instances, preference for a certain element or elements is commonly portrayed as an ongoing and ordinarily pleasant preoccupation; even for writers who are known for experimenting with form, many of the anecdotes in this subcategory indicate persistent privileging of a given element over a lengthy period of time. While references to structure dominate this subcategory, writers also designate theme and character as rich resources of first insight. Less frequently cited literary features include mood, plot and micro-level issues such as individual words, phrases or sentences.

Relevant to the most frequently referenced literary element, arrangement, Ted Hughes's interview transcript effectively represents the nature of this subcategory in a passage that weighs the facilitative powers of strictures defining "traditional" poetic forms (which he practiced for some time) in contrast to the liberties of free verse. Specifically, he attests that "it's not just that rhymes and the requirement of meter actually stimulate invention—which they obviously do, at certain levels—but it's the strange satisfaction of making that square treasure chest and packing it."[24] With this observation, Hughes credits a preexisting sense of structure with the genesis of his poetry by noting that the material to pack the container comes *after* identifying the container itself. Hughes's experience echoes that of T. S. Eliot, who acknowledges that, during a span of time working in formal verse, "form gave the impetus to content."[25] Haruki Murakami also finds structure facilitative, but with a notable twist: claiming that he's especially attuned to form, he works from the desire to undo the edifice of his previous book in search of a fresh approach.[26]

Next to structure, theme and character are the most prolific instigators of first insights in this subcategory. In fact, Gabriel Garcia Marquez outrightly attributes his inspirations to theme, contending that finding the right one

---

24. Hughes, *The Paris Review Interviews*, 273, 304.
25. T. S. Eliot, interview by Donald Hall, in *The Paris Review Interviews*, vol. 1, ed. Philip Gourevitch (New York: Picador, 2006), 70.
26. Haruki Murakami, interview by John Wray, in *The Paris Review Interviews*, vol. 4, ed. Philip Gourevitch (New York: Picador, 2009), 352.

facilitates the work yet to come."[27] Others demonstrate this connection by relating specific themes they turn to again and again because their fascination with them is enabling. Jan Morris, for example, credits continued rumination on empire with the genesis of her renowned works,[28] while Maya Angelou reports gravitating toward moments in her life marked by themes packing emotional significance, such as cruelty, generosity and so on.[29] Also musing on theme as an unending source of starting points for creative production, Orhan Pamuk recognizes how his writings about Turkey and its relationship to the West are reminiscent of his ongoing infatuation with the topic of competition between him and his brother.[30]

References to character are nearly as prolific as those to theme, but the former is rarely discussed separately from the latter. Furthermore, when character is mentioned, the depiction is typically nonspecific, possibly because returning again and again (as one might do with theme) to the same character wouldn't offer the same level of variability. Indicative of this pattern, Georges Simenon, within his highly methodical approach to composing (which involves "planning envelopes" documenting traits of protagonists and antagonists), discusses how the conception of characters in relation to largely unconscious notions of theme or atmosphere solidifies his direction.[31] In like fashion, Chinua Achebe observes that, ordinarily, "the general idea is the first [element to come], followed by the major characters." He proceeds to explain: "We live in a sea of general ideas. But the moment a particular idea is linked to a character, it's like an engine moves it. Then you have a novel underway."[32]

While references to structure, theme and character abound in this subcategory of first insight, they aren't necessarily the most striking or elaborated. With what reads primarily as a nod to plot, Eliot celebrates "Greek myth as a springboard of sorts," providing a "*situation*" (emphasis added) that the author can rethink in modern terms via fresh characters and events.[33]

---

27. Gabriel Garcia Marquez, interview by Peter H. Stone, in *The Paris Review Interviews*, vol. 2, ed. Philip Gourevitch (New York: Picador, 2007), 197.
28. Jan Morris, interview by Leo Lerman, in *The Paris Review Interviews*, vol. 3, ed. Philip Gourevitch (New York: Picador, 2008), 310.
29. Maya Angelou, interview by George Plimpton, in *The Paris Review Interviews*, vol. 4, ed. Philip Gourevitch (New York: Picador, 2009), 244.
30. Orhan Pamuk, interview by Angel Gurria-Quintana, in *The Paris Review Interviews*, vol. 4, ed. Philip Gourevitch (New York: Picador, 2009), 388.
31. Georges Simenon, interview by Carvel Collins, in *The Paris Review Interviews*, vol. 3, ed. Philip Gourevitch (New York: Picador, 2008), 26–27.
32. Chinua Achebe, interview by Jerome Brooks, in *The Paris Review Interviews*, vol. 3, ed. Philip Gourevitch (New York: Picador, 2008), 257.
33. Eliot, *The Paris Review Interviews*, 77.

More graphically representing the possibilities of a glimpse into plot, John Cheever relates the following: "There's a stock beginning that I've always had in mind: Someone is coming back from a year in Italy on a Fulbright scholarship. His trunk is opened in customs, and instead of his clothing and souvenirs, they find the mutilated body of an Italian seaman, everything there but his head." Cheever also alludes to the power of fully formed sentences as catalysts for composing, naming one that continually intrigued him: "The first day I robbed Tiffany's, it was raining."[34] Gabriel Garcia Marquez also talks about the power of first lines, but he needs an entire paragraph as opposed to sentences; for him, that initial paragraph functions as a roadmap for the entire novel, and, once he's got it, the remainder proceeds fairly easily.[35]

Regardless of the literary element or feature that a fiction writer or poet tends to privilege, this subcategory of first insight establishes that the tools of literary production, in and of themselves, are generative. Uniting all the anecdotes highlighted in this section is the idea that the whole of a product emerges from up-front and deep reflection on what are projected to be its essential parts. Writers who portray first insight in this way find solace in the promise that, once one or two of these parts are in place, the trajectory for the work in question is sound. Interviewees who speak of first insight in these terms seem to have a more definitive sense—in contrast to reflections on felt sense and cognitive dissonance—of where the proposed literary work is headed.

Specific Images

In sync with that trend, a particular literary element—one so liberally cited that it earned its own subcategory—provides additional examples of first insight that carries a comprehensive sense of the end product. Instances of that element, imagery, are overwhelmingly visual and singular in nature as reported in the interviews though, occasionally, they did visit in sets. Whatever their exact nature, while a few remain unnamed, sources for most of the images are identified as externally located (see the examples to come). Of course, all the images to be shared in this section coincide with the moment that the interviewee sensed a new project was at hand, but it must be stressed relevant to this study's coding scheme that an image's generative capacity doesn't necessarily translate to its being placed at the beginning of the final literary product. On the contrary, it might surface in the middle or end of a work, or it might not even survive the journey to the published version of a poem, short story or novel. The point

---

34. John Cheever, interview by Annette Grant, in *The Paris Review Interviews*, vol. 3, ed. Philip Gourevitch (New York: Picador, 2008), 160.
35. Garcia Marquez, *The Paris Review Interviews*, 196.

is, regardless of what ultimately happens to it, in order to be identified as first insight, an image must be paramount in originally conceiving the project.

For example, while commenting on the relationship between concepts and emotion in poetry, Robert Lowell offers the following example of the interplay between image and his polished verse: "Some little image, some detail you've noticed—you're writing about a little country shop, just describing it, and your poem ends up with an existentialist account of your experience. But it's the shop that started it off."[36] Another prolific poet, Ted Hughes, shares that, when he "look(s) for or get(s) hold of" an idea for a poem that integrates all of his "deepest feelings," it often coincides with the image of an animal, presumably because "that's the deepest, earliest language that [his] imagination learned." Having spent the better part of his childhood and teenage years utterly fascinated with them, he claims they "became a language—a symbolic language that is also the language of [his] whole life."[37]

Turning from poetry to fiction, one of the most vivid recollections of image-based first insight in *The PR* interviews sampled for this study surfaces in a conversation with William Faulkner about the impetus for *The Sound and the Fury*. Specifically, Faulkner recalls:

> It began with a mental picture. I didn't realize at the time it was symbolical. The picture was of the muddy seat of a little girl's drawers in a pear tree, where she could see through a window where her grandmother's funeral was taking place and report what was happening to her brothers on the ground below. By the time I explained who they were and what they were doing and how her pants got muddy, I realized it would be impossible to get all of it into a short story and that it would have to be a book. And then I realized the symbolism of the soiled pants, and that image was replaced by the one of the fatherless and motherless girl climbing down the drainpipe to escape from the only home she had, where she had never been offered love or affection or understanding.[38]—Copyright © by *The Paris Review*, used by permission of The Wylie Agency LLC. William Faulkner, "The Art of Fiction #12." Copyright © 1956 by Jean Stein. All rights not specifically granted herein are hereby reserved to the Licensor.

---

36. Robert Lowell, interview by Frederick Seidel, in *The Paris Review Interviews*, vol. 2, ed. Philip Gourevitch (New York: Picador, 2007), 95.
37. Hughes, *The Paris Review Interviews*, 293.
38. William Faulkner, interview by Jean Stein, in *The Paris Review Interviews*, vol. 2, ed. Philip Gourevitch (New York: Picador, 2007), 44.

Later in that same conversation, Faulkner affirms that, for him, "a story usually begins with a single idea or memory or mental picture" toward which he begins writing so as to explain how the event or situation it captures came to be.[39] Another vivid account of the capacity of imagery to initiate a project is John Gardner's depiction of the pre-composition agony that led to his writing the short story "Redemption." Portraying the project as one that wouldn't be ignored no matter how hard he tried, he describes a nightmarish scene that essentially assumed control over him:

> For instance, before I wrote the story about the kid who runs over his younger brother [...] always, regularly, every day I used to have four or five flashes of that accident. I'd be driving down the highway and I couldn't see what was coming because I'd have a memory flash. I haven't had it once since I wrote the story. You really do ground your nightmares, you name them. When you write a story, you have to play that image, no matter how painful, over and over until you've got all the sharp details so you know exactly how to put it down on paper.[40]—Copyright © by *The Paris Review*, used by permission of The Wylie Agency LLC and with permission of the Brockport Writers Forum.

This reflection, in concert with those shared by Lowell, Hughes and Faulkner, epitomizes the overriding nature of textual units coded to this subcategory; the images are visual and singular and collectively illustrate that, despite an image's generative power, its exact role in the final product may differ across writing situations.

The images in the previous paragraphs are rooted primarily in experience or author imagination—or at least the writer doesn't indicate otherwise. In contrast, Gabriel Garcia Marquez speaks openly about the contribution of other art forms in providing the images that stimulate his work. At his interviewer's prompting to speak about the way he tends to get started, Garcia Marquez responds as follows:

> I've got a photography book that I'm going to show you. I've said on various occasions that in the genesis of all my books there's always an image. The first image I had of *The Autumn of the Patriarch* was a very old man in a very luxurious palace into which cows come and eat the

---

39. Ibid., 48.
40. John Gardner, interview by Paul F. Ferguson, John R. Maier, Frank McConnell and Sara Matthiessen, in *The Paris Review Interviews*, vol. 2, ed. Philip Gourevitch (New York: Picador, 2007), 169.

curtains. But that image didn't concretize until I saw the photograph. In Rome I went into a bookshop where I started looking at photography books, which I like to collect. I saw this photograph, and it was just perfect. I just saw that was how it was going to be.[41]—Copyright © by *The Paris Review*, used by permission of The Wylie Agency LLC.

Similarly to Garcia Marquez, lyricist and musical composer Stephen Sondheim also looks to other art forms for inspiration, as displayed in the following anecdote summarizing a collaboration with experimental playwright James Lapine, in which the two turn to paintings for a possible way in to what might be the content of their next musical (*Sunday in the Park with George*):

We were talking one night about theme and variations, because that's a kind of show I had always wanted to do. I showed him a French magazine I had that was devoted to variations on the Mona Lisa. And we started talking about paintings. He had used the Seurat painting La Grande Jatte in a piece he had done up at Yale. And he said, Did you ever notice there are over fifty people in it and nobody's looking at anybody else? We started to speculate why. Suddenly I said, It's like a stage set, you know. It's like a French farce, isn't it? You know, maybe those people aren't supposed to be seen with each other. We started to talk about how it might make a story, and then James said the crucial thing: Of course, the main character's missing. I said, Who? He said, The painter. As soon as he said that, we knew we had a show.[42]—Copyright © by *The Paris Review*, used by permission of The Wylie Agency LLC and with permission of the estate of James Lipton.

Additional external forms touted in the interviews as wellsprings for images capable of germinating fiction and poetry include comic books, films and newspaper articles. But regardless of the source, perhaps the most distinct quality of textual units coded to the subcategory of images is their particularity, the kind of particularity that moves the writer more immediately to the substance of a poem or narrative, to what exactly will be described or what exactly will take place—in contrast to units constituting the other subcategories, which proffer more elusive starting points on the whole.

---

41. Garcia Marquez, *The Paris Review Interviews*, 194.
42. Stephen Sondheim, interview by James Lipton, in *The Paris Review Interviews*, vol. 4, ed. Philip Gourevitch (New York: Picador, 2009), 274.

An Additional Trend Worth Noting: Direct Experience and "Spontaneous Generation"

Although some of the images characterized in the previous section were borne of direct experience, it should be noted that sometimes, as opposed to crystallizing in mere snapshots requiring elaboration, direct experiences translate to surprisingly comprehensive renderings of a story or poem. Such instances didn't achieve the threshold of occurrences for surviving this study's coding process for subcategories of first insight.[43] Nevertheless, the phenomenon warrants mention as a way of ending this chapter because it is reminiscent of long-reigning Romantic takes on invention whereby, in a single moment, a project seems to burst forth in its entirety or, at least, in a way that immediately reveals and connects most of the dots required for bringing a poem or fictional piece to full fruition.[44] In one of the most impressive examples of spontaneous generation based on direct experience, Eudora Welty recalls writing her story "Powerhouse" in a single evening after feeling inspired by a concert she attended.[45] Similarly, E. B. White speaks about the swift arrival of a story based on a visit to the Bronx zoo where he witnessed a doe delivering a couple of fawns.[46] Though not referring to a wholly developed story per se, P. G. Wodehouse remembers conceiving characters and the entire plot for one of his books at the moment he received a new ledger in support of his work entering deposits at a bank that temporarily employed him.[47] And Stephen King suggests that the story "Cell" came to life in analogous fashion when he recalls that the simple experience of encountering a woman talking on her phone in front of a New York City hotel resulted in his instantly apprehending a protagonist, a riveting conflict and all eventualities that might proceed from them.[48]

Admittedly, for first insights stimulated by direct experience, there exists a rather thin line between those ushering in only parts of works and those spawning elaborated outlines of stories or even entire drafts in one fell swoop. Pertinent to the latter, however, it is noteworthy that there are very few such instances reported in the larger scheme of this discourse analysis—this despite

---

43. See discussion of the methodology in Chapter 1 for specifics.
44. This myth is also brought to mind relevant to other subcategories identified in this discourse analysis. See especially Chapter 5 on incubation and Chapter 6 on insight.
45. Eudora Welty, interview by Linda Kuehl, in *The Paris Review Interviews*, vol. 2, ed. Philip Gourevitch (New York: Picador, 2007), 132.
46. White, *The Paris Review Interviews*, 139.
47. P. G. Wodehouse, interview by Gerald Clarke, in *The Paris Review Interviews*, vol. 4, ed. Philip Gourevitch (New York: Picador, 2009), 163.
48. King, *The Paris Review Interviews*, 471.

the prevalence of the spontaneous generation myth in literary history and its detrimental effects on writers. Unfortunately, that myth has undermined many aspiring poets and novelists who fell prey to the age-old yarn that, for the truly gifted or capable, creativity is a matter of inexplicable inspiration as opposed to extensive groundwork, planning and mental and physical exertion. While in this study and elsewhere there do exist anecdotes of authors claiming to have received, in an instant, an entire poem or short story in perfected form,[49] the vast majority of writers cited in this chapter (actually, across the entire corpus of interviews sampled for this study) characterize creative activity as calculated and rigorous. This finding is in keeping with the current status of knowledge in the discipline of creativity studies, which long ago debunked the notion of "great works" (in any field) emerging from a vacuum.

In fact, most of the authors surveyed for this study view the birth of a piece or first insight as it is defined in the paradigmatic creative process model: that is, as the glimmer of an idea for a story or poem. And for most of the authors, that glimmer requires considerable follow-up work, sometimes in the form of strenuous, multilayered redrafting and sometimes in the form of extensive research or what the creative process model identifies as preparation. Accordingly, preparation is the subject of the next chapter, which clarifies how certain authors positioned themselves to elaborate their first insights through additional inquiry into the target subject matter or (in recursive fashion) through deeper reflection on personal and professional encounters and endeavors that gave life to first insights.

---

49. Of course, while the work may have felt spontaneously generated, the more likely explanation is that years of experience and thought abruptly converged with additional key stimuli—the sudden onset of flow in articulating the poem or story making it only seem spontaneously generated. Read more about such matters in subsequent chapters.

Chapter 4

PREPARATION, OR RESEARCH BROADLY CONCEIVED

In the trajectory of any given artistic or scientific endeavor, the sense of excitement attending first insight (see Chapter 3)—as well as the subsequent insights crucial to realizing an initial vision (see Chapter 6)—often gives way to memories of prolonged, unglamorous, mentally and physically taxing groundwork essential to creative achievement. Such groundwork falls under "preparation" in the paradigmatic creative process model, the term no doubt bringing to mind (in line with the definition in Chapter 1) images of lonely individuals locked in various modes of formal research: a chemist vetting the most recently published articles in her field to determine relevance for a current experiment, a painter meticulously observing the landscape he's decided to depict on canvas, a playwright devouring biographies of the famous character she's struggling to portray. All of these activities qualify as preparation, but this element of the creative process model is far more wide-ranging than these examples imply. In addition to formal research lies the instructive potential of virtually all experiences and relationships, both personal and professional. In the end, then, it is reasonable to assume that every aspect of an artist's or scientist's existence is a possible resource for preparation.

Excerpts classified as preparation from *The Paris Review* (*PR*) interviews sampled for this study demonstrate that poets and fiction writers rely on varied means of acquiring knowledge or information needed to satisfy their creative aspirations. As expected, these writers collectively reference a diversity of formal research strategies, as well as periods of deep reflection on significant life events from early childhood through late adulthood. Frequently, preparatory effort follows directly upon first insights; at other times, in recursive fashion, it commences or resurfaces when a project in question is well underway. Because the category of preparation is so sweeping and eclectic, it demonstrates more glaringly than any other category in this study the interpretive nature of the coding processes as recognized in the permeable boundaries of not only the subcategories to be identified but also the themes within those subcategories.

Despite the challenges of assigning textual units (a total of 490) relevant to preparation, they convincingly align in six viable, if admittedly overlapping, subcategories: mentorship, distinctive personal experiences, formal research, study of others' literary works, prewriting strategies and cross-pollination between disciplines. As noted above, while virtually every aspect of existence might be viewed as contributing to an artist's preparation, this analysis seeks to disaggregate strategies, and the most reliable avenue for doing so is isolating writer commentary that directly attributes literary success or progress in composing to a specific technique or occurrence. In accordance with that stipulation, then, the remainder of this chapter explores the remarkable array of phenomena that reportedly helped the interviewees acquire knowledge or understanding essential to realizing their professional goals.

Mentorship

This subcategory encompasses both informal and formal educational experiences that directly or indirectly supported the interviewees' early literacy development and/or their later composing endeavors. Such formative influences appear to have sparked special interest in the interviewees, as many of the transcripts reveal an eagerness to expound on memories of specific individuals and contexts for learning perceived as instrumental in bolstering their literary sensibilities and capabilities. These memories collectively span an interval of time from early childhood to young adulthood, capped in many cases by a college degree. Considering that no strict patterns emerge regarding the age at which a particular experience occurred or needed to occur to prove significant, the analysis to follow proceeds thematically as opposed to chronologically.

Turning to the most dominant theme, the interviewees' young lives were steeped in story. Many grew up in homes filled with books and with relatives who, regardless of profession, loved to read in their spare time, both classical and popular literature. This love of reading was passed on in some cases through passive example and, quite commonly, through the art of storytelling. Familial efforts to cultivate a love for literature often involved performance, whether poetic recitation, oral tale-spinning about family history or enactment of scenes from a favorite novel or play. Novelist John Gardner effectively represents the full tenor of such home-based learning in response to a question about his boyhood exposure to literature:

> We had a lot of books. My mother was a schoolteacher, and my father was a farmer who loved to read: classics, Shakespeare, and of course, the Bible. They were great reciters of literature, too. I've had visitors—sophisticated people—who've heard my father recite things, and have

been amazed at how powerfully he does it. It's an old country tradition, but my father was and is the best. We'd be put to bed with a recital of poetry, things like that. At Grange meetings, for instance, my mother and father would do recitations as part of the evening's entertainment. Or while my father was milking the cows my mother would come out and read something to him—Lear, say—leaving out the part of whomever my father felt like being that day.[1]—Copyright © by *The Paris Review*, used by permission of The Wylie Agency LLC and with permission of the Brockport Writers Forum.

Complementing a devotion to reading, the rich oral traditions exhibited by many of the interviewees' families served to secure access to and enliven works of literature that might otherwise have confounded the analytical capabilities of developing minds. Moreover, the penchant for storytelling exhibited by parents, siblings and grandparents transferred to the would-be authors themselves, with several connecting their desire to write with the joy they felt while entertaining friends and classmates in like manner. Importantly, these authors' home cultures, which so highly valued reading and storytelling, provided prolonged apprenticeships in matters of content, structure and style and paved the way for levels of enjoyment, intrigue and immersion that ignited lifelong dedication to craft.

The above overview of family initiated reading and storytelling portrays a sort of indirect mentorship, the type that doesn't necessarily set out to produce poets and fiction writers but that often does so by demonstrating an affinity for all things literary, for the entertainment value derived from sharing inspiring or instructive tales. Interspersed with such recollections of indirect mentorship in the interview transcripts are examples of direct mentorship by relatives who, with authorial ambitions of their own, were key in fostering the interviewees' understanding of what makes for publishable literature and what it takes to sustain an author's existence. In certain cases, these special mentors were interviewees' parents, some of who aspired to be published and some of who were already accomplished writers, as was the case with the fathers of Isak Dinesen, V. S. Naipaul and Martin Amis. More specifically, Dinesen considers her appetite for the adventure of living in and writing about Africa to be expected in the wake of her father's career,[2] and Naipaul praises the

---

1. John Gardner, interview by Paul F. Ferguson, John R. Maier, Frank McConnell and Sara Matthiessen, in *The Paris Review Interviews*, vol. 2, ed. Philip Gourevitch (New York: Picador, 2007), 160.
2. Isak Dinesen, interview by Eugene Walter, in *The Paris Review Interviews*, vol. 3, ed. Philip Gourevitch (New York: Picador, 2008), 54.

self-examination and cultural critique in his father's stories as having deeply impacted him.[3] Martin Amis speaks at length on what he views as a complicated yet ultimately edifying relationship with his famous father, whose frequently aloof demeanor spurred a critical detachment necessary to effectively rendering life in prose and whose status lent him a sense of security that his own work would be seriously regarded.[4]

Continuing with the theme of direct mentorship, several interviewees enjoyed the good fortune of crossing paths with renowned writers who, though unrelated, generously offered time, expertise and access to publishers. For example, as a young man working in New Orleans, William Faulkner befriended Sherwood Anderson, who, after mornings devoted to working on his latest novel, shared countless leisurely afternoons with the aspiring novelist, touring the city and talking. Reflecting on time spent with Anderson, Faulkner relays a humorous anecdote about the effect this famous author had on his career:

> I decided if that was the life of a writer, then becoming a writer was the thing for me. So I began to write my first book. At once I found that writing was fun. I even forgot that I hadn't seen Mr. Anderson for three weeks until he walked in my door, the first time he ever came to see me, and said, "What's wrong? Are you mad at me?" I told him I was writing a book. He said, "My God," and walked out. When I finished the book—it was *Soldiers' Pay*—I met Mrs. Anderson on the street. She asked how the book was going, and I said I'd finished it. She said, "Sherwood says that he will make a trade with you. If he doesn't have to read your manuscript he will tell his publisher to accept it." I said, "Done," and that's how I became a writer.[5]—Copyright © by *The Paris Review*, used by permission of The Wylie Agency LLC. William Faulkner, "The Art of Fiction #12." Copyright © 1956 by Jean Stein. All rights not specifically granted herein are hereby reserved to the Licensor.

While Anderson apparently didn't advise Faulkner regarding elements of the fiction he was drafting, he modeled the author-life, supplied intellectual companionship and smoothed the ordinarily rough journey toward seeing one's work in print. Another example of direct mentorship by an established

---

3. V. S. Naipaul, interview by Tarun Tejpal and Jonathan Rosen, in *The Paris Review Interviews*, vol. 4, ed. Philip Gourevitch (New York: Picador, 2009), 290.
4. Martin Amis, interview by Francesca Riviere, in *The Paris Review Interviews*, vol. 3, ed. Philip Gourevitch (New York: Picador, 2008), 339–40.
5. William Faulkner, interview by Jean Stein, in *The Paris Review Interviews*, vol. 2, ed. Philip Gourevitch (New York: Picador, 2007), 49.

author surfaces in an interview with Robert Lowell, who recounts the import of his relationship with Richard Eberhart, a professor at the university Lowell attended. Though he didn't have opportunity to take a class with Eberhart, Lowell regularly sought him out, and the professor responded graciously:

> He'd read aloud and we'd talk, he was very pleasant that way. He'd smoke honey-scented tobacco, and read Baudelaire and Shakespeare and Hopkins—it made the thing living—and he'd read his own poems. I wrote very badly at first, but he was encouraging and enthusiastic. That probably was decisive, that there was someone there whom I admired who was engaged in writing poetry.[6]—Copyright © by *The Paris Review*, used by permission of The Wylie Agency LLC.

In contrast with what Anderson did for Faulkner, Eberhart critically engaged Lowell's work, but whatever the exact contribution of such famed mentors, the attention of someone who has broken into the profession—the gift of an accomplished individual's serious regard for a developing writer's work—delivers an invaluable boost in confidence and the will to actually pursue what, for most, is a painfully elusive goal.

While parents and established writers served as fitting role models for a good number of the interviewees, others similarly benefited from acquaintance with talented classroom teachers who took great care in bolstering their students' faith in themselves and in channeling their innate abilities.[7] References in the interviews to the positive influence of formal education extend beyond tributes to individual instructors, focusing also or instead on particular classes or courses of study. As might be expected, literature classes and creative writing seminars elicit the most praise, but courses in translation, history, philosophy and religion also receive mention. Benefits associated with courses emphasizing literary analysis include greater familiarity with the parameters of the knowledge domain to which the interviewees were hoping to contribute (i.e., a sense of what had already been done), as well as wider exposure to literature of different eras and cultures. Relevant to the entirety of their time in college, several of the aspiring authors report treasuring the extensive time afforded to hone their writing talents in the presence of professors and talented peers in various courses across the disciplines.

---

6. Robert Lowell, interview by Frederick Seidel, in *The Paris Review Interviews*, vol. 2, ed. Philip Gourevitch (New York: Picador, 2007), 63.
7. Ted Hughes, interview by Drue Heinz, in *The Paris Review Interviews*, vol. 3, ed. Philip Gourevitch (New York: Picador, 2008), 273; Salman Rushdie, interview by Jack Livings, in *The Paris Review Interviews*, vol. 3, ed. Philip Gourevitch (New York: Picador, 2008), 371; Stephen Sondheim, interview by James Lipton, in *The Paris Review Interviews*, vol. 4, ed. Philip Gourevitch (New York: Picador, 2009), 264.

Whether initiated by informal or formal educational contexts, early and ongoing interaction with literature in the presence or under the tutelage of others who shared their passion motivated many of the interviewees to try their hand at writing poems, short stories and novels while still quite young. For these individuals, preparation in critically assessing and managing the elements of fiction (i.e., the tools of their knowledge domain) had been well underway before publishing works that eventually brought them fame. Examples include Dorothy Parker, Evelyn Waugh, John Gardner and Stephen King, who all were writing fiction by the time they entered grade school or shortly thereafter.[8] John Cheever invented serial stories at the age of eight; his, however, were delivered orally to classmates as approved by his teacher in the event that all finished their math lessons in timely fashion.[9] Though not quite as precocious given that he was ten before he began writing, Truman Capote had some of his short stories published at the age of seventeen, and Joyce Carol Oates was writing novels while still in high school.[10] Most of these early attempts at poetry and fiction were enabled by immersion in the literary arts, and they set a course for the future, functioning as experiments from which the authors learned valuable lessons on which they would build. As follows, they stand as check points along pathways of continued growth, where these aspiring writers could take stock of how well positioned they were to achieve their professional dreams and could identify avenues for augmenting their experience so as to ready themselves for the next level of success.

Study of Others' Literary Works

Several accounts of formative educational experiences discussed in the previous section are punctuated with references to specific reading materials that fed the authors' youthful literary zeal. For example, Ted Hughes, Gabriel Garcia Marquez and Stephen King claim that comics are what first attracted

---

8. Dorothy Parker, interview by Marion Capron, in *The Paris Review Interviews*, vol. 1, ed. Philip Gourevitch (New York: Picador, 2006), 7; Evelyn Waugh, interview by Julian Jebb, in *The Paris Review Interviews*, vol. 3, ed. Philip Gourevitch (New York: Picador, 2008), 66; Gardner, *The Paris Review Interviews*, 161; Stephen King, interview by Christopher Lehmann-Haupt and Nathaniel Rich, in *The Paris Review Interviews*, vol. 2, ed. Philip Gourevitch (New York: Picador, 2007), 465.
9. John Cheever, interview by Annette Grant, in *The Paris Review Interviews*, vol. 3, ed. Philip Gourevitch (New York: Picador, 2008), 152, 153.
10. Truman Capote, interview by Pati Hill in *The Paris Review Interviews*, vol. 1, ed. Philip Gourevitch (New York: Picador, 2006), 19–20; Joyce Carol Oates, interview by Robert Phillips, in *The Paris Review Interviews*, vol. 3, ed. Philip Gourevitch (New York: Picador, 2008), 186–87.

them to writing as youngsters, with King having composed stories to fit the colorful panels that he copied.[11] But, of course, strong feelings about particular works or bodies of work might emerge at any time during an author's education as sensibilities evolve and creative agendas assume more definite shapes. *The PR* interviews sampled for this study are rife with pronouncements of such indebtedness, rendering this subcategory one of the most dominant relevant to any element of the creative process model. This trend in the data is no doubt reflective of the interviewers' keen interest in literary influences, impetus for what appears to be a stock inquiry. In a few cases, queries of this nature elicit clipped responses (i.e., a list of names, maybe a few titles) that ultimately skirt any sort of elaboration. Representative of such vagueness, Earnest Hemingway proffers a sizable inventory of literary giants only to finally pronounce that the inventory is insufficient since sorting out all who impacted him and the manner in which they did so is a solemn exercise that "requires an examination of conscience."[12] The majority of responses, however, expound on particular lessons in content or style that laid groundwork for the interviewees' subsequent literary triumphs.

Regarding matters of content, several of the interviewees credit their forebearers with teaching them what counts as viable subject matter, having formerly believed that their unconventional perspectives or mundane personal circumstances were inappropriate or not adequately profound. Franz Kafka sparked this revelation in Gabriel Garcia Marquez, whose enthusiasm for pursuing a literary career solidified upon reading Kafka's "The Metamorphosis" as a college student. Recalling that moment, Garcia Marquez explains: "When I read the [first] line I thought to myself that I didn't know anyone was allowed to write things like that. If I had known, I would have started writing a long time ago. So I immediately started writing short stories."[13] With an interest in more realistic subject matter, Richard Price credits Hubert Selby's *Last Exit to Brooklyn* with helping him realize that much successful literature portrays people and experiences reminiscent of the environment he grew up in and that it was permissible to pull subject matter from his own life, to excavate the "diamonds in his own backyard."[14] Similarly inspired by Eudora Welty, Flannery O'Connor, Katherine Anne Porter and Carson McCullers, Alice

---

11. Hughes, *The Paris Review Interviews*, 272–73; Gabriel Garcia Marquez, interview by Peter H. Stone, in *The Paris Review Interviews*, vol. 2, ed. Philip Gourevitch (New York: Picador, 2007), 184; King, *The Paris Review Interviews*, 465.
12. Earnest Hemingway, interview by George Plimpton, in *The Paris Review Interviews*, vol. 1, ed. Philip Gourevitch (New York: Picador, 2006), 46.
13. Garcia Marquez, *The Paris Review Interviews*, 184.
14. Richard Price, interview by James Linville, in *The Paris Review Interviews*, vol. 1, ed. Philip Gourevitch (New York: Picador, 2006), 381.

Munro acknowledges that these authors of the American South introduced her to compelling possibilities for commenting on rural life, which she applied in writing about small-town existence in Ontario, Canada, where she resided most of her life.[15]

Others drew even more explicitly on the content of works they admired, specifically alluding to them in their own publications. Joyce Carol Oates, for instance, recognizes Lewis Carroll as a literary touchstone from whom she borrows titles and various other features for her stories.[16] More obviously derivative, John Gardner ties the substance of his work to classics and more contemporary models: his novel *Grendel* retells the legend of *Beowulf* from the monster's perspective, and *The Sunlight Dialogues* parodies "the whole idea of family and locale in Faulkner."[17] As if taking cues from Gardner's *Grendel*, Jean Rhys's *Wide Sargasso Sea* provides the back story of the madwoman in *Jane Eyre*, rectifying what she viewed as a disservice to Creole women.[18] (Rhys is one of a handful of interviewees who attributed their special interest in a particular piece or author to what they viewed as faults, thus opening avenues for their own advancement.) Also focused on matters of character, Haruki Murakami links all his protagonists to Nick Carraway in F. Scott Fitzgerald's *The Great Gatsby*; in particular, he points to Carraway's detached neutrality in observing the world around him, a quality dependent on freedom from a vertical family structure.[19] In this example, content and technical matters are clearly intertwined, and many passages in the interview transcripts address both simultaneously.

Be that as it may, a host of other passages concentrate exclusively on technique, as is the case in Joan Didion's transcript, which heaps appreciation on several of her literary precursors, including Melville, whose ability to harness ostensibly digressive language escaped her when she read *Moby Dick* as a teen; Theodor Dreiser, whose lack of a discernible style leveled a terrific power; and Earnest Hemingway, whose sentences' simplistic surface appearance belied an underlying complexity.[20] Also an admirer of Hemingway (there are many in the interview corpus, by the way), Ralph Ellison compliments his unparalleled

---

15. Alice Munro, interview by Jeanne McCulloch and Mona Simpson, in *The Paris Review Interviews*, vol. 2, ed. Philip Gourevitch (New York: Picador, 2007), 423.
16. Oates, *The Paris Review Interviews*, 185.
17. Gardner, *The Paris Review Interviews*, 154.
18. Jean Rhys, interview by Elizabeth Vreeland, in *The Paris Review Interviews*, vol. 3, ed. Philip Gourevitch (New York: Picador, 2008), 211.
19. Haruki Murakami, interview by John Wray, in *The Paris Review Interviews*, vol. 4, ed. Philip Gourevitch (New York: Picador, 2009), 359.
20. Joan Didion, interview by Hilton Als, in *The Paris Review Interviews*, vol. 1, ed. Philip Gourevitch (New York: Picador, 2006), 478–80.

ability to describe and explicate processes, such as those involved in hunting or art, and he remembers reading Hemingway's stories to absorb the sentence structures and methods of arrangement.[21] Marilynne Robinson identifies her locus of fascination in metaphor as deployed in American literature beginning with Emerson; this fascination led to a dissertation that set the stage for her novel, *Housekeeping*.[22] Apparently more interested in the musical qualities of language, Ted Hughes reports being captivated as a young man by "the rhythmical, mechanical drive" of Rudyard Kipling's verse and recalls penning several epics in that fashion.[23]

Though perhaps not as focused or detailed as those just summarized, there exist numerous additional references to stylistic influences in the data supporting this analysis. But whether the authors were enamored of the style of their forbearers, the content of their masterpieces or both, the interview corpus on the whole indicates that the works of other authors served as rich resources for aspiring writers. Manners of assistance might have been applied holistically or relevant to particular literary elements, and they might have suggested specific strategies for working through unique challenges the interviewees encountered in the quest to wrestle their own ideas and experiences into workable and engaging form. Whether discovered during childhood or later in life, these groundbreaking models of fiction and poetry broadened the interviewees' visions of the knowledge domains in which they were creating and expanded their repertoire of literary techniques, all of which prepared them to write their own masterpieces.

Formal Research

While reading and thinking about renowned poetry and fiction written by others is a useful exercise for aspiring authors, they may also need to engage in more formal types of research, including review of pertinent scholarship and even empirical methods such as observation, interviewing and ethnography. The majority of references relevant to this subcategory focus on the necessity of consulting academically oriented books for understanding that would enhance the authenticity of a poem or fictional work. Whether striving to accurately depict a historical figure, a setting from a past era, a plotline occurring in a specialized environment or even philosophical movements undergirding a given

---

21. Ralph Ellison, interview by Alfred Chester and Vilma Howard, in *The Paris Review Interviews*, vol. 3, ed. Philip Gourevitch (New York: Picador, 2008), 4.
22. Maryilynne Robinson, interview by Sarah Fay, in *The Paris Review Interviews*, vol. 4, ed. Philip Gourevitch (New York: Picador, 2009), 443.
23. Ted Hughes, *The Paris Review Interviews*, 273.

theme, those who spoke about conducting formal research made clear that the factual information they gathered lent credibility to those literary elements and, by extension, their own authorial voices. Peter Carey argues that such formal research establishes the right to assume some authority over subject matter that extends beyond direct experience.[24] Those who earned that right through reading collectively tapped a variety of disciplines as their special interests dictated, including, for a few representative examples, history (Munro), medicine (Oates) and philosophy (Gardner).[25] Of course, reading is by no means a passive endeavor, and a couple of authors emphasized the necessity of weighing book knowledge and the "conventional wisdom" typically taught in school against their own experience and imagination.[26]

Not surprisingly, some interviewees found book research insufficient to their plans, and so they ventured into the world around them, investigating it firsthand. Several who resorted to such methods assign particular importance to the power of observation, with William Faulkner going so far as to declare it one of three essential attributes for a successful writer, alongside experience and imagination,[27] and with Earnest Hemingway proclaiming that the writer who "stops observing is finished."[28] Most of the authors who comment on the ability to visually absorb people and places as a means of developing characters and setting treat it as a learned skill, an attitude eloquently expressed by James Baldwin in the following anecdote:

> I remember standing on a street corner with the black painter Beauford Delaney down in the Village, waiting for the light to change, and he pointed down and said, "Look." I looked and all I saw was water. And he said, "Look again," which I did, and I saw oil on the water and the city reflected in the puddle. It was a great revelation to me. I can't explain it. He taught me how to see, and how to trust what I saw.[29]—Copyright © by *The Paris Review*, used by permission of The Wylie Agency LLC.

---

24. Peter Carey, interview by Radhika Jones, in *The Paris Review Interviews*, vol. 2, ed. Philip Gourevitch (New York: Picador, 2007), 451.
25. Munro, *The Paris Review Interviews*, 413; Oates, *The Paris Review Interviews*, 178; Gardner, *The Paris Review Interviews*, 146.
26. Toni Morrison, interview by Elissa Schappell and Claudia Brodsky Lacour, in *The Paris Review Interviews*, vol. 2, ed. Philip Gourevitch (New York: Picador, 2007), 392–93; Robinson, *The Paris Review Interviews*, 463.
27. Faulkner, *The Paris Review Interviews*, 47–48.
28. Hemingway, *The Paris Review Interviews*, 57.
29. James Baldwin, interview by Jordan Elgrably, in *The Paris Review Interviews*, vol. 2, ed. Philip Gourevitch (New York: Picador, 2007), 243.

In contrast to this profound experience, education in recognizing detail resonated for some with substantial degrees of angst, even pain. Indeed, Stephen King honed his capacity to write about children among the trials and tribulations of raising his own son and daughter.[30] Vastly more distressing, when asked about white authors' accuracy in portraying "the black experience," Maya Angelou reminds her interviewer that slaves became extra-aware of white people's facial expressions and gestures as signs that they were going to be beaten or sold—a reality that caused black people to study white people to an extent and in different ways than the latter have had to study the former.[31] These thoughts about observation as a research strategy reveal that, while authors are commonly presumed to be gifted with an innate talent for gleaning the details of their surroundings, in actuality, that talent as it translates to their finished works signifies a lifetime of ongoing, purposeful effort.

When observation occurs over an extended period of time, perhaps supported by other research strategies, including interviews, it begins taking the shape of informal ethnography, which involves the researcher's immersion in an unfamiliar culture. The interviews analyzed for this study reveal that several authors pursued such lengths in constructing their literary worlds. Richard Price, for one, found the research for his novel *Clockers* about Jersey City housing projects to be quite addictive as he hung out with drug dealers, police officers and welfare moms for three years, compiling a two-foot-high stack of notebooks detailing various aspects of their lives. The author's transparency about his purpose and the subjects' desire to vent about the difficulties of their existence enabled his deep infiltration of their lives. Price views such measures as essential to representing the full measure of reality behind those lives so that his fictional account of them would be just.[32] This sentiment undoubtedly motivates most fiction writers who adopt ethnographic methods. In fact, it is salient in the words of David Grossman, whose interviewer questions him about the extent of his research in light of the author's statement in another setting regarding the importance of being "meticulous with facts." To that query, Grossman replies:

> If I am going to write about a man joining a shoal of salmon, as in *See Under: Love*, I have to start by making the reality of the salmon very concrete and credible. So I joined divers, I became a salmon. I was unable to eat salmon for years—really. I felt like a cannibal when I ate

---

30. King, *The Paris Review Interviews*, 474.
31. Maya Angelou, interview by George Plimpton, in *The Paris Review Interviews*, vol. 4, ed. Philip Gourevitch (New York: Picador, 2009), 256–57.
32. Price, *The Paris Review Interviews*, 391–92.

salmon. When I wrote *The Zigzag Kid*, I joined the detective squad of the Jerusalem police for six months, spending almost every night with them."[33]—Copyright © by *The Paris Review*, used by permission of The Wylie Agency LLC and with permission of Jonathan Shainin.

Grossman continues with insights about similarly dedicated research methods informing other novels he's written, noting that immersing himself in settings that he is writing about is a way of moving beyond his own limited perspective. Also a believer in the power of immersion, Isak Dinesen's perspective expanded significantly by traveling to Africa (as mentioned earlier, in the footsteps of her father) and joining a native community, experiences on which she based her highly acclaimed work of creative nonfiction, *Out of Africa*.[34]

In fact, travel in general (i.e., not necessarily tied to immersion) functioned as a mode of research—or exposure to facts and realities previously unencountered in quite the same way—that proved instrumental in forming, cultivating and sometimes shifting an author's outlook. Poet Jack Gilbert makes this point when he recalls the positive effect of living abroad as an American. You need to do so, he asserts, "so you have something to compare to what you think is normal, and you encounter things you aren't used to. One of the great dangers [to an author] is familiarity."[35] Joan Didion likely would agree with Gilbert regarding the danger he points to, but she apparently doesn't view overseas travel as a requirement for capitalizing on exposure to the unfamiliar. Although she traveled to other countries in support of her fictional and nonfictional works, she also spent time exploring a diverse swath of American cities, one of which she explicitly highlights as exemplifying the benefit Gilbert cites: "In New Orleans, you get a strong sense of the Caribbean. I used a lot of [a full] week in New Orleans in *Common Prayer*. It was the most interesting place I had been in a long time. It was a week in which everything everybody said to me was astonishing."[36] With these words, Didion joins the chorus of authors who sing the praises of travel in supplying new knowledge or fresh understanding that enabled particular works or more generally edified them in writing about certain people, places or themes with unique acuity.

As this subcategory of preparation reveals, direct research performed via travel, ethnography or simple yet close observation, coupled with or separate

---

33. David Grossman, interview by Jonathan Shainin, in *The Paris Review Interviews*, vol. 4, ed. Philip Gourevitch (New York: Picador, 2009), 415.
34. Dinesen, *The Paris Review Interviews*, 54.
35. Jack Gilbert, interview by Sarah Fay, in *The Paris Review Interviews*, vol. 1, ed. Philip Gourevitch (New York: Picador, 2006), 445.
36. Didion, *The Paris Review Interviews*, 488.

from more traditional "library research," snatched considerable amounts of time from the interviewees' lives. Although a few insist they write (or wrote) primarily, if not entirely, from imagination, a large faction acknowledges that formal research plays a crucial role in bringing their literary visions to completion. In some cases, it seems the research itself is the greatest source of joy associated with writing—a reprieve between or in the midst of certain projects, the actual drafting of which can be intimidating, exasperating and draining in comparison.

Distinctive Personal Experiences

The mantra "Write what you know," or some version of it, commonly surfaces in informal and formal contexts intended to guide aspiring writers. Whether delivered in casual conversation with an established novelist or in an undergraduate poetry seminar, these words underlie all the themes in the subcategory of preparation to be addressed in this section. While the formerly discussed subcategories might afford "distinctive personal experiences" that could become the basis for a story or poem, this subcategory addresses data that comments on literary works purposefully derived from *unusual or profound* incidents that the interviewee lived or learned about through family or acquaintances. As separate from immersion under formal research, this subcategory encompasses passages that stress the generative impact of personal experience as opposed to methods for investigating it.

Several of the passages coded to this subcategory find the interviewees simply reinforcing the aforementioned mantra. Among such general observations, a good number go so far as to insist that all writing is to some degree autobiographical, even if only for being filtered through the author's perspective. The extent to which the interviewees based their work on specific moments or persons in their lives varies dramatically, running the gamut from a plot line exactly replicating a particular incident (with names or places changed to protect the innocent) to a single composite character sporting qualities of appearance and personality drawn from two or more people (often outside the circumstances that originally introduced them to the author). Representing the former end of the spectrum, Stephen King, whose frightening encounter with a St. Bernard functioned as a stimulus for the novel *Cujo* (see Chapter 3), recalls that another of his novels, *Pet Sematary*, followed personal experience to the letter before reaching a significant turn in the plot: "Everything in it—up to the point where the little boy is killed in the road—everything is true."[37] On the opposite end of that spectrum, sometime autobiographer, Paul Auster, when asked about his fiction in particular, reveals that it selectively incorporates provocative details

---

37. King, *The Paris Review Interviews*, 474.

and incidents from his own life when serving the purpose of an otherwise unrelated plot.[38] Regardless of the amount of autobiographical material a writer employs, as the following paragraphs will illustrate, the mantra "Write what you know" has achieved its status for a reason: reflecting on personal experience is a highly productive means of preparation for writing, as evidenced in some of the greatest literary works ever produced.

As might be predicted, many of the interviewees affirmed that writing about personal experience enabled them to commemorate and illuminate aspects of their childhood or adolescence. Richard Price, whose intense investigative methods for *Clockers* are described above under "Formal Research," indicates that the drive for writing that novel was rooted in research for the screenplay *Sea of Love*, which compelled him to return to the Jersey City housing projects so that he could discern the underlying reasons for the stark contrast between his childhood and adolescent memories of them and the state they were in when he returned as an adult. In the following excerpt, while detailing the impetus for yet another of his novels, *The Wanderers*, Price eloquently explains this attraction to his younger years:

> Out there in Palo Alto [on a fellowship in Stanford's creative writing program], I felt so isolated from my past life that a great need came over me to crystallize my memories of the Bronx, my adolescence, the textures of a life to which I knew I'd never return. So my need to write about these mooks kicked into high gear—it was all tied into homesickness and disorientation. I was writing in the same manner and for the same reason that someone would whistle a tune as they navigated a dark and creepy forest.[39]—Copyright © by *The Paris Review*, used by permission of The Wylie Agency LLC and with permission of James Linville.

Though not necessarily as concrete as Price in explaining their motives, plenty of other interviewees acknowledge mining early life experiences for nuggets of literary gold, which include tales of young love, the joy of innocent pastimes, the beauty of one's birthplace or quaint ways of life defining a certain subculture.

Some of the most striking passages relevant to this theme chronicle episodes of trauma or intense struggle early in the authors' lives. For example, both James Baldwin and V. S. Naipaul lost friends to suicide in their teens and later modeled

---

38. Paul Auster, interview by Michael Woods, in *The Paris Review Interviews*, vol. 4, ed. Philip Gourevitch (New York: Picador, 2009), 322–23.
39. Price, *The Paris Review Interviews*, 394–95.

characters on them.⁴⁰ Also influenced by tragedy experienced at a young age, Paul Auster recalls a hiking expedition with some boyhood friends, during which one was struck by lightning. The story of that tragedy, which appears in *The Red Notebook*, reportedly changed Auster's life, as he explains in the following passage: "One moment the boy was alive and the next moment he was dead. I was only inches away from him. It was my first experience with random death, with the bewildering instability of things. You think you're standing on solid ground and an instant later the ground opens under your feet and you vanish."⁴¹ While not as emotionally searing an experience as losing a friend to suicide or an accident, growing up with a brother whose temperament was very different from his own stirred in Orhan Pamuk a "galaxy of nerve points" that he repeatedly confronted, as he does in the sadomasochistic relationship between two central characters in *The White Castle*.⁴² Other interviewees who spoke about struggles they experienced as children focused on fears and insecurities engendered by severe sociopolitical upheaval (e.g., discrimination, poverty, diseases raging out of control) in the countries where they were raised.

Struggles of adulthood also found voice in literature produced by the interviewees, with specific topics including spiritual conflict, seamy sides of existence associated with financial hardship, the undermining of political allegiances, disillusion with government and the horrors associated with war. However, as was the case with childhood experience, much adult experience that made it into the literature these authors composed had proven edifying. In *Pleasures of a Tangled Life*, for example, Jan Morris, takes up transsexuality, what she refers to as "'the conundrum experience.'" That book, she says, "tries to present [...] what kind of a sensibility has resulted from this sort of thing"; further, she explains that she recognizes "the pleasures, nearly all of them, are ones that I enjoy in a particular way because of 'the conundrum thing.'"⁴³ Similarly prone to emphasizing the positive, Maya Angelou (who also wrote about horrific traumas that she faced during childhood) agrees with her interviewer that the enduring themes in her work are love for her child and human resilience.⁴⁴ Other upbeat sentiments about specific adulthood experiences come from Philip Roth, as well as Evelyn Waugh. Roth shares that he draws pleasure from the grandeur of rural life, which enabled his representation of

---

40. Baldwin, *The Paris Review Interviews*, 254; Naipaul, *The Paris Review Interviews*, 289.
41. Auster, *The Paris Review Interviews*, 319.
42. Orhan Pamuk, interview by Angel Gurria-Quintana, in *The Paris Review Interviews*, vol. 4, ed. Philip Gourevitch (New York: Picador, 2009), 388.
43. Jan Morris, interview by Leo Lerman, in *The Paris Review Interviews*, vol. 3, ed. Philip Gourevitch (New York: Picador, 2008), 320–21.
44. Angelou, *The Paris Review Interviews*, 250.

a reclusive writer's existence in *The Ghost Writer*,[45] and Waugh, though admittedly giving his protagonist a hard time at the head of the classroom in *Decline and Fall*, reflects fondly on his stint as a teacher, experience which directly informed the novel.[46]

That authors draw upon personal experience comes as no surprise, to be sure. Nevertheless, the sample interviews provide a sense of the extent and varied manner of writers' reliance on this source of preparation. In some cases, the transcripts reveal that personal experience is merely suggestive of literary elements, while in others it provides specific models for them. Additionally, the transcripts collectively establish that certain memories of childhood are as accessible and productive as events occurring later in life while also emphasizing that talented writers can create engaging, resonant literature from both tragedy and triumph.

Prewriting Strategies

Creative writing seminars, composition courses and various publications on writerly advice from established authors regularly promote exercises designed for generating material in response to a given writing challenge. As discussed in Chapter 2, these exercises are sometimes referred to as "prewriting strategies" or "heuristics" and include, for example, activities like brainstorming and freewriting, as well as more structured devices. Writers typically employ them in hopes of sparking a first insight or fleshing out initial glimmers of direction for a project. The latter is most germane to this subcategory of preparation, which explores how the interviewed authors capitalized on prewriting strategies to elaborate early plans for composing. Given writing's recursive nature, coding passages relevant to prewriting strategies proved especially difficult. Nevertheless, with the goal of maintaining as discrete a classification system as possible across the study, the textual units assigned to this subcategory depict instances when the authors turned to prewriting strategies following first insight and prior to having developed a substantial draft of an eventually published work.[47]

Considering the scholarly attention devoted in the past few decades to the benefits of collaboration in writing and other creative activities, it seems

---

45. Philip Roth, interview by Hermione Lee, in *The Paris Review Interviews*, vol. 4, ed. Philip Gourevitch (New York: Picador, 2009), 225.
46. Waugh, *The Paris Review Interviews*, 67.
47. Textual units that did not fit these parameters were coded to either first insight (if the strategy was employed to spark the initial glimmer of a work) or insight (if the strategy was employed to work through a block when the author was deep into drafting).

important to note at this juncture that the prewriting strategies emphasized by interviewees in this study are largely solitary ventures. While it is true that a few of them do discuss conversation with others as facilitative of early ideas for writing,[48] on the whole, this group of authors attributes special value to prewriting strategies that enable focused concentration and quiet reflection. One such strategy is note-taking, sometimes in the form of lists or outlines and sometimes in the form of diaries or journals. This mode of preparation for elaborating first insights involves recording an array of events, sights, sounds and other impressions, as well as apt phrasings or snippets of dialog reflective of characters-to-be. The nature of some of these notes reportedly allowed dropping them into a developing draft verbatim while, in stark contrast, others assumed the form of instructions for how to proceed once the author began drafting. While reflections on note-taking pervade the interviews, the large majority merely mention the strategy as crucial in supporting projects they were planning.

Peter Carey breaks this mold in his response to a query about his means of preparation for drafting. Analyzing a picture taken of him while working on a screen play, he observes: "In the picture I'm using index cards and dividing up chapters and asking myself, What will happen in that chapter? I'll often look at those chapters as little boxes or rooms, and I'll start to ask myself what happens within each room."[49] Likewise, Stephen King details an orderly approach to note-taking through the example of one of his many novels, *Duma Key*. Referring to what he labels his "filing system," he explains: "I've actually codified the notes to make sure I remember the different plot strands. I write down birth dates to figure out how old characters are at certain times. Remember to put a rose tattoo on this one's breast, remember to give Edgar a big workbench by the end of February." King religiously maintains this intricate system to protect himself from expending labor on missteps that would likely prove difficult to solve.[50] Although most of the other authors appear not to harbor such fears, or at least refuse to quell them with systems as complex as King's, a few do report that their note-taking is equally extensive. Norman Mailer, for example, confesses to compiling copious notes upon which he broods before

---

48. Of course, the potential role of collaboration relevant to writing extends beyond prewriting strategies. In fact, collaboration is a notable theme to arise in this study pertinent generally to informal mentorship by family members, teachers and established authors and, more specifically, to verification—most significantly through feedback and conversation with editors in the context of revision (see Chapter 7).
49. Carey, *The Paris Review Interviews*, 444.
50. King, *The Paris Review Interviews*, 478.

drafting,[51] and P. G. Wodehouse puts a number on such preliminaries, claiming that he regularly scratches out four hundred pages of predrafting notes.[52] Ultimately though, regardless of the amount of prewriting they generate, many of the interviewees seem to share in Wodehouse's sentiment that, even if one's notes are incoherent to some degree, they typically lead to a moment when the author feels the novel is started and can project how it likely will end.[53]

As helpful as note-taking or journaling can be in formulating the substance of a poem or story, occasionally an author must resort to more inventive measures. As the interview transcripts reveal, many authors engage in literary experimentation as a means of developing their ideas. In other words, following upon an inclination to pursue a particular idea or project (i.e., first insight), they deliberately push themselves beyond their usual genres or structural preferences in order to spark their creative fires. Jorges Luis Borges provides a sense of how this strategy might work, contending that most poets, for instance, have only a few original ideas in them and they keep repackaging them, invoking various perspectives, eras, plots and characters to deliver those ideas in different ways.[54] Though perhaps not as pessimistic as Luis Borges about the capacity for original thought, Jack Kerouac talks of wrapping ideas for *October in the Railroad Earth* in prose that was "very experimental, intended to clack along all the way like a steam engine pulling a one-hundred-car freight with a talky caboose at the end." In contrast, the "spontaneous style" for *On the Road* resulted from Kerouac's desire to emulate the "fast, mad confessional" nature of letters written to him by his Beat Generation friend, Neal Cassady.[55] Eudora Welty also benefited from changing up her prose style, indicating that *Losing Battles* found expression in her desire to encapsulate all her ideas and feelings into action and dialogue—a departure from her formerly heavy reliance on description and character introspection.[56] While other authors addressed the value of experimentation, some of their recollections depicted activity more akin to first insight and are coded accordingly. Nevertheless, as this paragraph

---

51. Norman Mailer, interview by Andrew O'Hagan, in *The Paris Review Interviews*, vol. 3, ed. Philip Gourevitch (New York: Picador, 2008), 400.
52. P. G. Wodehouse, interview by Gerald Clarke, in *The Paris Review Interviews*, vol. 4, ed. Philip Gourevitch (New York: Picador, 2009), 156.
53. Ibid.
54. Jorge Luis Borges, interview by Ronald Christ, in *The Paris Review Interviews*, vol. 1, ed. Philip Gourevitch (New York: Picador, 2006), 151.
55. Jack Kerouac, interview by Ted Berrigan, in *The Paris Review Interviews*, vol. 4, ed. Philip Gourevitch (New York: Picador, 2009), 84.
56. Eudora Welty, interview by Linda Kuehl, in *The Paris Review Interviews*, vol. 2, ed. Philip Gourevitch (New York: Picador, 2007), 121.

portrays, a decision to escape the bounds of routine in response to first insight suggests all sorts of fresh possibilities for rendering the concepts one wishes to communicate.

Other prewriting activities, though failing to warrant status as freestanding themes, ostensibly boosted their respective authors' preparatory efforts. One of these practices, termed "warm-up writing" for purposes of this study, deserves mention in light of its astonishing nature. While there exist numerous anecdotes in the interview transcripts portraying how certain authors use writing to discover what they want to say or do (including journaling and note-taking discussed at the beginning of this section), many are coded as insight—the element of the creative process model discussed in Chapter 6— since the phenomenon occurred during drafting of a given publication. In contrast, warm-up writing may help authors discover what they want to say or do, but it does so indirectly; that is, it points them in new directions as opposed to supporting a publishable project in progress. Applying this prewriting exercise in the extreme are Joyce Carol Oates and Haruki Murakami, who maintain that they wrote entire novels as a means of readying themselves for what they deemed more serious or impressive works.[57] Composing an entire novel as practice for another attests to these authors' dedication and stamina. Collectively, though, the prewriting activities described in the sample interviews hint at a range of cognitive styles and underscore the observation in Chapter 2 that no single prescription for "the writing process" could adequately serve all writers.

Cross-Pollination between Disciplines

One of the most intriguing revelations in the discourse analysis informing this study is that so many of the subjects practiced or closely studied other art forms.[58] Several report being exposed to other arts by a relative (as is the case with reading as discussed earlier in this chapter), and still others report having received formal training outside the home. Pertinent to the subject of this chapter, preparation, the interview transcripts make clear that, in more than a few cases, immersion in another art form directly impacted development of the interviewees' prose or verse. Some authors, including Rebecca West, Elizabeth Bishop and Isak Dinesen, discuss the impact of another art form on the content of their work. Dinesen waxes more specific

---

57. Oates, *The Paris Review Interviews*, 186–87; Murakami, *The Paris Review Interviews*, 352.
58. A few reported being influenced by the sciences, but these instances were comparatively sparse.

than the other two, attributing her pattern of writing about past eras to her training as a visual artist, explaining that "a painter never wants the subject right under his nose; he wants to stand back and study a landscape with half-closed eyes."[59]

Other authors benefiting from cross-pollination appear more attuned to lessons learned about style and arrangement as opposed to content. Focusing, as does Dinesen, on the relevance of painting to writing, Georges Simenon insists that the general feeling he strives to convey in his literature "is nothing but the impressionism of the painter adapted to literature." Forever charmed by Impressionist masterpieces hanging in the museums he frequented as a child, he offers this analogy to explain the reason he deliberately set out to place "noncommercial" passages for inclusion in his "commercial" novels:

> A commercial painter paints flat; you can put your finger through. But a painter—for example, an apple by Cezanne has weight. And it has juice, everything, with just three strokes. I tried to give my words just the weight that a stroke of Cezanne's gave to an apple. That is why most of the time I use concrete words. I try to avoid abstract words, or poetical words.[60]—Copyright © by *The Paris Review*, used by permission of The Wylie Agency LLC.

While Simenon turned to the Impressionists in the quest to achieve dimension in his writing, several other writers added dimension to their work by employing techniques lifted from cinematic photography.[61]

Although references to visual arts dominate the subcategory of cross-pollination relevant to preparation, one of the most in-depth reflections on stylistic transfer between art forms comes from Toni Morrison explaining the influence of music on her writing. The following excerpt, focused on her novel *Jazz*, is a mere snippet of the insight she offers about the connection between these two art forms in her interview:

> I thought of the plot in that novel, the threesome, as the melody of the piece, and it is fine to follow a melody—to feel the satisfaction of

---

59. Dinesen, *The Paris Review Interviews*, 56.
60. Georges Simenon, interview by Carvel Collins, in *The Paris Review Interviews*, vol. 3, ed. Philip Gourevitch (New York: Picador, 2008), 38.
61. Price, *The Paris Review Interviews*, 397; King, *The Paris Review Interviews*, 465; Rushdie, *The Paris Review Interviews*, 390–91; Auster, *The Paris Review Interviews*, 327. A few textual units that mention transfer of technique from film to literature were coded elsewhere in line with the overriding tenor of the passage.

recognizing a melody whenever the narrator returns to it. That was the real art of the enterprise for me—bumping up against that melody time and again, seeing it from another point of view, seeing it afresh each time, playing it back and forth.

When Keith Jarret plays "Ol' Man River," the delight and satisfaction is not so much in the melody itself but in recognizing it when it surfaces and when it is hidden, and when it goes away completely, what is put in its place. Not so much in the original line as in all the echoes and shades and turns and pivots Jarret plays around it. I was trying to do something similar with the plot in *Jazz*.[62]—Copyright © by *The Paris Review*, used by permission of The Wylie Agency LLC and with permission of Claudia Brodsky.

Equally enamored and derivative of strategies associated with music, Haruki Murakami recognizes that both jazz and blues, which he began listening to as a teen, significantly impacted him, stoking ambitions to become a musician. When considering his lack of dexterity in handling instruments, however, he opted for writing through which he channels musical notes and cadences that he hears. In sum, he insists that the two arts are quite similar.[63]

Whatever discipline the author may have consulted, the potential of cross-pollination in figuring out how to execute a particular intention lies in the benefits of escaping habitual ways of thinking about subject matter, organization and linguistic choices. As Chapter 2 exemplifies, juxtaposing knowledge domains promotes fresh connections as analytical lenses typically employed in one field are purposefully trained on another (see Chapter 6 for more on connection-making).

Some Closing Observations

This chapter illustrates that authors draw on a variety of resources in preparing themselves to elaborate their literary visions. The frequent and detailed references to preparatory activity across the interview corpus reinforce the notion that writers typically expend considerable energy between first insight and formal drafting activity in researching, planning and note-taking, often building on years of studying literature and honing their literary sensibilities. The painstaking labor of compiling information, the many false starts and the challenges of experimenting with one's composing preferences, for example, indicate the level of perspiration that

---

62. Morrison, *The Paris Review Interviews*, 380.
63. Murakami, *The Paris Review Interviews*, 366.

follows upon the initial inspiration for writing. All the labor, though, is well worth it since the creative process elements to be discussed in Chapters 5 and 6—incubation and insight, respectively—depend on the richness and complexity of the "conceptual matrix"[64] related to both content and style in which the project is grounded.

---

64. Rosemary L. Gates, "Applying Martin Greenman's Concept of Insight to Composition Theory," *Journal of Advanced Composition* 9, no. 1–2 (1989): 64.

Chapter 5

INCUBATION, OR BREAKS FROM CONSCIOUS ATTENTION

As the previous chapter establishes, the second element in the paradigmatic creative process model, preparation, may consume weeks, months or years and may involve diverse modes of inquiry. In some cases, preparation on the heels of a promising first insight immediately yields more substantial insights that advance a project. In other cases, the well-prepared mind becomes saturated, having reached a point where additional research holds little promise, and yet still it cannot conceive a productive pathway forward, cannot grasp how the accumulated knowledge should be combined or reenvisioned in the quest for a solution to the creative problem. Of course, given its recursive nature, creative activity may be arrested at any moment, and history portends that scientific and artistic endeavors of any consequence rarely proceed in seamless fashion, free of obstructions that threaten to undermine them. It is in these disheartening moments of stagnation that the value of incubation—the third element listed in the creative process model and the subject of this chapter—can be fully appreciated.

In practical terms, incubation (not to be confused with procrastination[1]) is defined as the interval of time between the onset of a break from deliberate work on a creative problem and the achievement of insight (the fourth element of the creative process model). Given that incubation occurs entirely within the mind and is, therefore, difficult to study directly,[2] researchers typically infer its nature and usefulness from behaviors and happenings surrounding it, either by observing people at

---

1. Incubation is distinct from procrastination, which denotes a putting off of responsibilities and all subtasks associated with them. Moreover, procrastination implies a distaste for the looming task. In contrast, incubating artists and scientists are not putting off responsibilities. Indeed, in most cases, they have voluntarily pursued them and demonstrated initiative in starting them. They walk away from projects not to avoid them but because they desire so desperately to finish them and make them as perfect as possible.
2. Science in this area is advancing by means of MRI studies, but applications for creativity studies at this time are fledgling.

work[3] or by listening to or reading accounts of creative accomplishment. Empirical investigations regularly label the most significant of those happenings, the arrival of insight, as an "incubation effect," thereby positing a direct cause–effect relationship between the two constructs. While the insight-stimulating benefits of incubation are widely associated with unique powers of the unconscious, they have also been linked to fringe consciousness (e.g., daydreaming) and to what Robert M. Olton dubs "creative worrying"[4] (i.e., alternating bouts of conscious and unconscious mentation) on grounds that both enable the sort of loose, uninhibited thinking attributed to the unconscious and thus liberate the mind from cognitive fixations that impede original or fresh perspectives. On the other hand, some researchers correlate incubation effects with ordinary thinking processes undertaken during states of full awareness, including trial and error,[5] selective forgetting (a weakening of the mind's propensity for traveling familiar pathways)[6] and connection-making relevant to fresh intellectual or environmental stimuli.[7]

Clearly, these different theories regarding the locus of successful incubation are not mutually exclusive, and, in the end, the question of whether incubation effects depend on wholly unconscious, partially conscious or entirely conscious mental activity matters little to creative individuals seeking a breakthrough. Rather, they are content simply to know that incubation delivers results, and there exists plenty of published research, both qualitative and quantitative, suggesting that it does. Introductions to incubation scholarship commonly relay dramatic tales of artists or scientists in the midst of infertile periods or debilitating mental blocks who, after interrupting focused attention on their work, are suddenly struck by insights that spark profound triumphs. One of the most famous episodes of this phenomenon stars seventeenth-century

---

3. Incubation has been studied empirically by presenting subjects with a problem, allowing them to work on it for a while, imposing some sort of break in conscious attention to the problem (with no break for the control group in an experimental design), directing subjects to resume attempts to solve the problem and, then, measuring in some fashion whether the subjects have solved or are closer to solving the problem as a result of the break.
4. Robert M. Olton, "Experimental Studies of Incubation: Searching for the Elusive," *Journal of Creative Behavior* 13, no.1 (1979): 11.
5. Daniel S. Schubert, "Is Incubation the Silent Rehearsal of Mundane Responses?" *Journal of Creative Behavior* 13, no. 1 (1979): 37.
6. Colleen Seifert et al., "Demystification of Cognitive Insight: Opportunistic Assimilation and the Prepared-Mind Perspective," in *The Nature of Insight*, ed. Robert J. Sternberg and Janet E. Davidson (Cambridge, MA: MIT Press, 1995), 82.
7. Steven M. Smith, "Fixation, Incubation, and Insight in Memory and Creative Thinking," in *The Creative Cognition Approach*, ed. Steven M. Smith, Thomas B. Ward and Ronald S. Finke (Cambridge, MA: MIT Press, 1995), 147–48.

organic chemist August Kekule von Stradonitz, who was struggling to envision the molecular structure of Benzene. After years of pondering the conundrum and reaching a few preliminary insights, he finally experienced his Eureka moment while dozing one evening in a chair by his fireplace. During this light slumber, he began dreaming of snakes (later interpreted to be carbon chains) and eventually witnessed one of the slithery creatures swallowing its own tail. Upon awakening, Kekule realized this dream-image held the solution to his problem: benzene, contrary to expectations for similar compounds at that time, should be represented in the shape of a ring as opposed to a string.

Moving to the realm of writing, the birth of Robert Louis Stevenson's *The Strange Case of Dr. Jekyll and Mr. Hyde* is an equally astounding story. Having been frustrated in ongoing attempts to write about the "double being which must at times come in upon and overwhelm the mind of every thinking creature," a worsening financial situation intensified Stevenson's fervor to concoct a plot suitable for conveying that universal theme. After two intense days of "racking his brains," he recalls that "on the second night I dreamed the scene at the window, and a scene afterward split in two, in which Hyde, pursued for some crime, took the powder and underwent the change in the presence of his pursuers." Reflecting on those dream-images, he explains that "all the rest was made awake, and consciously, although I think I can trace in much of it the manner of my Brownies" (the author's name for his unconscious collaborators).[8] Exhilarating tales such as those imparted by Stevenson and Kekule abound in histories of creative achievement, including fiction and poetry writing. However, as noted above and illustrated in subsequent sections of this chapter, dream states are by no means prerequisites for incubation effects.

Whatever the precise catalyst for incubation, writers' retrospective reports of behaviors and happenings surrounding the phenomenon have been published in a number of edited collections, ordinarily embedded in narratives of larger creative acts. *The Paris Review* (*PR*) interviews are rich resources of commentary on incubation, with analysis of those sampled for this study producing a total of 181 textual units. These units disperse across two distinct subcategories. The first to be addressed speaks to the nature of incubation and how the interview subjects purport to experience it. The second takes up widely recognized precursors of incubation (blocks and breaks)—harbingers of the construct that represent some of the only accessible routes for making sense of it given the challenges of directly studying the unconscious. Of course, to qualify as

---

8. Robert Louis Stevenson, "A Chapter on Dreams," in *Across the Plains* (New York: Charles Scribner's Sons, 1892), https://etc.usf.edu/lit2go/110/selected-essays-of-robert-louis-stevenson/5111/a-chapter-on-dreams/.

incubation, these precursors must be followed by the construct's other concrete indicator, insight. Although references to this phenomenon inevitably surface in allusions to incubation in the sampled *PR* interviews, a close analysis of insight as a separate element of the creative process model is deferred to Chapter 6.

The Nature of Incubation

Roughly half of the textual units coded as incubation serve to characterize its essence, and most of those units portray it as a wholly or largely unconscious mental state,[9] the first of two themes constituting this subcategory. The prevalence of interview passages relevant to this theme suggests that writers are highly aware of and quite comfortable with the notion that the mind is especially fertile when operating below the threshold of full-blown awareness. John Cheever is particularly complimentary of the mind's inexplicable depths, claiming (in agreement with novelist Raymond Chandler) that writing enables elemental access of the subconscious and that the most beloved books are those that, at first encounter, purvey a sense of having visited there.[10] Echoing such sentiments, Jan Morris contends that the gifts of the unconscious typically transcend the efforts of the conscious.[11] Those inclined to credit the unconscious with their most impressive creative feats ascribe such appraisals to its transformative capacity, its unique facility for fashioning a stagnated thought into something they could not otherwise have imagined. Ostensibly, T. S. Eliot holds this capacity of the unconscious in high esteem, noting that, as opposed to storing partially conceived works on paper to gather dust in their inherently static form, he prefers entrusting them to the recesses of his mind where they have occasion to evolve.[12]

The transformative potential of the unconscious inspires so much awe that writers frequently cloak it in religious terminology, characterizing it as a miracle, some sort of god-speak or the influence of demons (the latter term denoting its frustratingly fickle nature). Other writers, though relying on less pious language, attribute the unconscious with mysterious, even magical,

---

9. Although a few references to the unconscious in the interview corpus ended up in subcategories under the umbrella of first insight (as they depicted cognitive moves tied to the genesis of a work), the large majority recalled episodes that followed preparation and/or, in recursive fashion, occurred after drafting was well underway or certain insights had already been achieved.
10. John Cheever, interview by Annette Grant, in *The Paris Review Interviews*, vol. 3, ed. Philip Gourevitch (New York: Picador, 2008), 161.
11. Jan Morris, interview by Leo Lerman, in *The Paris Review Interviews*, vol. 3, ed. Philip Gourevitch (New York: Picador, 2008), 321–22.
12. T. S. Eliot, interview by Donald Hall, in *The Paris Review Interviews*, vol. 1, ed. Philip Gourevitch (New York: Picador, 2006), 73.

properties. Such personifications and attributions to inexplicable forces might, at first glance, seem to bolster the spontaneous generation myth discussed near the end of Chapter 3. Upon closer scrutiny, however, these passages make clear that, when in the grips of a formidable and prolific unconscious, writers seldom abdicate their conscious responsibility in bringing a project to fruition. Take Saul Bellow, for example. Referring to a personified inner being (which, incidentally, isn't necessarily holy or evil), he offers a detailed portrayal of roles played by both the unconscious and conscious relevant to the unusual difficulty he encountered in authoring the novel *Herzog*:

> I suppose that all of us have a primitive prompter or commentator within, who from earliest years has been advising us. [...] There is such a commentator in me. I have to prepare the ground for him. From this source come words, phrases, syllables; sometimes only sounds, which I try to interpret, sometimes whole paragraphs, fully punctuated.[13]—Copyright © by *The Paris Review*, used by permission of The Wylie Agency LLC.

In this interview excerpt, Bellow recognizes that he must actively prepare for and respond to contributions of the unconscious, even while placing considerable responsibility on his "primitive prompter" to provide general guidance as well as polished prose. Personifications pervade portraits of the unconscious in *The PR* interviews consulted for this study, but many authors shy away from such fanciful depictions, opting instead for language that highlights its emanation from unfamiliar recesses of the brain and/or its abruptness in presenting unexpected solutions. Along these lines, as might be expected given the historical prevalence and status of experiences like those of Kekule and Stevenson, insight-facilitating dream states punctuate stories of the unconscious at work in the interview corpus, with talk of daydreams, in particular, conjuring associations with meditation and trance-like reverie.

Beyond these largely laudatory reflections on the general nature of the unconscious, an additional, more specific refrain pervades this incubation subcategory: lack of author awareness about eventual particularities of a piece. Pertinent to this refrain, many of the interviews reveal that fiction writers and poets often enjoy great successes during invention and drafting that are workable and in line with their plans, only to find that their end products contain features or effects that they didn't recognize while those works were in progress. For a couple of writers in the sampled interviews

---

13. Saul Bellow, interview by Gordon Lloyd Harper, in *The Paris Review Interviews*, vol. 1, ed. Philip Gourevitch (New York: Picador, 2006), 95.

(Jorge Luis Borges, Graham Green), validation of the unconscious manifests in acknowledgment that, though they didn't set out to emulate other authors, the influences of those they admire are discernible.[14] Other interviewees connect lack of awareness about aspects of their own work to isolated literary elements, collectively referencing character, plot, theme, voice, symbolism, rhythm and even humor.

To summarize a few of the most striking examples addressing isolated literary elements, Alice Munro, while contemplating character during her interview, struggles to grasp why, as a 25-year-old, she kept writing about aging spinsters, especially since she wasn't acquainted with any.[15] Eudora Welty reveals that she was not conscious when writing her early stories that she was applying physical traits to her characters as a way of exposing their inner beings.[16] Regarding plot, V. S. Naipaul admits being shocked by the violence in one of his own novels, insisting that he was not conscious of it until performing a public reading of said novel for an audience of New Yorkers.[17] Similarly unaware of the nature of actions driving his novels, Haruki Murakami observes that, when he drafts, he is just as anxious to know how events will unravel as his readers will be.[18] According to Robert Lowell and James Baldwin, theme is yet another elusive element. More specifically, Lowell implies that he may not realize he has something to say until that message finally emerges in a finished poem,[19] and Baldwin flatly denies knowing exactly how he goes about asserting literary theses despite his interviewer's query assuming the presence of sociopolitical viewpoints in certain works.[20]

Regardless of whether the unconscious is hammering out literary elements or solving larger creative problems in the context of dreams or daytime

---

14. Jorge Luis Borges, interview by Ronald Christ, in *The Paris Review Interviews*, vol. 1, ed. Philip Gourevitch (New York: Picador, 2006), 138; Graham Greene, interview by Martin Shuttleworth and Simon Raven, in *The Paris Review Interviews*, vol. 2, ed. Philip Gourevitch (New York: Picador, 2007), 8.
15. Alice Munro, interview by Jeanne McCulloch and Mona Simpson, in *The Paris Review Interviews*, vol. 2, ed. Philip Gourevitch (New York: Picador, 2007), 401.
16. Eudora Welty, interview by Linda Kuehl, in *The Paris Review Interviews*, vol. 2, ed. Philip Gourevitch (New York: Picador, 2007), 131.
17. V. S. Naipaul, interview by Tarun Tejpal and Jonathan Rosen, in *The Paris Review Interviews*, vol. 4, ed. Philip Gourevitch (New York: Picador, 2009), 296.
18. Haruki Murakami, interview by John Wray, in *The Paris Review Interviews*, vol. 4, ed. Philip Gourevitch (New York: Picador, 2009), 365.
19. Robert Lowell, interview by Frederick Seidel, in *The Paris Review Interviews*, vol. 2, ed. Philip Gourevitch (New York: Picador, 2007), 95.
20. James Baldwin, interview by Jordan Elgrably, in *The Paris Review Interviews*, vol. 2, ed. Philip Gourevitch (New York: Picador, 2007), 248. Baldwin's key statement references the "how" of writing, but the context makes clear he is discussing thematic development.

reverie, the textual units coded to this theme land there as a result of phrasing in the interviewees' remarks establishing that the mind reached key insights at times when the author had been entirely or largely unaware that progress was underway. Stated more precisely, inclusion in this theme required that the mental activity perceived as most crucial to advancing a project was obviously more unconscious than it was conscious. Incubation's association with the unconscious or fringe conscious is well established in the creativity scholarship, but, as noted near the beginning of this chapter, it can also manifest in what Robert Olton terms "creative worrying," or alternating bouts of unconscious and conscious mentation, the focus of another theme defining this subcategory.

Indeed, Olton maintains that the time between a creative block and an insight is frequently occupied by an *evenhanded exchange* between the unconscious and the conscious—an exchange during which the conscious is more consistently and aggressively involved in solving the problem at hand, as opposed to merely executing the solution after the unconscious has formulated it, as implied by anecdotes cited in previous paragraphs.[21] In applied language, creative worrying can be understood as the decision to temporarily abandon a problem for other activities, only to find that it is constantly darting in and out of mind. Of course, one doesn't need to be a famous innovator to understand this phenomenon. Especially in contemporary society with its increased dependence on the ability to multitask, people are used to placing professional problem-solving on hold to address the demands of personal life, while the time constraints imposed by those demands necessitate stealing moments here and there to contemplate career-related work in the interest of completing it on schedule.

Beyond the partnership between conscious and unconscious cognition that characterizes creative worrying, it can be further distinguished from wholly or primarily unconscious cognition for the fact that insights produced by the latter ordinarily arrive quite abruptly, whereas insights produced by the former tend to materialize more gradually. Of course, the comparatively more gradual and wakeful nature of productive creative worrying increases appreciation of—or, more likely, panic over—passing time. In fact, numerous passages from the interview transcripts coded as creative worrying in this study indicate that the incubation period for novels could be years or even decades long. Even if not excessively lengthy, periods of creative worrying, by definition, exhibit incessant interruptions amidst personal and professional obligations.

These interruptions might reasonably be construed as breaks (a theme discussed in the next section) as opposed to creative worrying; however, the key

---

21. Olton, "Experimental Studies of Incubation," 11.

to identification with the latter theme is that the time away is marked by continual interplay between conscious and unconscious cognition relevant to the targeted project. Further complicating coding processes for creative worrying, it seems a few authors refer to the phenomenon simply as "thinking." But that word connotes full consciousness, and so the balanced exchange between consciousness and lack of consciousness portrayed in the passages coded to this section warrants invoking the more technical terminology. Moreover, such passages coded as creative worrying, in contrast to mere thinking, pinpoint special problems or projects the artists are stewing over, in contrast to more random or generic cognitive activity.

Despite the challenges of coding certain passages that imply creative worrying, more than a few offer quintessential illustrations of the construct. Consider James Thurber, for example, who catches himself suddenly attending to projects at inopportune moments, when he hasn't been expecting to work beyond what might occur subconsciously. Thurber explains, "Sometimes my wife comes up to me at a party and says, 'Dammit, Thurber, stop writing.' She usually catches me in the middle of a paragraph. Or my daughter will look up from the dinner table and ask, 'Is he sick?' 'No,' my wife says, 'he's writing something.'" Though the author's way of composing had been impacted to some degree by the fact that he was losing his eyesight, these recollections exemplify creative worrying in stark contrast to his deliberate, focused work dictating to a secretary during regularly assigned writing hours.[22] Jack Kerouac offers a similarly vivid account of creative worrying in response to an interview question about the extent to which he calculates the content of a novel before he begins drafting: "You think out what actually happened, you tell friends long stories about it, you mull it over in your mind, you connect it together at leisure, then when the time comes to pay the rent, you force yourself to sit at the typewriter."[23] The intermittent bouts of conscious, intentional treatment of the proposed project (sharing it with friends, actively pondering it, testing possible links between ideas), while taking advantage of leisure time as he reportedly does, classify this excerpt from Kerouac's interview as an instance of creative worrying.

Appearing to have much in common with Kerouac when it comes to formulating a piece, Alice Munro observes that she ordinarily has "a lot of acquaintance with the story" before she drafts it. She continues by noting that "when I didn't have regular time to give to writing, stories would just be working

---

22. James Thurber, interview by George Plimpton and Max Steele, in *The Paris Review Interviews*, vol. 2, ed. Philip Gourevitch (New York: Picador, 2007), 31.
23. Jack Kerouac, interview by Ted Berrigan, in *The Paris Review Interviews*, vol. 4, ed. Philip Gourevitch (New York: Picador, 2009), 109.

in my head for so long that when I started to write I was deep into them."[24] In addition to providing a readily identifiable account of creative worrying, Munro's remarks contain phrasing that represents a significant trend in this theme—that is, many writers who talk about creative worrying articulate it as some version of entertaining an idea or plan for a literary work *in one's head* over *a significant expanse of time*. In line with the definition of the phenomenon proffered earlier, that phrasing indicates deliberate, though occasional, contemplation of the idea or plan as other aspects of the authors' lives would intervene and compel the unconscious to take over for a while. (In contrast, the earlier remark from Eliot about storing gems of thought in the back of his mind makes no mention of his actively contemplating them; thus, that passage was coded differently.)

Overall, findings of this study relevant to the nature of incubation establish that it may unfold in a variety of ways. Whether the authors' breakthroughs or insights in composing are depicted as resulting from the unconscious, from the fringe conscious or from an equal exchange between the unconscious and the conscious, their words make clear that relaxed, unfocused mental states are highly facilitative in the context of sophisticated problem-solving activities like writing. Having become increasingly enlightened about the nature and capability of incubative processes, these writers apparently understand that letting go of a piece and submitting it to the unconscious, even sparingly, can move them more quickly and efficiently than conscious rigor through some of their darkest professional hours. Even when insight is long in coming, the authors' words convey optimism that incubation time will elucidate avenues around a creative block, a notable precursor of incubation and the focus of the following section.

Precursors of Incubation

To repeat an observation already made, it is very difficult to study incubation directly; therefore, its nature and impact must be gleaned from occurrences and behaviors surrounding it. One significant occurrence to be observed in this respect is a creative block, known in literary circles as writer's block. Published lore and empirical research about creative and expository writing brim with tales of writer's block, and this study of *PR* interviews reflects that trend. The prolific body of scholarship on the ailment establishes that it is widespread, and this scholarship, though discouraging, allows individuals to share in and draw strength from a community's collective suffering. Not unexpectedly, the sheer agony of writer's block is acknowledged in most of the passages assigned

---

24. Munro, *The Paris Review Interviews*, 407.

to this theme, the extent of which is summed up succinctly by John Cheever, who contends that "there is nothing more painful to a writer than an inability to work."[25] Precise expressions attached to the mental and emotional distress associated with writer's block invoke references to depression, desperation, disappointment, disintegration, hopelessness, irritability, impatience, misery and paralysis. One author even admits suicidal thoughts.[26]

The most intense of these emotions are rooted in dread that this time the block (even though blocks have come and gone throughout a career) might prove to be permanent, thus ending one's personal and professional livelihood. T. S. Eliot, for example, when questioned about a lull in his output following "Prufrock," confessed that, during that period, he feared he had run out of ideas for writing.[27] In like fashion, Philip Larkin laments that years of failed efforts to craft another novel after the success of his first two led him to believe that he had lost all ability to write, and Paul Auster claims that, when he became blocked after composing poetry for 10 years, he feared his writing life had come to an end (he later switched genres, becoming an acclaimed novelist).[28] James Baldwin's struggles in this regard are especially poignant, revealing that, following the assassination of Martin Luther King Jr., his outlook deteriorated to the extent that he "couldn't write at all"—he no longer saw any reason for it. Responding to his interviewer about the matter, he states, "I was hurt […] I can't even talk about it. I didn't know how to continue, didn't see my way clear." Fortunately, he reached out to his brother who helped him reengage the novel he was writing when the block occurred (i.e., *No Name in the Street*).[29]

While most of the commentary on the pain of writer's block focuses on its emotional toll, Ralph Ellison suggests that its negative effects can attack the body as well as the spirit. Reflecting on advice that he "get some rest" upon becoming physically sick in the months preceding work on *The Invisible Man*, Ellison contends that "part of [his] illness was due, no doubt, to the fact that [he] had not been able to write a novel for which [he'd] received a Rosenwald Fellowship the previous winter."[30] To be accurate, not all of the

---

25. Cheever, *The Paris Review Interviews*, 165.
26. Richard Price, interview by James Linville, in *The Paris Review Interviews*, vol. 1, ed. Philip Gourevitch (New York: Picador, 2006), 397.
27. Eliot, *The Paris Review Interviews*, 71.
28. Phillip Larkin, interview by Robert Phillips, in *The Paris Review Interviews*, vol. 2, ed. Philip Gourevitch (New York: Picador, 2007), 217, 225; Paul Auster, interview by Michael Wood, in *The Paris Review Interviews*, vol. 4, ed. Philip Gourevitch (New York: Picador, 2009), 316.
29. Baldwin, *The Paris Review Interviews*, 251.
30. Ralph Ellison, interview by Alfred Chester and Vilma Howard, in *The Paris Review Interviews*, vol. 3, ed. Philip Gourevitch (New York: Picador, 2008), 11.

interviewees who talk about creative blocks communicate levels of distress as intense as those experienced in the anecdotes just reviewed. Nevertheless, even for authors who suffer less over writer's block, it's no stretch to imagine that months or years of being stuck while composing a single work would lead to considerable anxiety and doubt about one's skills.

On that point, even when not explicitly attached to acute pain, weak or waning confidence is an oft-cited source of writer's block in the interviews consulted for this study.[31] Robert Lowell, for instance, remembers "giving up" for a while when the kind of poetry he hoped for and tried to produce "became so cluttered and overdone that it wasn't really poetry."[32] Gabriel Garcia Marquez reports being inhibited for having lost sight of his audience, for not being able, after completing *One Hundred Years of Solitude*, to discern anymore what his intended readers were likely to respond to.[33] More baldly critical in his self-assessment regarding sources of writer's block, Harold Pinter relates the following when considering the prospect of composing another play: "Something people don't realize is the great boredom one has with oneself, and just to see those words come down again on paper, I think: Oh Christ, everything I do seems to be predictable, unsatisfactory, and hopeless."[34] Expanding the list of perceived inadequacies already documented, certain authors suggest that they believed they had nothing of importance left to share with the world. Embodying this attitude is Richard Price, who claims to have suddenly run out of autobiography, a predicament that left him treading water, refusing to finish two books that he started because they felt vapid.[35] Still other writers blame their blocks on aspects of drafts in progress that just didn't seem to be working and that left them feeling unsettled for long periods of time.

Regardless of its cause, writer's block can be debilitating, as the above review of pertinent *PR* interview excerpts attests. To be sure, most anyone who has written anything of relative length or complexity has experienced the feelings of frustration, and even desperation, that some of these writers portray. The groundwork laid earlier in this chapter establishes that the essential

---

31. Confidence levels are also addressed in Chapter 8 on emergent patterns, but, there, the issue is treated more generically—that is, it is not tied to a specific element of the creative process model but, rather, to the larger concern of making it as a professional writer.
32. Lowell, *The Paris Review Interviews*, 64.
33. Gabriel Garcia Marquez, interview by Peter H. Stone, in *The Paris Review Interviews*, vol. 2, ed. Philip Gourevitch (New York: Picador, 2007), 187.
34. Harold Pinter, interview by Lawrence M. Bensky, in *The Paris Review Interviews*, vol. 3, ed. Philip Gourevitch (New York: Picador, 2008), 140.
35. Price, *The Paris Review Interviews*, 396.

remedy for writer's block is to release the project at hand from fully conscious attention, paving the way for the benefits of loose thinking. The aforementioned vehicle for doing so is break-taking, a second theme to surface in data coded to the subcategory of incubation precursors.

As indicated at the beginning of this chapter, the exact route to successful incubation is less important to individuals caught in debilitating creative struggles than is the likelihood that incubation will deliver results. Several of the interviewees who extol the advantages of interrupting concentrated work on a project collectively allude to a variety of mechanisms that might have facilitated their Aha! moments. Of course, the very definition of incubation ensures that every passage coded as such at least implies a break preceding insight. In the interest of strictly distinguishing textual units assigned to this theme, then, coding procedures sought to cull only those passages in which the break-taking itself was emphasized, as opposed to a particular apparatus of incubation or the block that compelled it, as in the previous sections.

Whatever the combination of unconscious and conscious mentation, the recursivity of creative endeavor predicts that productive breaks might occur at any time. Pertinent to this observation, the interview sample represents a wide spectrum of composing processes, with some writers apparently suspending projects for years after initially conceiving them, some delaying engagement with a text at multiple junctures while drafting and still others insisting on leaving fully articulated drafts alone for weeks at a time before revising or editing them. As for breaks surrounding invention, Saul Bellow indicates that he must find ways of detaching for a while from his fledgling ideas.[36] Likewise focusing on the gestation period, William Styron acknowledges the necessity of attaining some distance from especially emotional events before writing about them.[37] And, rather dauntingly, Jean Rhys recalls needing two decades to finally detangle an intricate web of thoughts that eventually spawned her novel, *Voyage in the Dark*.[38] All of these examples reinforce understanding that, while first insights can strike seemingly in an instant as illustrated in Chapter 3, initial ideas for literary works regularly require extensive research and rumination before they are developed enough for drafting to begin.

Relevant to more fully conceived projects, breaks in the midst of drafting manifest on occasion in a visceral reluctance to reengage a text in progress, presumably because translating ideas into prose or verse—that is, turning

---

36. Bellow, *The Paris Review Interviews*, 96.
37. William Styron, interview by George Plimpton and Peter Matthiessen, in *The Paris Review Interviews*, vol. 4, ed. Philip Gourevitch (New York: Picador, 2009), 11.
38. Jean Rhys, interview by Elizabeth Vreeland, in *The Paris Review Interviews*, vol. 3, ed. Philip Gourevitch (New York: Picador, 2008), 199–200.

one type of symbolic representation into another—is the most taxing activity involved in writing. Cases in point, both Robert Stone and Richard Price admit to actively dawdling between work sessions, and Price goes so far as to list some specific delay tactics, such as reading the newspaper, fielding phone calls and playing with paper clips.[39] On the other hand, certain writers exhibit intense discipline in their approach to drafting, seeking the most extreme focus possible. T. S. Eliot is one such writer; he strictly limits drafting to only three hours per day, forcing breaks at the end of that time allotment since, when he produces beyond it, the results tend to be less than satisfactory.[40] Maya Angelou also drafts in accordance with strict guidelines, forcing breaks through a regimen she has established for combating the exhaustion experienced during prolific bouts of literary production. This regimen includes composing in the morning followed by showering, grocery shopping, preparing a hearty dinner for herself (and maybe some friends), clearing the table and, finally, evaluating the text she produced earlier in the day.[41] Cooking may be Angelou's diversion of choice, but Philip Roth prefers reading. He claims that he "reads all the time while he's working," an inclination he views as a way of "keeping the circuits open," of "thinking about [his] *line* of work while getting a little rest from [it]," of "fuel[ing] the overall obsession" with writing.[42]

The above interview excerpts suggest that breaks during gestation and drafting tend to accompany a lack of preparedness to initially commit, or continue committing, words to paper or screen. As drafts reach completion, the source of blocks seemingly shifts to a conviction that first stabs at proposed products are always inadequate and they cannot be improved without applying break-induced, refreshed literary sensibilities at the whole-text level. Authors who acknowledge the import of taking breaks at this juncture are apparently so committed to the strategy that it assumes the status of habit or ritual (much as taking breaks during drafting in the context of Angelou's experience). Truman Capote, for instance, makes a habit of filing away his fully developed drafts for weeks, months, maybe longer before revising them, while Jorge Luis Borges settles for approximately two

---

39. Robert Stone, interview by William Crawford Woods, in *The Paris Review Interviews*, vol. 1, ed. Philip Gourevitch (New York: Picador, 2006), 308. Price, *The Paris Review Interviews*, 384.
40. Eliot, *The Paris Review Interviews*, 75.
41. Maya Angelou, interview by George Plimpton, in *The Paris Review Interviews*, vol. 4, ed. Philip Gourevitch (New York: Picador, 2009), 241.
42. Philip Roth, interview by Hermione Lee, in *The Paris Review Interviews*, vol. 4, ed. Philip Gourevitch (New York: Picador, 2009), 207.

weeks.[43] Another voice of experience on this front, Stephen King insists that a complete rough draft should "sit and breathe" for six weeks at the minimum before the author returns to it.[44] And Toni Morrison so earnestly values the act of taking breaks late in her composing ventures that she teaches the tactic to students in her creative writing courses.[45] E. B. White would undoubtedly approve Morrison's advice for aspiring novelists given that, after spending two years drafting the entirety of *Charlotte's Web*, he set it aside for some time to let it percolate, convinced that something was still awry.[46] These representative examples of late-breaking break-taking point to the importance of delaying closure,[47] even when the impetus to finally be finished with such a labor-intensive quest must be at its strongest. It seems the professional success of these artists hinges on their patience in waiting for the sharpening of critical acuity through extended mental detachment from a project, detachment that can produce both minor and major insights about comprehensive initial drafts.

As indicated near the beginning of this chapter, theories accounting for the mind's activity during incubation are various, one being that the breaks initializing its onset afford opportunities for exposure to fresh intellectual or environmental stimuli, thus enabling novel connections in thought that directly stimulate insight. One productive route for such connection-making is cross-pollination, introduced in Chapter 4 (relevant to preparation) as the act of engaging in cognitive or physical activities different from the creative endeavor itself. While, assuredly, cross-pollination is shown to be helpful in priming writers to commence a draft, the phenomenon is also evident in textual units coded as breaks relevant to incubation—but with a unique twist: writers who capitalize on cross-pollination during breaks tend to do so by switching writing projects as opposed to exploring comparatively remote disciplines or pastimes, as is relatively common during preparation. Indeed, more than a few break-related passages indicate that some poets and novelists believe the most promising method for pushing through a block is to write something else, possibly

---

43. Truman Capote, interview by Pati Hill, in *The Paris Review Interviews*, vol. 1, ed. Philip Gourevitch (New York: Picador, 2006), 30–31; Luis Borges, *The Paris Review Interviews*, 128.
44. Stephen King, interview by Christopher Lehmann-Haupt and Nathaniel Rich, in *The Paris Review Interviews*, vol. 1, ed. Philip Gourevitch (New York: Picador, 2007), 480.
45. Toni Morrison, interview by Elissa Schappell and Claudia Brodsky Lacour, in *The Paris Review Interviews*, vol. 2, ed. Philip Gourevitch (New York: Picador, 2007), 365.
46. E. B. White, in *The Paris Review Interviews*, vol. 4, ed. Philip Gourevitch (New York: Picador, 2009), 139.
47. Donald Murray, "The Essential Delay," in *When a Writer Can't Write*, ed. Mike Rose (New York: Guilford, 1985), 219–26.

even dabbling in other genres for a while, a technique that allows one work to "shape and qualify" the other.[48] In such instances, the secondary project, which serves as a source of cross-pollination for the primary project, suggests the authors' break-time preferences for linguistic diversions in contrast to other artistic or leisure activities. While references to cross-pollination during incubation are not prolific enough to earn their own subcategory as they did in Chapter 4 on preparation, the references are plentiful enough to warrant treatment here since their ties to breaks are so explicitly established by the interviewees.

Commenting on breaks between novels, John Gardner affirms the need to "get in enough life and enough thinking about things to have anything to say, any clear questions to work through." He engages various other genres to do so, including book reviews, children's stories and scholarly articles and books.[49] Stephen King also believes in cross-pollinating between major projects, noting that composing short stories helps revive him, helps him recover when he falls flat after exerting so much energy on a novel. Joyce Carol Oates attributes the rejuvenating impact of cross-pollination to a need for consistently being in a writer's frame of mind so that, even as a fully drafted novel is awaiting her final approval, she'll work on a short story and another novel.[50] Celebrating the benefits of *within-draft* cross-pollination, Paul Auster recounts one of the most striking instances of the phenomenon in the interview corpus informing this analysis:

> I started writing *Oracle Night* before *The Book of Illusions*. I had twenty pages or so, but then I stopped. I realized that I didn't quite understand what I was doing. *The Book of Illusions* took me three years to write, and all during that time I continued thinking about *Oracle Night*. When I finally returned to it, it came out with remarkable speed.[51]—Copyright © by *The Paris Review*, used by permission of The Wylie Agency LLC.

Of course, though the "continued thinking" about *Oracle Night* while working on *The Book of Illusions* might point to creative worrying, this passage was coded as cross-pollination given its specific reference to a purposeful (as opposed to

---

48. Paul F. Ferguson, John R. Maier, Frank McConnell and Sara Matthiessen, "John Gardner," in *The Paris Review Interviews*, vol. 2, ed. Philip Gourevitch (New York: Picador, 2007), 144.
49. John Gardner, interview by Paul F. Ferguson, John R. Maier, Frank McConnell and Sara Matthiessen, in *The Paris Review Interviews*, vol. 2, ed. Philip Gourevitch (New York: Picador, 2079), 145.
50. Joyce Carol Oates, interview by Robert Phillips, in *The Paris Review Interviews*, vol. 3, ed. Philip Gourevitch (New York: Picador, 2008), 173.
51. Auster, *The Paris Review Interviews*, 332.

casual), significant (as opposed to intermittent) break from one novel to pursue focused work on another novel (as opposed to random, unrelated pastimes).

The passages just reviewed suggest that, while any intellectual or environmental change of pace affords opportunities for cross-pollination, for many writers, even a relative tweak in focus will facilitate adjustments capable of overcoming a creative block. Furthermore, these passages, in tandem with those cited in Chapter 4, demonstrate that cross-pollination can be beneficial at virtually any stage of composing. Despite their nature, catalysts or timing, one axiom about breaks arising from *The PR* discourse coded as germane to incubation is that they are valuable, if not essential, in the context of creative activity. While sometimes they are forced—that is, the writer wants to continue working but cannot move forward—the reality that so many writers willfully build them into professional life is a testament to their perceived payoff. Whatever they allow the mind to do (unleash the unconscious, rest and refresh itself, escape ruts in thinking, build connections through cross-pollination), breaks tend to elicit insight in a much more efficient manner than would a relentless sense of discipline that, although it may feel noble in the moment, is likely to prove deflating and possibly even defeating. Most assuredly, the mind locked in the rigors of creativity needs breaks, maybe even frequent breaks, depending on the nature of the project.

Some Incubated Closing Remarks

The primary objective of this chapter is to stress that creative achievement results from an intricate dance of focused and unfocused, conscious and unconscious cognitive activity. Unfortunately, the grueling work of steeping oneself in the knowledge base essential to elaborating a brilliant first insight seldom leads, in and of itself, to the kind of groundbreaking revelation that would sustain an effortless drafting experience. Rather, as exemplified in the words of the writers whose voices support this study, the act of composing most often proceeds in fits and starts, interrupted as it is by breaks that are not merely helpful but crucial to problem-solving and originality. Though what exactly occurs in the mind during these breaks can't be verified in any positivistic sense, empirical research on incubation effects, bolstered by author testimony reviewed in this chapter and elsewhere, leaves little room for doubting the cliché that all work and no play makes for dull minds. Contrary to the conviction that interrupting focus is evidence of mental weakness or lack of commitment, pulling oneself away from a creative problem can actually stimulate insights and expedite productive drafting in the long run.

Chapter 6
INSIGHT, OR THE EUREKA EXPERIENCE

The Eureka experience, the Aha! moment, the incubation effect—all are synonyms for insight, the fourth element of the paradigmatic creative process model introduced in Chapters 1 and 2 as the emergence of a solution to a creative problem. As Chapters 3, 4 and 5 collectively indicate, insight typically follows upon considerable labor and frustration associated with defining the parameters of a particular challenge, gathering background information essential to undertaking it, managing the stress of mental blocks, as well as locating and applying strategies for breaking through them. In response to all the effort and vexation, insight is an exhilarating reward that keeps creators engaged with their work despite the intense cognitive, emotional and physical endurance it requires.

Relevant to writing, insight is most reasonably linked with drafting. In other words, the solution to a creative problem reveals itself in the execution of a concept or plan for a literary work in the form of easily and smoothly expressed phrases, sentences, paragraphs and even larger sections of text, accompanied by a feeling that the draft in progress is an apt realization of that concept or plan. These circumstances often result in a state of "flow," defined in Chapter 2 as "an almost automatic, effortless, yet highly focused state of consciousness" in the midst of "painful, risky, difficult activities that stretch [personal] capacity and [involve] an element of novelty and discovery."[1] This definition is worth repeating here since it previews the vast majority of references to insight in *The Paris Review* (*PR*) interviews sampled for this study as will become clear in the remainder of this chapter. References coded as insight total 136 and fall into four subcategories that clarify how the interview subjects experience insight: effortless drafting, autonomous literary elements, discovery writing and sudden connections. Each of these subcategories

---

1. Mihaly Csikszentmihalyi, *Creativity: Flow and the Psychology of Discovery and Invention* (New York: HarperCollins, 1996), 110. Read more about flow specific to writing in Chapter 2.

contains passages that communicate a sense of how Eureka moments feel and/or how they come to be.

Special difficulties in coding this element of the creative process model involved distinguishing it from first insight. Readers will recall that first insight is the initial vision for a project, usually a vague and underdeveloped notion merely suggestive of a direction or final destination. By contrast, insight comes later in reaction to refining the initial vision, solidifying parameters of the creative task and performing essential research. At times during transcript analysis, it was difficult to discern from an author's remarks whether an insight originated a creative act or occurred once it was underway; in most cases, however, interviewers' questions and the conversations surrounding troublesome passages proved helpful in making such distinctions. The following discussion, then, provides an overview of passages indicating breakthroughs in the midst of creative struggle, after the poet or fiction writer had initiated a project and engaged in some level of preparation as characterized in Chapter 4.

Effortless Drafting

As previewed in the introduction to this chapter, most definitions of "flow," a common manifestation of insight in writing, equate the construct with ease of production. In this vein, flow has long been a staple of the layperson's lexicon for characterizing activities or processes that proceed with unusual fluidity, unhampered by distractions or glitches that can delay, or even foil, progress toward an anticipated goal. During his interview, Gabriel Garcia Marquez actually invokes the term, indicating that "there is a special state of mind in which you can write with great ease and things just flow."[2] Most of the writers, however, defer to language reminiscent of the construct's formal definitions, with several portraying the outcomes associated with flow as everything suddenly "falling into place," an adeptness for composing a greater-than-usual number of pages in a relatively short time span or the stamina to compose for longer periods of time in one sitting because focus is so intense and ideas are coming so readily. In most of these instances, the authors also report a sense of excitement or joy, with Marilynne Robinson observing that such feelings bolster her willingness to seclude herself for her work and explain why she becomes ill-humored when she's expected to deal with the tedious demands of daily existence.[3]

---

2. Gabriel Garcia Marquez, interview by Peter H. Stone, in *The Paris Review Interviews*, vol. 2, ed. Philip Gourevitch (New York: Picador, 2007), 196.
3. Marilynne Robinson, interview by Sarah Fay, in *The Paris Review Interviews*, vol. 4, ed. Philip Gourevitch (New York: Picador, 2009), 456.

Certain authors waxed more specific about their flow experiences, offering alternative metaphors for the sensations that accompany them. For example, after struggling for some time with the narrative mode for *Midnight's Children*, Salman Rushdie recalls suddenly hitting upon an option that allowed him to quickly spin out what survives nearly intact as the novel's first page. Alluding to Muses or divine intervention (more prevalently associated with first insight or incubation), Rushdie recalls the "arrival" of his protagonist's savvy, humorous voice, explaining further that he "was electrified by what was coming out of [his] typewriter" and that "it was one of those moments when you believe that the writing comes through you rather than from you."[4] In concert with Rushdie's assessment, Paul Auster describes insight as a trance-like sensation,[5] while Maya Angelou compares it to scudding in the context of sailing, indicating that she might glide smoothly for up to three days propelled by insight-generated winds. Further, she shares that flow is her favorite aspect of writing—that is, the moment when language finally bends its will to the writer.[6]

While Angelou's depiction of insight hints at a symbiosis between her ideas and an authentic voice, several of the interviews render the connection more explicit, so much so that it is a notable theme within transcripts that comment on the nature of insight. Such is the case with Phillip Larkin's transcript, which reveals that after a lengthy dry spell during which he thought his career was effectively finished, he changed environments and suddenly came to life. At this point, he was able to compose a second poetry collection, one that his interviewer describes as being fresher and more sophisticated. Of this experience Larkin claims that all aspects of his art—his ideas, his feelings, words appropriate to capturing them—were thriving in unison and in such a way that he discovered an authentic voice.[7] Gabriel Garcia Marquez and V. S. Naipaul share memories quite similar to Larkin's, as they recount extended bouts of writer's block that finally ended with discovery of a voice fitting to their intentions. Garcia Marquez contends that this breakthrough enabled him to move from writing nothing of any consequence for five years to writing every day straight for 18 months, eventually penning *One Hundred Years of Solitude*.[8] And Naipaul remembers emerging from a period of deep depression (caused

---

4. Salman Rushdie, interview by Jack Livings, in *The Paris Review Interviews*, vol. 3, ed. Philip Gourevitch (New York: Picador, 2008), 376.
5. Paul Auster, interview by Michael Woods, in *The Paris Review Interviews*, vol. 4, ed. Philip Gourevitch (New York: Picador, 2009), 332.
6. Maya Angelou, interview by George Plimpton, in *The Paris Review Interviews*, vol. 4, ed. Philip Gourevitch (New York: Picador, 2009), 257, 258.
7. Philip Larkin, interview by Robert Phillips, in *The Paris Review Interviews*, vol. 2, ed. Philip Gourevitch (New York: Picador, 2007), 225.
8. Garcia Marquez, *The Paris Review Interviews*, 188.

by harsh criticism leveled at one of his manuscripts) to a position where he was able to begin his famed short story collection, *Miguel Street*.⁹

As the passages just reviewed imply, insight turns frustration and hardship into delight and confidence. In many cases, the authors state or suggest that the phenomenon streamlines the notoriously taxing business of drafting (see more on such challenges in Chapter 8), if only for a short time. Occasionally, writing from insight is so effortless that it feels as if the book or poem is developing itself, that it or some element of it has taken control of the author, dictating subsequent moves. Such depictions of insight are so abundant in the interview corpus that they earned their own subcategory, which is explored in the following section.

Literary Work or Elements as Autonomous

One of the most intriguing findings of this study is the regularity with which authors delegate responsibility over their writing to characters, plot or, in some cases, a poem, story or novel in its entirety. These references distinguish themselves from those alluding to supernatural intervention tied to other subcategories in the coding scheme as the authors' words leave no doubt that they perceived the literary elements *that they created* took charge, as opposed to some force external to the creative act. As might be expected, there are a few skeptics, the most vehement being John Cheever, who takes offense at the notion that authors are servants to their "cretinous inventions."¹⁰ Martin Amis and Toni Morrison also relay reservations though they are ultimately tempered by their acknowledgment that, while they, as authors, remain in command, the characters can get out of hand. More specifically, Amis speaks of giving them "a bit of license," listening to their ideas while poised to "slap them down" if need be.¹¹ In agreement with the gist of Amis's observation, Morrison locates a need for author assertiveness in her characters' wild independence rooted in all-consuming self-centeredness; in fact, one of her characters (Pilate in *Song of Solomon*) became so troublesome in this regard that the author confesses to actively stifling her.¹²

Despite the reservations and qualifications, an impressive majority of authors whose words are coded to this subcategory seem resigned, if not quite

---

9. V. S. Naipaul, interview by Tarun Tejpal and Jonathan Rosen, in *The Paris Review Interviews*, vol. 4, ed. Philip Gourevitch (New York: Picador, 2009), 291.
10. John Cheever, interview by Annette Grant, in *The Paris Review Interviews*, vol. 3, ed. Philip Gourevitch (New York: Picador, 2008), 146.
11. Martin Amis, interview by Francesca Riviere, in *The Paris Review Interviews*, vol. 3, ed. Philip Gourevitch (New York: Picador, 2008), 352.
12. Toni Morrison, interview by Elissa Schapell and Claudia Brodsky Lacour, in *The Paris Review Interviews*, vol. 2, ed. Philip Gourevitch (New York: Picador, 2007), 376–77.

willing, to follow the lead of the beings inhabiting their poetry and prose. This disposition translates in nonmetaphoric language to acceptance of inevitabilities engendered by interactions between the literary elements they are manipulating. Adding to Amis's and Morrison's observations, authors represent their characters' independent streaks in a variety of ways. Following is a sample:

> There is always a point in the book where the characters themselves rise up and take charge and finish the job.[13]—Copyright © by *The Paris Review*, used by permission of The Wylie Agency LLC. William Faulkner, "The Art of Fiction #12." Copyright © 1956 by Jean Stein. All rights not specifically granted herein are hereby reserved to the Licensor.

> I let [the characters] go where they have to go, and analyze as I'm going along what's involved, what the implications are.[14]—Copyright © by *The Paris Review*, used by permission of The Wylie Agency LLC and with permission of the Brockport Writers Forum.

> I don't know what kind of characters my plays will have until […] they indicate to me what they are.[15]—Copyright © by *The Paris Review*, used by permission of The Wylie Agency LLC.

> […] a character determines his or her own "voice" and I must follow along."[16]—Copyright © by *The Paris Review*, used by permission of The Wylie Agency LLC.

> […] highly intuitive characters […] tend to perceive the contours of the literary landscape in which they dwell and […] try to guide or even take over the narrative.[17]—Copyright © by *The Paris Review*, used by permission of The Wylie Agency LLC.

---

13. William Faulkner, interview by Jean Stein, in *The Paris Review Interviews*, vol. 2, ed. Philip Gourevitch (New York: Picador, 2007), 43.
14. John Gardner, interview by Paul F. Ferguson, John R. Maier, Frank McConnell and Sara Matthiessen, in *The Paris Review Interviews*, vol. 2, ed. Philip Gourevitch (New York: Picador, 2007), 157.
15. Harold Pinter, interview by Lawrence M. Bensky, in *The Paris Review Interviews*, vol. 3, ed. Philip Gourevitch (New York: Picador, 2008), 128.
16. Joyce Carol Oates, interview by Robert Phillips, in *The Paris Review Interviews*, vol. 3, ed. Philip Gourevitch (New York: Picador, 2008), 183.
17. Ibid., 183.

[...] I tend to think of them as autonomous beings with their own opinions and their own ways of expressing themselves.[18]—Copyright © by *The Paris Review*, used by permission of The Wylie Agency LLC.

Several of the authors citing character autonomy explore the phenomenon beyond such general statements, demonstrating that the relationships they developed with these ink-and-paper personalities were not only confrontational at times (as in the cases of Amis and Morrison) but also disappointing or depressing.

Richard Price's characters, for example, persist in self-destructive behavior, causing him to complain: "I can't stop them. It's getting ridiculous. I get laughed at for the volume of chemicals that gets consumed, the amount of dope and booze."[19] The fact that Price would defer to his characters over critics is a testament to how forceful he found them to be, with one of them, Ray Hicks in *Dog Soldiers*, shooting a buddy without the author's anticipating it.[20] On another melancholy note, after explaining that he eradicated larger portions of his original draft of *Shalimar the Clown* at the characters' insistence, Salman Rushdie recalls breaking into tears and wondering what he was doing when the father of his protagonist's love interest died in a fruit orchard.[21] More irritated than disheartened, David Grossman confesses being initially put off by the character, Etsi, who boldly interjected herself into his novella, *Frenzy*, even though she proved to be the perfect foil for the obsessive and jealous main character whose difficult behavior confounded the author for 11 years.[22] Grossman's anecdote about *Frenzy* is arguably the most dramatic example of character-induced insight in the interview sample, as it memorializes the solution to a problem that launched a gut-wrenchingly lengthy period of writer's block.

As suggested near the beginning of this section, however, the contributions of characters are occasionally overshadowed by the contributions of other literary elements, most commonly plot. Eudora Welty identifies plot as a rich resource of Eureka moments, explaining that, even when she had an outline of a novel's action well in mind before drafting, "events proliferated" as she worked herself further into the narrative. Commenting on the novel *Losing Battles*, she claims: "I thought all the action in the novel would be contained in one day and night, but a folder started to fill up with things marked 'Next A.M.' I didn't foresee the stories that grew out of the stories." Those unforeseen

---

18. Paul Auster, *The Paris Review Interviews*, 328.
19. Richard Price, interview by William Crawford Woods, in *The Paris Review Interviews*, vol. 1, ed. Philip Gourevitch (New York: Picador, 2006), 320.
20. Ibid., 324.
21. Rushdie, *The Paris Review Interviews*, 362–63.
22. David Grossman, interview by Jonathan Shainin, in *The Paris Review Interviews*, vol. 4, ed. Philip Gourevitch (New York: Picador, 2009), 413.

stories, or insights extending the original plotline, expanded her original vision for a short book to one that in her estimate is nearly four times longer than her usual output.[23] A similar deference for plot infiltrates the musings of John Gardner, the following observation indicating that, for him, the action driving a story can be just as domineering as characters can be for other authors:

> One plot will just sort of rise above all the others for reasons that you don't fully understand. All of them are interesting, all of them have interesting characters, all of them talk about things that you could talk about; but one of them catches you like a nightmare. Then you have no choice but to write it; you can't forget it. It's a weird thing.[24]—Copyright © by *The Paris Review*, used by permission of The Wylie Agency LLC and with permission of the Brockport Writers Forum.

Martin Amis also depends on plot to illuminate his way through a novel (although, as noted earlier, he also depends on characters at times). He revels in the moments when a book comes to him "pretty consecutively" (i.e., flows) and it feels "like a journey in that you get going and the plot, such as it is, unfolds and you follow your nose."[25] While plot and characters elicit more praise than other literary elements in spawning solutions to problems or igniting flow, others do receive mention, including setting, technique and theme, with the authors who cite them reporting Aha! experiences similar to those stimulated by action and people.

The beginning of this section previews the final theme in this subcategory—that is, certain authors' perception that insights result not from the seeming autonomy of single literary elements but from their symbiosis, which manifests in the sensation that the story or poem essentially composes itself. Authors who tend to describe their progress on a work in this manner report a lot of waiting in the midst of their efforts (possibly incubating?) for it to progress of its own accord (again, instead of by some ethereal being). Sounding a little like Amis and Morrison discussing the need to rein in their characters, Jack Gilbert focuses on the genre at large, insisting that his verse became less decorous and more heartfelt when he began listening to what his poems had to say.[26] Also viewing composing acts as a collaboration between the author and a draft in progress, Richard Price suggests that a novel can shape him as much as he shapes it.[27]

---

23. Eudora Welty, interview by Linda Kuehl, in *The Paris Review Interviews*, vol. 2, ed. Philip Gourevitch (New York: Picador, 2007), 122.
24. Gardner, *The Paris Review Interviews*, 168.
25. Amis, *The Paris Review Interviews*, 335.
26. Jack Gilbert, interview by Sarah Fay, in *The Paris Review Interviews*, vol. 1, ed. Philip Gourevitch (New York: Picador, 2006), 452.
27. Price, *The Paris Review Interviews*, 391.

Stephen King, on the other hand, proves more willing to relinquish control of his books; referencing science fiction writer Alfred Bester, who insists "the book is boss," King insists that his novel *Lisey's Story* started and proceeded of its own volition and that *Cell* "announced" that it must be written at once after he had spent a good amount of time incubating ideas for it.[28] Implicit in several passages constituting this theme is recognition that, even though an intention may be in place at the outset of drafting, the landscape of a work constantly evolves, often surprising the author as it twists and turns. David Grossman sums up this reality nicely, observing that he always learns from the experience of drafting a novel as he absorbs "what it wants to tell [him]."[29]

In essence, insight is a mode of learning; it marks the moment when creative individuals finally realize the answers to questions that have been preoccupying them. In the interview passages coded to this subcategory of insight, the authors place themselves in a passive role, avowing at least partial subservience to the literature they are composing or some aspect of it. To the extent that the very act of fashioning poetry, fiction or their elements teaches the writers where they need to go, one might reasonably conclude that this is a form of discovery writing, the topic of the next section. Nevertheless, the perceived autonomy of a literary work and its parts deserves its own subcategory on grounds that it is a unique form of discovery writing. In contrast, the following subcategory is reserved for references to discovery writing that produced insights when, according to the authors, they were in full control of their faculties, as well as the destinations of their projects.

Discovery Writing

As is emphasized throughout this book, creative processes are recursive, proceeding in cyclical as opposed to linear fashion. Relevant to drafting in the context of composing, this inevitable recursivity results in an ongoing reconsideration of a text in progress. Most writers accept this state of affairs as endemic to their craft, willingly and frequently reviewing already articulated ideas in exchange for the productive leaps or insights that such activity stimulates. Often, the insights occur in the throes of forming sentences, as the very act of placing words on the page helps crystallize and guide the author's intentions and drives the text's subsequent development. This is the very definition of discovery writing.

One particularly dramatic instance of this type of insight comes from Salman Rushdie. As noted in the previous section, Rushdie is in the camp of authors who acknowledge the autonomy of the literature they create (in fact,

---

28. Stephen King, interview by Christopher Lehmann-Haupt and Nathaniel Rich, in *The Paris Review Interviews*, vol. 2, ed. Philip Gourevitch (New York: Picador, 2007), 480, 482, 498.
29. Grossman, *The Paris Review Interviews*, 420.

he is quite vocal on this front). Nevertheless, he is aware of his own agency in the enterprise, as exemplified in the following anecdote regarding difficulties he encountered in effecting an appropriate tone of voice: "Each book has to teach you how to write it, but there's often an important moment of discovery. [...] There was a particular day when, after some false starts, I wrote what is now the beginning of [*Haroun and the Sea of Stories*]." Rushdie continues this tale of discovery writing by comparing himself in the following observation to Joseph Heller in the midst of penning *Catch-22*. Referring to "the moment he [Heller] wrote the sentence about Yossarian falling in love with the chaplain," Rushdie claims: "That sentence told him where the rest of the novel was going. That happened to me when I wrote the beginning of *Midnight's Children* and *Haroun*. I had that lightbulb moment."[30] Clearly in this passage, Rushdie credits himself, as opposed to one of his typically headstrong characters, with writing the sentence in question. More to the point of this subcategory of insight, he clarifies that the act of producing that particular string of words, one that fit his intentions better than other combinations he tried, produced a profound insight, the magnitude of which cut a clear pathway through a cluttered thicket of confusion and failed attempts.

A more gradual revelation than Rushdie's single sentence produced, William Gaddis's drafting efforts for *The Recognitions* resulted in an ongoing elaboration of his original focus, as he reveals in response to a question about the novel's genesis:

> *The Recognitions* started as a short piece of work, quite undirected, but based on the Faust story. Then as I got into the idea of forgery, the entire concept of forgery became—I wouldn't say an obsession—but a central part of everything I thought and saw; so the book expanded from simply the central character of the forger to forgery, falsification, and cheapening of values and what have you, everywhere.[31]—Copyright © by *The Paris Review*, used by permission of The Wylie Agency LLC and with permission of Zoltan Abadi-Nagy.

These remarks depict Gaddis unearthing a better sense of what he really wants to write about in the act of executing his original plan. In broadening the scope of the project as he "got into" it (apparently the result of a succession of small insights as opposed to a single earthshaking breakthrough), he could more fully engage the theme on which he became progressively fixated. Peter Carey's drafting processes mimic Gaddis's, though the former unpacks them

---

30. Rushdie, *The Paris Review Interviews*, 377.
31. William Gaddis, interview by Zoltan Abadi-Nagy, in *The Paris Review Interviews*, vol. 2, ed. Philip Gourevitch (New York: Picador, 2007), 276.

more specifically. Speaking about his typical approach to a project's initial iteration, he clarifies:

> It's like standing on the edge of a cliff. This is especially true of the first draft. Every day you're making up the earth you're going to stand on. Normally I know what I want to achieve in a chapter, and I have an idea about where events should take place and I'll have some rough idea of the characters involved. But I might not have fully invented the place. And I certainly won't fully know the characters. So in the first draft, I'm inventing people and place with a broad schematic idea of what's going to happen. In the process, of course, I discover all sorts of bigger and more substantial things. Within those successive drafts, my characters keep on doing the same things over and over; it's like some hellish repetition of events. But the reasons they do them gradually become more complex and layered and deeply rooted in the characters. Every day's a miracle: Wow, I did that, I didn't know any of that yesterday.[32]—Copyright © by *The Paris Review*, used by permission of The Wylie Agency LLC and with permission of Radhika Jones. Copyright © Peter Carey. Reproduced by permission of the author c/o Rogers, Coleridge & White Ltd., 20 Powis Mews, London W11 1JN

Carey follows this summary of his insight-filled drafting processes with a more focused discussion of discoveries surrounding characters, in particular. More specifically, he explains that certain actions driving the storyline require repeated reworking of characters' motivations, causing him to gradually discover who those people really are and leading to their more complex representation.[33] Of course, poets also may experience insight(s) while drafting, including Philip Larkin, who emphasizes the significance of last lines in completing his longer works. Although sometimes the last line came before any other and he had to write himself into it, usually it came about two-thirds of the way through a draft and all he had left to do was fill the gap.[34]

Rushdie, Gaddis and Larkin are representative of numerous authors in the interview corpus who report that their plans for a literary work shifted or expanded while drafting (again, divorced from the sensation that the work itself or one of its elements had taken charge). In some cases, however,

---

32. Peter Carey, interview by Radhika Jones, in *The Paris Review Interviews*, vol. 2, ed. Philip Gourevitch (New York: Picador, 2007), 442.
33. Ibid., 442–43.
34. Philip Larkin, interview by Robert Phillips, in *The Paris Review Interviews*, vol. 2, ed. Philip Gourevitch (New York: Picador, 2007), 211.

the in-progress discoveries appear to have occurred less organically, relevant to larger portions of text or even via gimmicks the author employed. Stephen Sondheim, for example, divulges that he and his collaborator, Jim Goldman, wrote multiple drafts of *Follies* before understanding that the solution to their unsound script lay in the plot's undermining of atmosphere. Consequently, they trimmed the former and enhanced the latter.[35] Upping the ante relevant to Sondheim and Goldman's experience, Philip Roth wrote literally boxes of drafts, which collectively yielded a solution to the creative problem he wrestled with in composing *My Life as a Man*—that is, finding an appropriate setting for an acutely unpleasant event he'd imagined.[36] Another example of Roth's drafting-induced insights occurring at the whole-draft level surfaced relevant to *The Anatomy Lesson* when, between full iterations of the story, he decided to switch the original positions and behaviors of the protagonist and his girlfriend in the context of an argument they were having, an insight that enabled him to enliven an exchange that was lagging.[37] Finally, relevant to this theme, David Grossman shares a unique strategy for prompting draft-in-progress insights that is somewhat akin to prewriting techniques as defined in Chapter 4 on preparation. That strategy (coded here instead for its application well after the author is firmly invested in the trajectory of a project) involves writing letters to his main characters as a means of learning more about them, of generating information that typically fuels more productive approaches to the creative problems he has set for himself.[38]

As this subcategory of insight makes clear, once drafting is well underway, breakthroughs may occur at any time and by various means. In reaction to these insights, several authors celebrate the fact that, though they had exerted plenty of energy up front on charting the course of a poem or work of fiction, the unexpected turns they wrote themselves into were quite gratifying. Some even highlight potentiality as strong motivation for writing and imply that they would be less committed to their art if not for the exciting surprises that awaited them during drafting. Authors also express appreciation for the element of surprise in the previous section, in reference to the literary work or certain elements taking command of the project, and they do so in the following section in reference to Eureka moments sparked by the juxtaposition of seemingly unrelated phenomena.

---

35. Stephen Sondheim, interview by James Lipton, in *The Paris Review Interviews*, vol. 4, ed. Philip Gourevitch (New York: Picador, 2009), 270.
36. Philip Roth, interview by Hermione Lee, in *The Paris Review Interviews*, vol. 4, ed. Philip Gourevitch (New York: Picador, 2009), 224–25.
37. Ibid., 228.
38. Grossman, *The Paris Review Interviews*, 415.

Sudden Connections

Whether between plot lines, character traits, images, even words or phrases, associations of disparate elements rest at the core of many literary achievements and provide some of the most dramatic accounts of creativity in action.[39] For example, consider Stephen King's description of events that birthed his novel *Carrie*, as detailed in his memoir *On Writing*. During his brief tenure as a high school janitor, one of his tasks being to clean the girls' locker room, he conjured an image of several young women demeaning and physically bullying a meek classmate. Almost simultaneously, he remembered having read a *Life* magazine article about the possibility of telekinetic powers (a theory proffered in explanation of reported poltergeist activity) in young teenagers, especially girls. All at once: "Pow! Two unrelated ideas, adolescent cruelty and telekinesis, came together, and [he] had an idea."[40] As in King's case, fresh visions forged by unlikely connections frequently stimulate first insight, as has been established in creativity scholarship at large; however, anecdotes of this nature aren't plentiful enough to survive as a subcategory of first insight in this study. On the other hand, such anecdotes relevant to works in progress are plentiful enough and range from commentary on the general facilitative capacity of unlikely associations to memories of sudden connection-making incidents related to particular poems or stories.

Asserting the general facilitative capacity of unlikely associations, Marianne Moore invokes ancient philosophy to help make her case when replying to an interview question with a question of her own about incongruity between literary works published in a journal she edited: "Didn't Aristotle say that it is the mark of a poet to see resemblances between apparently incongruous things."[41] Orhan Pamuk supports Moore's implication, observing that the recipe for originality is to "put together two things that were not together before."[42] Though not as broadly prescriptive as Moore and Pamuk, Robert Stone enjoys juxtaposing unrelated entities, testifying that he's always been

---

39. Arthur Koestler, *The Act of Creation* (London: Penguin Books, 1664), 211. This celebrated creativity scholar offers some of the earliest extended commentary on the role of connection-making in achieving insight. He labels the phenomenon "bisociation," which is achieved through any of a number of devices including "the substitution of vague visual images for precise verbal formulations; symbolization, concretization, and impersonation; mergers of sound and sense, of form and function; shifts of emphasis, and reasoning in reverse gear; guidance by nascent analogies."
40. Stephen King, *On Writing: A Memoir of the Craft* (New York: Scribner, 2000), 75.
41. Marianne Moore, interview by Donald Hall, in *The Paris Review Interviews*, vol. 4, ed. Philip Gourevitch (New York: Picador, 2009), 39.
42. Orhan Pamuk, interview by Angel Gurria-Quintana, in *The Paris Review Interviews*, vol. 4, ed. Philip Gourevitch (New York: Picador, 2009), 398.

enamored of the process, so much so that it guided his entertainment choices, drawing him to the radio program *Tell Me a Story*, which involved presenting guests with three isolated elements that they were to integrate in an original tale.[43] Juxtapositions of this nature are implicit in Dadaistic literary collage, referenced by both Pamuk and Jack Kerouac relevant to their composing practices.[44]

In addition to these general observations about the creative potential of disparate connections, several of the interviews elicited reflections on particular literary pieces that benefited from concepts or language merging in unexpected ways while authors were drafting or redrafting. John Cheever, after commenting on unlikely associations at the point of conception, also considers their efficacy in the context of fully developed drafts:

> What I love is when totally disparate facts come together. For example, I was sitting in a café reading a letter from home with the news that a neighboring housewife had taken the lead in a nude show. As I read I could hear an Englishwoman scolding her children. "If you don't do thus and so before Mummy counts to three" was her line. A leaf fell through the air, reminding me of winter and of the fact that my wife had left me and was in Rome. There was my story. I had an equivalently great time with the close of "Goodbye, My Brother" and "The Country Husband." [...] I had everything in there: a cat wearing a hat, some naked women coming out of the sea, a dog with a shoe in his mouth, and a king in golden mail riding an elephant over some mountains.[45]—Copyright © by *The Paris Review*, used by permission of The Wylie Agency LLC.

Also celebrating the insight-inducing power of connecting disparate phenomena, David Grossman reminisces that, when walking with a friend one day and talking excitedly about salmon moving upstream as he was in the midst of drafting *See Under: Love*, he suddenly realized that what he was actually doing in the novel was analyzing similarities between the fish's life cycle and his experience as a Jewish person. As soon as he recognized this, he achieved a greater degree of flow.[46] Poets also benefit from unexpected

---

43. Robert Stone, interview by William Crawford Woods, in *The Paris Review Interviews*, vol. 1, ed. Philip Gourevitch (New York: Picador, 2006), 324.
44. Orhan Pamuk, *The Paris Review Interviews*, 387; Jack Kerouac, interview by Ted Berrigan, in *The Paris Review Interviews*, vol. 4, ed. Philip Gourevitch (New York: Picador, 2009), 124.
45. Cheever, *The Paris Review Interviews*, 162.
46. Grossman, *The Paris Review Interviews*, 414.

combinations of ideas as exemplified by T. S. Eliot, who recalls that, in "Ash Wednesday" and "The Hollow Men," he joined parts of other poems he had written, apparently no rare occurrence: "That's one way in which my mind does seem to have worked throughout the years poetically—doing things separately and then seeing the possibility of fusing them together, altering them, and making a kind of whole of them."[47] More focused on language as the source of insights and flow, Marianne Moore speaks about her processes for translating ideas into stanzas, indicating that they are driven by words that "cluster like chromosomes." Though spontaneously generated and ordinarily effective in their original forms, she does refine them in ways that guide her drafting of subsequent stanzas.[48]

Summarizing Authors' Insights about Insight

All of the chapters preceding this one emphasize the strenuous nature of creativity as it involves chasing and concretizing first insights, preparing oneself with information and skills, enduring and overcoming writer's block and arranging and expressing concepts in ways suitable to one's purposes. Insights are brief but welcome moments—inspirations that, amidst all the effort and frustration of creative problem-solving, encourage writers to continue facing down the challenges that come with articulating the ideas and experiences that define, educate and edify humanity. As the interview transcripts analyzed for this study demonstrate, insights may be grand or small, singular or successive, quick or agonizingly slow in arriving. Regardless of their varied catalysts, insights ultimately manifest in a similar outcome: the sudden solution to a creative problem, the most extreme manifestation of which is flow in drafting. Of course, while flow states are pretty accurate signs that a creative problem has been effectively addressed, they are by no means foolproof in this respect, nor are they necessarily indicative of the finished product's quality or reception by intended audiences. Such assurances require additional forms of verification, which are explored in the next chapter.

---

47. T. S. Eliot, interview by Donald Hall, in *The Paris Review Interviews*, vol. 1, ed. Philip Gourevitch (New York: Picador, 2006), 73–74.
48. Moore, *The Paris Review Interviews*, 35–36.

Chapter 7

VERIFICATION, OR EVALUATION

For all the excitement and relief that accompany insights as depicted in Chapter 6, wizened artists and scientists live with the reality that the high of those Aha! moments may be short-lived, that ostensible solutions to creative problems they've posed may, in hindsight, be deemed inadequate or even false. Hindsight in this context equates with verification, the fifth element of the paradigmatic creative process model, which involves further reflection on proposed solutions in the interest of testing their viability. Tests for viability of insights in writing may occur relevant to various elements of the paradigmatic composing process model. At times, an insight's efficacy is borne out in the maintenance of flow during drafting; put another way, a break in flow could signal that the supposed insight is erroneous or inadequate. Most commonly, however, efficacy is determined in the analysis of all the inner workings of a text during revision and editing processes.

While certain measures of viability are performed by writers as they are engaged in their craft, verification eventually extends beyond authors' assessments of their own works as they are subjected to the judgments of individual readers, target audiences, the publishing industry and professional critics. Along these lines, the 434 references to verification in the transcripts of *The Paris Review* (*PR*) interviews examined for this study break neatly into two subcategories: self-evaluation and evaluation by others. The first subcategory to be addressed explores authors' reflections on their drafting and revision processes, but it also acknowledges the significance of individual artistic sensibility. The second subcategory focuses on the estimation of others, not only those whose opinions the authors especially value, including family members and close friends, but also members of the literary establishment.

Self-Evaluation

Three manifestations of self-evaluation as a mode of verification appear in the interview data, including the writer's identification as a professional, revision practices and the author's sense of "rightness" regarding a text under review.

It seems appropriate to begin this section with the theme of professional identity since, separate from it, the other modes of self-evaluation would essentially become moot. Indeed, an individual's sense of identity as an author—as someone who was destined to become a literary artist or write for a living—provides impetus for committing long term to a career that, despite its many rewards, is undeniably demanding, often demoralizing and relatively tenuous. Authorial identity functions as verification insofar as it represents a constellation of factors communicating to aspiring writers that they are right to pursue such a career, that they possess the rare talent for succeeding at it.

Sources of validation contributing to authorial identity vary in nature, as suggested in *The PR* interview transcripts supporting this study. For many interviewees who commented on their beginnings as writers, the source was a precocious desire to write or an intuition that they were fated to do so. In this camp are Truman Capote, James Baldwin, Alice Munro, Raymond Carver, Ted Hughes, P. G. Wodehouse, V. S. Naipaul and John Ashbery, all of whom trace the roots of their identity as writers to childhood, with Ashbery, as a high school student, being the slowest to recognize his lot in life.[1] Other interviewees who were asked to broach the topic of author identity, including James M. Cain, Richard Price, Gabriel Garcia Marquez, Orhan Pamuk and Peter Carey, report finding their purpose in their early- to mid-twenties,[2] while E. B. White and Haruki Murakami were closing in on 30 before they felt

---

1. Truman Capote, interview by Pati Hill, in *The Paris Review Interviews*, vol. 1, ed. Philip Gourevitch (New York: Picador, 2006), 19–20; James Baldwin, interview by Jordan Elgrably, in *The Paris Review Interviews*, vol. 2, ed. Philip Gourevitch (New York: Picador, 2007), 265; Alice Munro, interview by Jeanne McCulloch and Mona Simpson, in *The Paris Review Interviews*, vol. 2, ed. Philip Gourevitch (New York: Picador, 2007), 402; Raymond Carver, interview by Mona Simpson and Lewis Buzbee, in *The Paris Review Interviews*, vol. 3, ed. Philip Gourevitch (New York: Picador, 2008), 219; Ted Hughes, interview by Drue Heinz, in *The Paris Review Interviews*, vol. 3, ed. Philip Gourevitch (New York: Picador, 2008), 273–74; P. G. Wodehouse, interview by Gerald Clarke, in *The Paris Review Interviews*, vol. 4, ed. Philip Gourevitch (New York: Picador, 2009), 163; V. S. Naipaul, interview by Tarun Tejpal and Jonathan Rosen, in *The Paris Review Interviews*, vol. 4, ed. Philip Gourevitch (New York: Picador, 2009), 292; John Ashbery, interview by Peter Stitt, in *The Paris Review Interviews*, vol. 4, ed. Philip Gourevitch (New York: Picador, 2009), 176.
2. James M. Cain, interview by David L. Zinsser, in *The Paris Review Interviews*, vol. 1, ed. Philip Gourevitch (New York: Picador, 2006), 208; Richard Price, interview by James Linville, in *The Paris Review Interviews*, vol. 1, ed. Philip Gourevitch (New York: Picador, 2006), 381–82; Gabriel Garcia Marquez, interview by Peter H. Stone, in *The Paris Review Interviews*, vol. 2, ed. Philip Gourevitch (New York: Picador, 2007), 186; Peter Carey, interview by Radhika Jones, in *The Paris Review Interviews*, vol. 2, ed. Philip Gourevitch (New York: Picador, 2007), 440; Orhan Pamuk, interview by Angel Gurria-Quintana, in *The Paris Review Interviews*, vol. 4, ed. Philip Gourevitch (New York: Picador, 2009), 380.

assured their course was decided.[3] Outlier Toni Morrison claims that, despite having already written two novels, she didn't feel validated until she was writing her third book, *Song of Solomon*, the publication date of which establishes that Morrison was in her mid-forties before she considered herself an author. She attributes her reluctance to claim that title to the societal strictures placed on women of her generation, along with those imposed by race and socioeconomic status.[4] (Incidentally, Richard Price also laments barriers erected by socioeconomic status, remarking that his working-class background brought suspicion upon anyone who chased what was thought to be a financially unstable career.[5])

While a strong general desire or an intuition about destiny defines the authorial identity of several interviewees, others, especially people of color, attach that identity to other internal forces, a common one being the need to answer a "call to duty." Chinua Achebe, for instance, poignantly recalls such a need in response to a question about childhood experiences that led him toward becoming a novelist. Though reporting no special affinity for writing as a young boy, he always took great joy in hearing and reading stories. As he progressed through school, however, he began reading adventure tales that revealed "the danger of not having your own stories," which eventually turned his joy to concern. Specifically, he recalls:

> I didn't know that I was supposed to be on the side of those savages who were encountered by the good white man. I instinctively took sides with the white people. They were fine! They were excellent. They were intelligent. The others were not. [...] There is that great proverb—that until the lions have their own historians, the history of the hunt will always glorify the hunter. That did not come to me until much later. Once I realized that, I had to be a writer. I had to be that historian. [...] it is something we have to do so that the story of the hunt will also reflect the agony and the travail—the bravery, even, of the lions.[6]—Copyright © by *The Paris Review*, used by permission of The Wylie Agency LLC.

---

3. E. B. White, interview by George Plimpton and Frank H. Crowther, in *The Paris Review Interviews*, vol. 4, ed. Philip Gourevitch (New York: Picador, 2009), 132; Haruki Murakami, interview by John Wray, in *The Paris Review Interviews*, vol. 4, ed. Philip Gourevitch (New York: Picador, 2009), 342.
4. Toni Morrison, interview by Elissa Schappell and Claudia Brodsky Lacour, in *The Paris Review Interviews*, vol. 2, ed. Philip Gourevitch (New York: Picador, 2007), 367.
5. Price, *The Paris Review Interviews*, 381–82.
6. Chinua Achebe, interview by Jerome Brooks, in *The Paris Review Interviews*, vol. 3, ed. Philip Gourevitch (New York: Picador, 2008), 247–48.

For Achebe then, despite his insecurities and the challenges he encountered,[7] the need to preserve the experiences and voices of underrepresented cultures was evidently validation enough to risk submission of his first novel, *Things Fall Apart*.

Likewise viewing writing as a duty, V. S. Naipaul posits that it is the "only noble calling" equating it with a "constant striving after deeper understanding," not only of one's own experience but also of the world at large. He ties this profound sense of responsibility to values he internalized growing up with a father who wrote for a living, a father who conveyed through his stories of the harshness he associated with his Hindu upbringing that it is vital to scrutinize oneself in relation to the external world and its perceived enemies.[8] Similarly, Toni Morrison feels validated as a writer, feels "sovereign" and a part of this world, only through writing, when she is actively working to impose some order on the chaos represented in tragic, irreconcilable happenings that she simply can't ignore.[9] On a less global plane, James Baldwin's sense of assurance for finally pursuing the path he felt destined for as a child was reinforced by the need to support his family following the death of his father. In that moment, he realized he had no choice but to reach for that goal even in the face of the difficulties of being a black writer in the United States at that time.[10] While Achebe, Naipaul, Morrison and Baldwin are by no means the only interviewees to connect writing with admirable motivations, they are some of the most emphatic in associating those ends with their authorial identity, with the sense that they were doing what they were meant to be doing with their lives.

As prevalent as the theme of authorial identity is as a form of self-evaluation within the sampled interview transcripts, references to revision practices are even more prolific, as well as a more conventional way of thinking about verification relevant to the creative process model. What's more, this theme breaks into three equally dominant subthemes, including goals of revising, mechanisms of revising and extent of revising. Before considering these subthemes, however, readers should be reminded that, like all elements of the creative and composing process models, revision is a recursive activity. Most writers will revise to some degree as they draft, even while also invoking the term to describe final passes through their manuscripts before submitting them to publishers and after receiving feedback from them. The references to revision practices in *The PR* interview transcripts analyzed for this study focus

---

7. Ibid., 251–53.
8. Naipaul, *The Paris Review Interviews*, 290.
9. Morrison, *The Paris Review Interviews*, 366.
10. Baldwin, *The Paris Review Interviews*, 241–42.

primarily on final passes prior to submission when the authors had a full draft in hand.

Beginning with goals of revising, the interview transcripts display a diversity of concerns, with many of the authors seeming to equate "revision" (more precisely, editing) with low-order or surface-level rehashing of a text.[11] A sample of such issues includes replacing/eradicating overused, imprecise or superfluous words; rethinking punctuation choices; reworking sentence rhythms; and correcting simple errors (a couple of authors appeared to do a little of each). Nevertheless, several authors who comment on revision practices do engage at the whole text level, with organization surfacing as a common higher-order concern, especially with respect to the logical continuity between a work's ending and all that proceeds it. Certainly, the most elaborate accounts of postdrafting revision practices surface in the interviews with John Gardner, John Ashbery and Raymond Carver. Gardner attests that, whenever he is reviewing a draft, he notices previously unperceived symbols that he subsequently works to develop.[12] Ashbery often goes so far as to abandon the idea that initially stimulated the piece, explaining that he finds the interaction between ideas more engaging than any single concept.[13] Viewing revision as more extensively recursive than the other authors, Raymond Carver notes that he often leaves certain scenes underdeveloped or merely marked in the text since the meticulous care they require would consume too much time while drafting,[14] presumably breaking his flow.

The nature of Gardner's, Ashbery's and Carver's revision practices hints at the substantial time and attention that authors may devote to acts of verifying that their work lives up to the standards they've set for themselves. In fact, the majority of interviewees who comment on revision reveal that it consumes extensive amounts of time and attention, even for those who equate it with surface-level or other lower-order matters. While some of those authors remain a bit vague in communicating how much effort they expend, opting instead for generic phrasing that indicates it is estimable, others actually quantify their revision efforts in terms of drafts or pages or in a total

---

11. Contemporary composition classrooms stress the distinction between revision (large-scale changes) and editing (small-scale changes) to discourage developing writers from fixating on superficial errors once drafting is concluded when in all likelihood (even for experienced writers) an initial full draft will contain more serious and demanding weaknesses to contend with.
12. John Gardner, interview by Paul F. Ferguson, John R. Maier, Frank McConnell and Sara Matthiessen, in *The Paris Review Interviews*, vol. 2, ed. Philip Gourevitch (New York: Picador, 2007), 156.
13. Ashbery, *The Paris Review Interviews*, 198.
14. Carver, *The Paris Review Interviews*, 231.

of months/years expended, with some reporting staggering numbers. For example, short story master James Thurber professes that he completely reworked "The Train on Track Six" 15 times.[15] Turning to longer works, though Joyce Carol Oates and Robert Stone commonly compose three drafts for each novel, both acknowledge that certain scenes require highly concentrated attention. Toward that end, Stone rewrote Naftali's suicide in *A Flag for Sunrise* eight times, reducing it to a fourth of its original length, while Oates contends that she rehashed certain pages of her later novels up to 17 times.[16] Additional novelists who report fastidious treatment of at least portions of initial drafts include Toni Morrison, who recalls producing up to 13 versions of certain paragraphs within multiple works she's produced,[17] and Earnest Hemingway, who claims to have rewritten the final page of *A Farewell to Arms* 39 times.[18]

Stressing her dedication to revision, Maya Angelou notes that for every nine pages she drafts, she discards at least six.[19] Throwing away significant portions of early drafts is also common practice for Robert Stone, Eudora Welty and David Grossman, while Truman Capote confesses to discarding an entire novel as well as a number of short stories.[20] Likewise commenting on short stories, Raymond Carver attests that he will keep roughly half of the first pass on a 40-page manuscript, the final product representing many additions as well as deletions.[21] Rounding out representative commentary on the extent of revision are those who measure it relevant to time expended, with Richard Price laboring for 18 months on his novel *Clockers*, and Haruki Murakami for around 7 or 8 on most every novel he undertakes.[22]

---

15. James Thurber, interview by George Plimpton and Max Steele, in *The Paris Review Interviews*, vol. 2, ed. Philip Gourevitch (New York: Picador, 2007), 22.
16. Robert Stone, interview by William Crawford Woods, in *The Paris Review Interviews*, vol. 1, ed. Philip Gourevitch (New York: Picador, 2006), 307, 325; Joyce Carol Oates, interview by Robert Phillips, in *The Paris Review Interviews*, vol. 3, ed. Philip Gourevitch (New York: Picador, 2008), 171, 174.
17. Morrison, *The Paris Review Interviews*, 361.
18. Earnest Hemingway, interview by George Plimpton, in *The Paris Review Interviews*, vol. 1, ed. Philip Gourevitch (New York: Picador, 2006), 39.
19. Maya Angelou, interview by George Plimpton, in *The Paris Review Interviews*, vol. 4, ed. Philip Gourevitch (New York: Picador, 2009), 241.
20. Stone, *The Paris Review Interviews*, 325; Eudora Welty, interview by Linda Kuehl, in *The Paris Review Interviews*, vol. 2, ed. Philip Gourevitch (New York: Picador, 2007), 122; David Grossman, interview by Jonathan Shainin, in *The Paris Review Interviews*, vol. 4, ed. Philip Gourevitch (New York: Picador, 2009), 416; Capote, *The Paris Review Interviews*, 31.
21. Carver, *The Paris Review Interviews*, 233.
22. Price, *The Paris Review Interviews*, 384; Murakami, *The Paris Review Interviews*, 350.

A third and final theme to arise from the data on revision practices broaches the mechanics of a given author's approach. Many authors detail these mechanics for their respective interviewers, and, as would be expected given the idiosyncratic nature of composing processes, cognitive styles and logistical preferences vary widely. One of the most unique approaches to revision surfaces in the musings of Eudora Welty, who reveals that, after typing a draft, she "revise[s] with scissors and pins," the benefit of which she describes as follows: "Pasting is too slow, and you can't undo it, but with pins you can move things from anywhere to anywhere, and that's what I really love doing—putting things in their best and proper place, revealing things at the time when they matter most."[23] Highly regimented in her composing schedule, Maya Angelou dedicates herself to revising what she has written on any given day before she goes to bed each night.[24] Apparently as habitual as Angelou, Truman Capote transfers second drafts (which are always written in longhand) to typescript on a unique brand of yellow paper, which he loads into a typewriter that he balances on his knees while reclining in bed.[25]

Despite these examples of idiosyncrasies relevant to the mechanics of revising, commonalities of note did emerge from the data. One of those patterns is predicted by the data reviewed in Chapter 5 on incubation—that is, numerous authors report setting their drafts aside for a while before revising because the distance helps them review their work more objectively. A second pattern has to do with the advantages of rewriting (in longhand or typescript) entire portions of drafts up to the point where the writer left off on the previous day; doing so assists in identifying mistakes, as Earnest Hemingway implies, or in recapturing the rhythm of the story, as Joan Didion typically experiences.[26] Peter Carey engages in similar practice, ordinarily when he has already drafted a third of a novel, when he feels that he must bolster its as-of-yet unstable scaffolding.[27] Committed to drafting on computer, Stephen King's revision processes are most successful when he retypes entire drafts of novels into empty documents—this in contrast to revising in the moment, as a draft unfurls on-screen. In particular, he compares the former strategy to swimming and the latter to ice-skating, insinuating that they instigate differing levels of engagement.[28]

---

23. Welty, *The Paris Review Interviews*, 139.
24. Angelou, *The Paris Review Interviews*, 241.
25. Capote, *The Paris Review Interviews*, 30–31.
26. Earnest Hemingway, interview by George Plimpton, in *The Paris Review Interviews*, vol. 1, ed. Philip Gourevitch (New York: Picador, 2006) 39; Joan Didion, interview by Hilton Als, in *The Paris Review Interviews*, vol. 1, ed. Philip Gourevitch (New York: Picador, 2006), 476.
27. Carey, *The Paris Review Interviews*, 443.
28. Stephen King, interview by Christopher Lehmann-Haupt and Nathaniel Rich, in *The Paris Review Interviews*, vol. 2, ed. Philip Gourevitch (New York: Picador, 2007), 481.

A final salient pattern relevant to revision mechanics rests in the many reflections on the effects of altering drafts in longhand in contrast to altering them by means of keyboarding. Regardless of the era during which they were writing (i.e., whether personal computers were even available), several interviewees express strong opinions about the differences between the two methods of preserving their ideas in language. For example, Martin Amis unabashedly argues for the superiority of writing by hand:

> It's all nonsense about how wonderful computers are because you can shift things around. Nothing compares with the fluidity of longhand. You shift things around without shifting them around—in that you merely indicate a possibility while your original thought is still there. The trouble with a computer is that what you come out with has no memory, no provenance, no history—the little cursor, or whatever it's called, that wobbles around the middle of the screen falsely gives you the impression that you're thinking. Even when you're not.[29]—Copyright © by *The Paris Review*, used by permission of The Wylie Agency LLC.

Though it's unclear whether Amis intends to draw a distinction between revising and editing, he does ultimately acknowledge that the act of typing helps in identifying surface error[30]; thus, perhaps begrudgingly, he joins a chorus of authors who tout certain advantages of keyboarding. Beyond some general statements along these lines, T. S. Eliot, Philip Larkin, Eudora Welty and Paul Auster specifically state or strongly imply that typewriting actually facilitates corrections or alterations. Elaborating on this point despite his affinity for drafting in longhand,[31] Auster observes that, in the period of time when he's finalizing a manuscript for submission, "typing allows [him] to experience the book in a new way, to plunge into the flow of the narrative and feel how it functions as a whole," something he calls "reading with his fingers." He continues by exclaiming: "It's amazing how many errors your fingers will find that your eyes never noticed. Repetitions, awkward constructions, choppy rhythms. It never fails. I think I'm finished with a book and then I begin to type it up and I realize there's more work to be done."[32]

---

29. Martin Amis, interview by Francesca Riviere, in *The Paris Review Interviews*, vol. 3, ed. Philip Gourevitch (New York: Picador, 2008), 348.
30. Ibid., 349.
31. Paul Auster, interview by Michael Woods, in *The Paris Review Interviews*, vol. 4, ed. Philip Gourevitch (New York: Picador, 2009), 310.
32. Ibid., 313.

Regardless of divergent preferences or practices that the interviewees equate with revision, the data show that those who comment about that mode of verification believe that the extensive amount of time and attention they devote to it is crucial for achieving their artistic visions. The bright spot in all this taxing and often tedious rehashing of texts is that many authors appear to have a secure sense of rightness that signals when their visions and products are in sync. This sense of rightness, or lack thereof, the third and final theme to be addressed in the subcategory of self-evaluation, often mimics felt sense in the context of first insight as discussed in Chapter 3, and it manifests in different standards for different writers. Beginning with how certain interviewees experience this sense of rightness, E. B. White's account of the phenomenon is quite dramatic. Reflecting on his rigorous revision practices, he insists that he knows when his writing is working because "bells begin ringing and lights flash." Further in reaction to his interviewer's prompting about the tools of self-evaluation, he posits that some authors "are equipped with extrasensory perception."[33]

Whether extrasensory or not, many interviewees do invoke the word "feeling," or some synonym, in reference to the moment when they discern their goals for writing have been met. John Ashbery declares shifting assessments of his own work, observing that, though some of his poetry doesn't seem to fit that genre label, at times he "feel[s] very much at home with it." Further, he explains: "It's a question of a sudden feeling of unsureness at what I am doing, wondering why I am writing the way I am, and also not feeling the urge to write in another way."[34] Exceedingly hard on himself, William Faulkner knows when his writing is moving along in acceptable fashion because it makes him feel good, the same way reading admirable works of literature, such as *La Tentation de Saint Antione* and the Old Testament, makes him feel.[35] Also hard on himself, John Cheever nonetheless admits that several of his works produced a "great sensation"—"they were absolutely Bang! [He] loved them."[36] Poet Robert Lowell talks of last lines seeming "felt" and details "seem[ing] right," while playwright Harold Pinter cites "pure instinct" about "the rhythm seem[ing] right" as the force that lets him know when the curtain should fall.[37] To offer a few examples from the opposite vantage point, James Baldwin and Alice Munro speak of their novels or aspects of them as

---

33. White, *The Paris Review Interviews*, 140.
34. Ashbery, *The Paris Review Interviews*, 187.
35. William Faulkner, interview by Jean Stein, in *The Paris Review Interviews*, vol. 2, ed. Philip Gourevitch (New York: Picador, 2007), 42.
36. John Cheever, interview by Annette Grant, in *The Paris Review Interviews*, vol. 3, ed. Philip Gourevitch (New York: Picador, 2008), 165.
37. Robert Lowell, interview by Frederick Seidel, in *The Paris Review Interviews*, vol. 2, ed. Philip Gourevitch (New York: Picador, 2007), 73,74; Harold Pinter, interview

not "feeling" right,[38] and Georges Simenon "[has] always the impression" that he has failed in some respect that another chance at revision might help him overcome.[39] Reporting similar experience relevant to a particular work, E. B. White, "feeling that something was wrong" upon finishing a draft of *Charlotte's Web*, detached from it for a while before refining it.[40]

Whether or not they had experienced a visceral reaction regarding the perceived worth of a text they produced, many authors demonstrate a keen awareness of the standards they apply in judging their writing. Commenting generally on the quality of a work, William Faulkner measures his novels against those he deems the greatest examples in history.[41] Likewise occupying lofty ground, John Gardner invokes morality, which he defines in literary terms as telling the truth, as "making" rather than "destroying," as creating "dreams of what is possible" or "ways of living."[42] More practical in his estimations, William Styron's test for the success of his own writing is whether or not he likes reading it.[43] Given the fact that most authors, including those already mentioned, maintain nearly impossible standards for themselves, it's not surprising that a number of interviewees—including Eudora Welty, William Carlos Williams, Harold Pinter and Maya Angelou—report that they stop laboring on a project not because they've achieved some version of perfection but, rather, because they believe they have done all they can do with it[44] (or a highly similar version of that phrasing).

The majority of authors who speak about exercising their own sense of rightness in terms of standards do so holistically, in the fashion of those mentioned in the previous paragraph. A few, however, set their sights on specific literary elements when determining if a manuscript has achieved its promise. For example, James M. Cain, reflecting specifically on concocting a suspenseful plot, likens the activity to solving a math problem but in a unique way.[45] Focusing on the "shape" of a story, Truman Capote asserts that this

---

by Lawrence M. Bensky, in *The Paris Review Interviews*, vol. 3, ed. Philip Gourevitch (New York: Picador, 2008), 129.

38. Baldwin, *The Paris Review Interviews*, 252, 254; Munro, *The Paris Review Interviews*, 405.
39. Georges Simenon, interview by Carvel Collins, in *The Paris Review Interviews*, vol. 3, ed. Philip Gourevitch (New York: Picador, 2008), 33.
40. White, *The Paris Review Interviews*, 139.
41. Faulkner, *The Paris Review Interviews*, 42.
42. Gardner, *The Paris Review Interviews*, 173.
43. William Styron, interview by George Plimpton and Peter Matthiessen, in *The Paris Review Interviews*, vol. 4, ed. Philip Gourevitch (New York: Picador, 2009), 13.
44. Welty, *The Paris Review Interviews*, 121; William Carlos Williams, interview by Stanley Koehler, in *The Paris Review Interviews*, vol. 3, ed. Philip Gourevitch (New York: Picador, 2008), 111; Pinter, *The Paris Review Interviews*, 130; Angelou, *The Paris Review Interviews*, 240.
45. Cain, *The Paris Review Interviews*, 224.

mode of verification boils down to the following considerations: "After reading it, can you imagine it differently, or does it silence your imagination and seem to you absolute and final. As an orange is final. As an orange is something that nature made just right."[46] Paul Auster also concentrates on the shape of a piece, but with greater emphasis on style as he methodically drafts and revises each paragraph before moving to another. For him, a paragraph is not complete until it conveys "the right music," until it is "transparent and effortless."[47]

In the end, whether they feel the quality of their writing or subject it to particular assessment criteria, a sense of rightness about a work in the wake of intense revision efforts is requisite for sharing it with others, especially others who will be deciding its efficacy for publication. The specter of agents, editors and marketers who might tear the manuscript apart is ominous and explains why professional identification as an author—the first theme addressed in this section on self-evaluation as a mode of verification—is helpful in weathering the often stormy journey toward seeing a work in print. Of course, once the publishing houses are pleased, the audience and critics await. All three, as well as some other modes of evaluation by others, are discussed in the next section.

Evaluation by Others

Authors want and need an audience not only to supply income but also to identify with, or at least thoughtfully receive, the experience and knowledge that they communicate through their work. *The PR* interview transcripts sampled for this study reveal that appreciation and respect for audience run deep. For Jack Gilbert and Richard Price, the appreciation is a visceral reaction, a high of sorts in response to positive audience reaction during poetry readings.[48] John Cheever feels tremendous gratification upon receiving praise from his fans, as he reveals in response to his interviewer's inquiry about the author's projected readers: "All sorts of pleasant and intelligent people read the books and write thoughtful letters about them. I don't know who they are, but they are marvelous and seem to live quite independently of the prejudices of advertising, journalism, and the cranky academic world."[49] Likewise appreciative of his readers, James M. Cain admits that his feelings are rooted in pragmatics. When asked by his interviewer which of his books "stand up"

---

46. Capote, *The Paris Review Interviews*, 21.
47. Auster, *The Paris Review Interviews*, 330.
48. Jack Gilbert, interview by Sarah Fay, in *The Paris Review Interviews*, vol. 1, ed. Philip Gourevitch (New York: Picador, 2006), 464; Price, *The Paris Review Interviews*, 380.
49. Cheever, *The Paris Review Interviews*, 152.

the best, Cain admits that the only gauge he applies in making that determination is the number of people who buy them. (At the time of his interview, the winner was *The Postman Always Rings Twice*.[50]) While esteem for audience, as represented in the words of these authors, pervades the interview transcripts, in practice it manifests in a variety of ways—a reality alluded to by Ralph Ellison, who observes: "All the agony that goes into writing is borne precisely because the writer longs for acceptance—but it must be on his own terms."[51] In other words, while most authors crave validation from readers, they don't necessarily sanction the dispositions or practices that will earn it with some.

For a few of the interviewees, the best approach is to largely disregard audience, the presumption being that privileging their own personal standards and the integrity of their art ensures a level of quality that will naturally draw readers. Among writers who express such sentiments are Orhan Pamuk and Stephen King, who set readers aside while composing out of respect for them. More specifically, Pamuk recognizes that, though he can't completely escape awareness of eventual readers, he never caters to them, implying that they would be offended if they sensed he was playing to their expectations.[52] Although King insists that his avowed interest in readers' thinking will not affect his decision-making about any project, he encourages them to interact with him, to express opinions about what should or should not have happened in a given work.[53] As these representative citations illustrate, setting aside audience is not an expression of disdain; rather, the act often resides in the opposite emotion—emotion that guarantees readers remain at the forefront of writers' quests for validation through the literature they produce.

In fact, the transcripts show that many authors in the data pool foreground attention to audience as they plot and execute their poetry, plays, short fiction or novels. Robert Lowell, for instance, believes that seeking feedback from smart people who are not professional writers can be constructive.[54] Though T. S. Eliot disagrees with Lowell on the subject of poetry, asserting that the poet's primary audience is the self, he does believe that writing plays requires authors to remember from inception to completion that they will be read by others with an eye toward performance.[55] Screenplay author Billy Wilder likely would

---

50. Cain, *The Paris Review Interviews*, 223.
51. Ralph Ellison, interview by Alfred Chester and Vilma Howard, in *The Paris Review Interviews*, vol. 3, ed. Philip Gourevitch (New York: Picador, 2008), 6.
52. Pamuk, *The Paris Review Interviews*, 397.
53. King, *The Paris Review Interviews*, 478.
54. Lowell, *The Paris Review Interviews*, 76.
55. T. S. Eliot, interview by Donald Hall, in *The Paris Review Interviews*, vol. 1, ed. Philip Gourevitch (New York: Picador, 2006), 77.

appreciate the wisdom of this claim as he indicates in an anecdote about the last line of the final scene of *Some Like It Hot*: "Nobody's perfect." During the film's screening, that line, about which the filmmakers were generally unenthused, elicited a huge laugh from the audience, and thus it remained where it originally served as a placeholder, the audience's validation ultimately eclipsing the filmmakers' concerns.[56] Many authors, of course, don't have opportunity for adjusting a text to live consumers and are consequently having to project how their readers will react to certain aspects of a manuscript in question.

Anticipating the reactions of an audience that expanded to numbers he never expected, Gabriel Garcia Marquez bore a heavy weight of literary and political responsibility toward his readers.[57] John Ashbery adopts a somewhat narrower focus, striving to satisfy readers through the element of surprise, which requires an artful setup, along with considerable care in handling potentially shocking material.[58] Also preoccupied with plot, Kurt Vonnegut stresses reader inclusion, insisting that you hold readers at bay if the story fails to establish the setting and introduce the characters early on and if it doesn't involve the fulfillment of character desire. Moreover, he argues, you will bore readers if the characters do not face each other in conflict at some point.[59] Moving to surface-level concerns, David Grossman obsesses over words, always wondering if a particular language choice will be broadly comprehended since colorless expression makes for a similar sense of reality.[60] Indeed, for Grossman, as well as for Jorge Luis Borges and Salman Rushdie, clarity of expression seems to be a central concern.[61] Together, these audience-aware passages from the interview transcripts suggest the degree of attention that certain authors exercise in securing validation from their readers. They also illustrate the diversity of concerns an author may be juggling at any given time in the interest of drawing readers and maintaining their allegiance, not only in the context of a given text but also across an entire career.

---

56. Billy Wilder, interview by James Linville, in *The Paris Review Interviews*, vol. 1, ed. Philip Gourevitch (New York: Picador, 2006), 424.
57. Garcia Marquez, *The Paris Review Interviews*, 183.
58. Ashbery, *The Paris Review Interviews*, 179.
59. Kurt Vonnegut, interview by David Hayman, David Michaelis, George Plimpton and Richard L. Rhodes, in *The Paris Review Interviews*, vol. 1, ed. Philip Gourevitch (New York: Picador, 2006), 195.
60. Grossman, *The Paris Review Interviews*, 428.
61. Jorge Luis Borges, interview by Ronald Christ, in *The Paris Review Interviews*, vol. 1, ed. Philip Gourevitch (New York: Picador, 2006), 144; Salman Rushdie, interview by Jack Livings, in *The Paris Review Interviews*, vol. 3, ed. Philip Gourevitch (New York: Picador, 2008), 361.

In addition to those who engage poetry and fiction primarily for pleasure, members of the literary establishment render significant impact on the birth, health and length of an author's career. The heft of their verifying influence through discriminating response to and/or promotion of an author's efforts is reflected in the number of passages in the interview transcripts that reference relationships with editors or critics. A quick glance at the coding table for this study (Appendix A) makes clear that literary establishment is the most populated theme under verification and one of the most heavily populated in the entire discourse analysis. That many of the editors and critics referenced by the interviewees are established authors themselves deserves mention here since that finding belies the lore about pervasive competition between authors.[62]

On the subject of editors in particular, author commentary is overwhelmingly positive, displaying a profound sense of gratitude and indebtedness for incisive feedback, revision advice, promotional efforts and even emotional support. One of the most detailed accounts of what an author needs in terms of feedback and revision advice comes from Toni Morrison, whose description of and tribute to her editor, Bob Gottlieb, embodies many of the traits mentioned in more piecemeal fashion across the data pool. Specifically, Morrison explains:

> What made him good for me was a number of things—knowing what not to touch; asking all the questions you probably would have asked yourself had there been the time. Good editors are really the third eye. Cool. Dispassionate. They don't love you or your work; for me that is what is valuable—not compliments. Sometimes it's uncanny; the editor puts his or her finger on exactly the place the writer knows is weak but just couldn't do any better at the time. Or perhaps the writer thought it might fly, but wasn't sure. Good editors identify that place and sometimes make suggestions. Some suggestions are not useful because you can't explain everything to an editor about what you are trying to do. I couldn't possibly explain all of those things to an editor, because what I do has to work on so many levels. But within the relationship if there is some trust, some willingness to listen, remarkable things can happen.[63]—Copyright © by *The Paris Review*, used by permission of The Wylie Agency LLC and with permission of Claudia Brodsky.

---

62. While the data pool does contain some commentary on competition between authors and a few do admit feeling envious or being envied, most who address the matter downplay it.
63. Morrison, *The Paris Review Interviews*, 363.

Morrison's depiction of an ideal editor (whom she apparently met in Gottlieb) represents a trend in what several authors most appreciated relevant to their own editors—objective yet incisive advice for improving their work delivered in a spirit of cooperation.

With that objective in sight, Alice Munro insists that she and her editor have to interact from a place of agreement about what is possible within the genre she favors (short fiction) and, furthermore, that the editor must bring "a very sharp eye for the ways that [she] could be deceiving herself."[64] In answer to a question from his interviewer about Ezra Pound's editing of *The Waste Land*, T. S. Eliot expresses appreciation for Pound's determination in figuring out what a poet was trying to do, as opposed to forming that poet into an image of himself.[65] Joan Didion also appreciates an unimposing response style, speaking of how her editor encouraged (rather than demanded) changes and highlighted "weaker" material (presumably in contrast to the unqualified adjective "weak").[66] Yet another example of this trend surfaces in Robert Lowell's interview in which he praises his editor's practice of asking questions without passing judgment one way or the other about the object of those questions.[67]

As important as a nonjudgmental tone proved to be for some authors, others actually craved judgment—as long as it was affirming. In fact, several authors in response to questions about relationships with their editors mention the positive impact of genuinely felt expressions of admiration for works in progress. In some cases, the compliments reportedly expedited the acquisitions stage of the publishing process as editors garnered special attention for particular manuscripts. In other cases, the compliments afforded reassurance during later stages of that process when the authors were grappling with a variety of creative challenges. For a couple of authors, Toni Morrison and Richard Price, the support was so intensive that they likened it to psychiatric treatment,[68] with Price relaying a humorously self-deprecating anecdote about the effects of his editor's validation during the long and tedious birth of the novel *Clockers*:

> Writing the first draft, I went through a process with him in which every day for a solid year I read to him over the phone everything I wrote. It seems I needed to do that [...] to hear "good dog." [...] For him it must

---

64. Munro, *The Paris Review Interviews*, 400.
65. Eliot, *The Paris Review Interviews*, 68.
66. Joan Didion, interview by Hilton Als, in *The Paris Review Interviews*, vol. 1, ed. Philip Gourevitch (New York: Picador, 2006), 487.
67. Lowell, *The Paris Review Interviews*, 92.
68. Morrison, *The Paris Review Interviews*, 362.

have been like talking to a head-job or a child, coaxing and comforting, saying, Ooh, that's good. Wow. Oh, you're such a good writer. Very good. What page are we on? How many pages do you think you have left? What time is it? March?[69]—Copyright © by *The Paris Review*, used by permission of The Wylie Agency LLC and with permission of James Linville.

Certainly, this is one of the most colorful portrayals of an editor's personal devotion, but this excerpt from Price's interview transcript also speaks to his editor's fierce dedication to the work, which he lauds in an earlier exchange about revision, where the author notes that they labored through the thousand-page first draft of *Clockers* three times.[70] Though not as dramatic as Price's anecdotes, several authors express tremendous appreciation for the time and careful attention expended by their editors while simultaneously illustrating that praise is not the only form of helpful feedback.

Though having interacted with several different editors across his career, Peter Carey highlights the ultrameticulous nature of Gary Fisketjon, whose advice he especially welcomed in the context of writing *The Kelly Gang*. Carey reports that when Fisketjon returned the manuscript, each page was brimming with commentary, obviously having been scrutinized even at the sentence level. He was obsessed with chronology and rules, claims Carey, and even engaged the author one night in a four-hour phone conversation about ampersands.[71] Also grateful for a meticulous second set of eyes, John Cheever shares that his editor, Harold Ross, though difficult, had earned his genuine affection. Although he may have been deemed by many writers as overzealous in his response (lodging around 36 queries per short story) and he strove to agitate them in service of their art, Ross could be inspiring, brags Cheever, noting that the editor taught him quite a bit about the craft.[72] Jack Kerouac joins these two authors in voicing appreciation for the painstaking care editors bring to their work, complimenting his own editor's acutely honed proofreading skills and his ability to keep on top of seeming contradictions regarding dates and names of places.[73]

In the midst of all the positive commentary about editors represented in the previous paragraphs, a few negative remarks do surface, but mostly among those who ultimately voice gratitude for the assistance despite their bruised egos. When conversation turns to professional critics, however,

---

69. Price, *The Paris Review Interviews*, 385.
70. Ibid., 384.
71. Carey, *The Paris Review Interviews*, 447.
72. Cheever, *The Paris Review Interviews*, 154–55.
73. Jack Kerouac, interview by Ted Berrigan, in *The Paris Review Interviews*, vol. 4, ed. Philip Gourevitch (New York: Picador, 2009), 83.

author commentary registers as largely negative, countered by occasional recognition of an essential or helpful contribution to the author or to the discipline at large. Frustrations over critics are variously expressed but converge around a sense of disconnect between the motivations of authors and those who review them. This impression is summed up succinctly in the words of William Faulkner, who observes: "The artist is writing something which will move the critic. The critic is writing something which will move everybody else."[74] Examples of the "everybody else" Faulkner is referring to presumably would include the publishing industry and academia; certainly, other authors state or imply one or the other of those audiences in their appraisals of professional critics. Kurt Vonnegut alludes to both audiences while reflecting on multiple bad reviews across reputable venues in response to one of his later novels:

> Judging from the reviews of [...] *Slapstick*, people would like to bounce me out of the literary establishment. [...] All of a sudden, critics wanted me squashed like a bug. [...] The hidden complaint was that I was barbarous, that I wrote without having made a systematic study of great literature, that I was no gentleman since I had done hack writing so cheerfully for vulgar magazines—that I had not paid my academic dues.[75]—Copyright © by *The Paris Review*, used by permission of The Wylie Agency LLC.

The idea of paying dues may be rooted in what John Cheever identifies as the academy's commercial bent. Specifically, he argues: "The vast academic world exists like everything else, on what it can produce that will secure an income. So we have papers on fiction, but they come out of what is largely an industry. In no way does it help those who write fiction or those who love to read fiction."[76] With this remark, Cheever makes clear that a critic's audience is not writers or readers; as if in direct response, Marilynne Robinson suggests that the primary audience for critics is other critics.[77] This theme is further borne out by the opinion of several interviewees that critics place too much emphasis on pigeonholing authors into theoretical camps, efforts that are reductive, at best, and inaccurate, at worst.

But ostensibly more harmful than pigeonholing is the impact of hostile criticism on the writer's psyche—at least for those who pay attention to

---

74. Faulkner, *The Paris Review Interviews*, 53.
75. Vonnegut, *The Paris Review Interviews*, 186.
76. Cheever, *The Paris Review Interviews*, 151.
77. Marilynne Robinson, interview by Sarah Fay, in *The Paris Review Interviews*, vol. 4, ed. Philip Gourevitch (New York: Picador, 2009), 455.

reviews of their work, and it should be noted that many claim not to. Those who do pay attention and who admit they are not immune to the sting of harsh critique cover a diversity of emotions in describing its effects. James Baldwin felt surprise, pain and bewilderment at the unflattering labels applied to him as a young, black male writing in the 1960s.[78] Alice Munro charges that critics can be quite hurtful, subjecting authors to tremendous embarrassment before potential readers.[79] Stephen King anticipates occasional ugliness from critics and compares the experience of a bad review to hearing someone behaving hatefully toward a loved one.[80] Also the victim of a bad review now and again, Harold Pinter recalls one of his early plays, *The Birthday Party*, being ravaged by the critics, whose reactions really shook him and sent him into a deep depression.[81] As this sampling of comments about the emotional effects of negative criticism reveals, critics' capacity to demoralize authors is considerable, especially during the early stages of their careers. For these authors, lack of validation and harsh invalidation are difficult to tolerate. That being said, data relevant to this theme suggest that poets and fiction writers do tend to develop thicker skins as they evolve within the profession, and some are seemingly born with thick skins that brace them for bad press.

Despite all the naysaying about those who make their living criticizing others' work, some interviewees recognize that critics can play a vital role in forwarding a career and in advancing understanding of craft. Truman Capote believes this to be the case, but he is careful to note that there are good critics and bad critics and that writers should listen only to those who have earned their trust,[82] a conviction shared by Norman Mailer.[83] In spite of reservations about critics cited earlier, James Baldwin concedes that reviews can attract readers and that critics are illuminating to the extent that they help authors understand where their work is overwritten or confusing.[84] Joyce Carol Oates agrees with Baldwin about the potential for attracting readers, appearing to appreciate the attention critics may bring to a work,[85] and P. G. Wodehouse endorses Baldwin's view about critics' potential for refining an author's talents, claiming that one can learn from critics through occasional gems of advice.[86]

---

78. Baldwin, *The Paris Review Interviews*, 268.
79. Munro, *The Paris Review Interviews*, 422.
80. King, *The Paris Review Interviews*, 498.
81. Pinter, *The Paris Review Interviews*, 125.
82. Capote, *The Paris Review Interviews*, 32.
83. Norman Mailer, interview by Andrew O'Hagan, in *The Paris Review Interviews*, vol. 3, ed. Philip Gourevitch (New York: Picador, 2008), 429.
84. Baldwin, *The Paris Review Interviews*, 258, 269.
85. Oates, *The Paris Review Interviews*, 171.
86. Wodehouse, *The Paris Review Interviews*, 164.

In the end, however, those inclined to compliment professional critics are few and far between in the interviews analyzed for this study. Starkly contrasting the small group who feel they can learn from published reviews, most contend that reviews teach them nothing about their work.

Verifying Values about Verification

Arriving at the closing paragraphs of this chapter on verification, some readers may be wondering about one of the most emblematic modes of verification—awards. While some authors do mention awards in conversation with their interviewers, the bulk of information about such prizes in the anthologies consulted for this study is embedded in the biographical sketches preceding the interview transcripts, not in the transcripts themselves. Therefore, information about awards is not considered part of the data pool.[87] Nevertheless, a comprehensive account of verification as manifest in an author's experience begs mention of the shelves full of honors that the authors received for their work, ranging from scholarships and grants to Pulitzer Prizes.

If fact, the variety of awards they received mirrors the variety characterizing other modes of verification discussed in this chapter. No matter their level of fame, these authors continually subjected their special talents and the literature they produced to exceptionally rigorous standards of evaluation. As this chapter establishes, these standards translate to exacting revision and editing processes in the authors' quest to ensure that their poetry and fiction represent their artistic visions as closely as possible. For several of these authors, the level of dedication to their work and the quality they demand of it reflect their calling to write. This pursuit of excellence drives many of the interviewees to capitalize on the critical feedback and advice of trusted editors and other members of the literary establishment. But, when all is said and done, it seems the validation they most desire comes from their readers, who serve as ongoing sources of inspiration to sustain the tenuous, rigorous and isolating career of an author.

With the various modes of validation addressed, this study's treatment of the paradigmatic creative process model as embedded in the interview corpus comes to an end. Nevertheless, as previewed in Chapter 1, this discourse

---

87. The transcripts proper contain 11 references to awards scattered across the interview corpus. Those that afforded financial support are mentioned in Chapter 8 on emerging patterns. Including the biographical sketches that introduce each interview, passages referencing awards of various kinds total 31, with some denoting multiple awards per author.

analysis unearthed a number of patterns across the authors' reported experience that didn't neatly conform to the model's parameters, that didn't easily fit the definitions of first insight, preparation, incubation, insight or verification. Even so, these patterns are undeniable and enhance understanding of the model, particularly as they elaborate contextual phenomena that influence composing processes. Chapter 8 will characterize, illustrate and consider the significance of these patterns.

Chapter 8

EMERGENT PATTERNS

As established in the first two chapters of this book, the paradigmatic creative process model is a long-standing template for understanding and categorizing activities involved in a variety of creative endeavors. Of course, most (if not all) models are flawed to some degree as their inherent economy prevents them from fully accounting for the phenomena they represent. In keeping with that observation, the model applied in analyzing data for this study does not, by itself, automatically call to mind the rich array of contextual factors that may influence creativity. While Chapters 3 through 7 of this study do entertain contextual factors that affect the model's elements as illustrated in the sampled *Paris Review* (*PR*) interviews, the model does not readily subsume all salient themes that emerge through close reading of the data. To that point, the outlying patterns addressed in this chapter have less to do with particular composing subprocesses and their immediate stimuli and more to do with acts of composing on the whole. In metaphorical terms, while Chapters 3 through 7 zoom in on specific writing practices and matters that directly influence them, Chapter 8 adopts a wide-angle lens, revealing how a number of environmental, economic and sociocultural circumstances can impact the larger experience of becoming and living as a professional writer.

Data addressed in this chapter, a total of 651 passages, ultimately disperse across six subcategories: reasons for writing; role of art, including writing; difficulty of writing; confidence, or lack thereof; conditions for writing; and attitudes toward creative writing courses. Further, the data relevant to each of these subcategories fall into themes that lend those subcategories an illuminating level of detail. The themes attributed to conditions for writing are especially significant in terms of the number of data points that cluster around each of them (which might have justified them as subcategories in their own right). While readers may take issue with the assignment of some of the data presented in this chapter, it bears emphasizing, as mentioned in previous chapters, that qualitative research is not and does not purport to be an exact science. On the contrary, it is highly interpretive and embraces that trait as reflective of the complexity of human behavior and experience. Regardless, every effort has been taken in this chapter to clarify, when not obvious, the rationale for assigning data to certain subcategories or themes as opposed to others.

Reasons for Writing

In Chapter 7 on verification, relevant to the theme of authorial identity, several authors are cited as feeling validated in their choice of profession because they believe they were destined to write. Data assigned to this subcategory on reasons for writing find the interviewees ruminating more generally on their careers, sharing motivations for their long-standing commitment to such a demanding, often daunting, pursuit. While the data in this subcategory demonstrate an impressive level of variety, the majority gather into five dominant themes. The first theme to be discussed—authors' need to satisfy their egos— is referenced briefly in Chapter 7, where a couple of interviewees mention a desire for fame as an aside to the notion of fulfilling their destiny. In contrast, the ego-based passages to be discussed in this chapter foreground that desire.

To that point, John Cheever boldly contends that, while accomplished writers are often gifted in myriad areas of potential achievement, they gravitate toward writing because it allows more room for them to entertain their egos.[1] In a similar vein, Richard Price recognizes the need for being considered exceptional as one of two primary reasons for continuing as a writer (the other is a need to immerse oneself in genuinely intriguing subject matter).[2] As it turns out, Price ultimately privileges ego, acknowledging that his wish to be recognized as special is what keeps him going.[3] Also crediting fame with the generative power to sustain a career, Raymond Carver shares that, even though he didn't feel all that remarkable upon publication of his early works, the positive and validating attention he eventually received spurred him on.[4]

Putting an altruistic spin on the quest for fame, several other passages coded to this subcategory portray the interviewees naming and applying their talents out of a sense of obligation. Kurt Vonnegut, for example, indicates that, in contrast to his uniquely gifted sister and daughters, it never occurred

---

1. John Cheever, interview by Annette Grant, in *The Paris Review Interviews*, vol. 3, ed. Philip Gourevitch (New York: Picador, 2008), 149.
2. Richard Price, interview by James Linville, in *The Paris Review Interviews*, vol. 1, ed. Philip Gourevitch (New York: Picador, 2006), 396.
3. Ibid., 408.
4. Raymond Carver, interview by Mona Simpson and Lewis Buzbee, in *The Paris Review Interviews*, vol. 3, ed. Philip Gourevitch (New York: Picador, 2008), 238.

to him that he shouldn't exercise his own gifts to their limits.[5] James Baldwin did just that at the height of the civil rights movement. While he didn't view himself as a public speaker, Baldwin realized upon meeting Martin Luther King, Malcolm X and Medgar Evers that it was incumbent upon him to use his ability to get his work published in support of the movement.[6] Similarly to Baldwin, Toni Morrison feels a sense of obligation to channel her gifts in the direction of improving the world, asserting that, if she didn't, she would be complicit in the chaos surrounding her—"the incredible violence, the willful ignorance, the hunger for other people's pain."[7] Like the authors cited in the previous paragraph, Vonnegut, Baldwin and Morrison sport a healthy sense of ego; however, they distinguish themselves in naming their gifts by making clear that they carry a responsibility. While Vonnegut's sense of responsibility may be more generally articulated, all of the authors in this camp insist that the gift of writing must not be wasted. In the interest of transparency, it should be noted that a few other passages coded to reasons for writing speak of lofty altruistic purposes, but those passages do not overtly attach altruism to the authors' recognition that they possess unusual talent.

Beyond the psychological need for propping the ego, several other writers reveal that they remain devoted to their craft out of a need to maintain psychological balance. Some of these authors go so far as suggesting that their mental health would be in serious jeopardy if they didn't write. Several in that group speak about the capacity of writing to help them escape the pain of living, including Toni Morrison, who began pursuing her craft as a way of combating loneliness following divorce.[8] Also pointing to the capacity of writing to alleviate emotional pain, Jean Rhys reflects on a life filled with sadness, for which composing served as the only consistent antidote. Specifically, Rhys recounts: "I wrote because it relieved me. [...] I've never written when I was happy. I didn't want to. But I've never had a long period of being happy. [...] What came first with most of [my books] was the wish to get rid of this awful sadness that weighed me down. I found when I was a child that if I could put the hurt into words, it would go."[9] With motivations similar to those of

---

5. Kurt Vonnegut, interview by David Hayman, David Michaelis, George Plimpton and Richard L. Rhodes, in *The Paris Review Interviews*, vol. 1, ed. Philip Gourevitch (New York: Picador, 2006), 191.
6. James Baldwin, interview by Jordon Elgrably, in *The Paris Review Interviews*, vol. 2, ed. Philip Gourevitch (New York: Picador, 2007), 250.
7. Toni Morrison, interview by Elissa Schappell and Claudia Brodsky Lacour, in *The Paris Review Interviews*, vol. 2, ed. Philip Gourevitch (New York: Picador, 2007), 366–67.
8. Ibid., 366.
9. Jean Rhys, interview by Elizabeth Vreeland, in *The Paris Review Interviews*, vol. 3, ed. Philip Gourevitch (New York: Picador, 2008), 200–201.

Rhys, Joyce Carol Oates turns to writing even when she is "exhausted, when [she's] felt her soul as thin as a playing card, when nothing has seemed worth enduring for another five minutes." In such moments, she finds that "the activity of writing changes everything," or so it seems to.[10] Though not quite as dynamic in expressing like sentiments, David Grossman also associates writing with happiness or escape from emotional pain, suggesting that he might be abnormal if he didn't write.[11]

While the authors just cited regard writing as an escape from emotional pain, others coded to the theme of maintaining psychological balance appear to be struggling with a different kind of distress, the deleterious effects of anxiety. V. S. Naipaul and Raymond Carver, for example, contend that they feel edgy when they aren't writing.[12] Philip Roth describes this state of being as rooted in provocation to publicly communicate personal crisis.[13] But perhaps most forthcoming on this front is William Styron, who elaborates in the following passage on his observation that writing is a way of keeping himself calm:

> When I'm writing I find it's the only time that I feel completely self-possessed, even when the writing itself is not going too well. It's fine therapy for people who are perpetually scared of nameless threats as I am most of the time—for jittery people. Besides, I've discovered that when I'm not writing I'm prone to developing certain nervous tics, and hypochondria. Writing alleviates those quite a bit.[14]—Copyright © by *The Paris Review*, used by permission of The Wylie Agency LLC.

Collectively, Styron's reflections, along with other representative comments about the stabilizing impact of writing on mental health, underscore the promise of contemporary composition workshops and self-help seminars intended to promote recovery from traumatic experiences. In light of such opportunities for those who are suffering to work through psychological bruises, the assertion that writing can be healing is not necessarily unexpected;

---

10. Joyce Carol Oates, interview by Robert Phillips, in *The Paris Review Interviews*, vol. 3, ed. Philip Gourevitch (New York: Picador, 2008), 173.
11. David Grossman, interview by Jonathan Shainin, in *The Paris Review Interviews*, vol. 4, ed. Philip Gourevitch (New York: Picador, 2009), 436.
12. V. S. Naipaul, interview by Tarun Tejpal and Jonathan Rosen, in *The Paris Review Interviews*, vol. 4, ed. Philip Gourevitch (New York: Picador, 2009), 306; Carver, *The Paris Review Interviews*, 237.
13. Philip Roth, interview by Hermione Lee, in *The Paris Review Interviews*, vol. 4, ed. Philip Gourevitch (New York: Picador, 2009), 212.
14. William Styron, interview by George Plimpton and Peter Matthiessen, in *The Paris Review Interviews*, vol. 4, ed. Philip Gourevitch (New York: Picador, 2009), 5–6.

the fact that so many famous authors locate their reasons for writing in that healing power might be.

Of course, authors are undoubtedly learning about themselves while engaged in such psychological journeys, but several interviewees attribute their reasons for writing to a more general type of self-education about the world and what it means to be human. While this theme is not as robust as the previous two, it is populated enough to merit separate mention (as well, it dovetails with the discovery-writing theme relevant specifically to drafting oneself into an insight as discussed in Chapter 6). Most of the references constituting this theme—writing to educate oneself—stress the fresh perspective or understanding that serious authors aspire to, a goal that rests at the very core of creativity. Some of the interviewees who pinpoint this goal as the source of their drive report having moved outside of their comfort zones, the result being that they were compelled to revise their belief systems or to confront intimidating or frightening subject matter.[15]

The final theme pertinent to reasons for writing harkens to an ideal that many people would ascribe to their chosen profession: they engage in the work they do for the sheer joy of it. The data informing this study show that many authors write solely, or at least primarily, for amusement. Words (or forms thereof) encapsulating this theme in the interview transcripts include pleasure, fun, excitement and entertainment. One of the most detailed ruminations on this theme comes from Orhan Pamuk, who states: "I'm in love with what I do. I enjoy sitting at my desk like a child playing with his toys. It's work, essentially, but it's fun and games also."[16] Likewise unveiling his playful side, Philip Roth notes that the "pleasure" in writing derives from "go[ing] around in disguise," from "pass[ing] oneself off as what one is not," from pulling off "the sly and cunning masquerade."[17] While David Grossman doesn't label the type of amusement that writing brings him, he does equate composing with physical pleasure in response to his interviewer's question about leaving another career path to become a full time author. Specifically, he explains: "I always compare it to discovering sex. The moment before you do it, you have only a vague notion of what it will be like. It's threatening, it's attractive, it's everything. The

---

15. Baldwin, *The Paris Review Interviews*, 242; Morrison, *The Paris Review Interviews*, 364; Grossman, *The Paris Review Interviews*, 430; Marilynne Robinson, interview by Sarah Fay, in *The Paris Review Interviews*, vol. 4, ed. Philip Gourevitch (New York: Picador, 2009), 458, 459.
16. Orhan Pamuk, interview by Angel Gurria-Quintana, in *The Paris Review Interviews*, vol. 4, ed. Philip Gourevitch (New York: Picador, 2009), 377.
17. Roth, *The Paris Review Interviews*, 210.

moment after, you don't understand how you lived all your life without it. You immediately become an addict. You know that this is what you want to do."[18]

Although these example remarks about amusement as a motivator for and sustainer of composing energy may not fit stereotypical images associated with famous creators, their message seems almost a given when considering the challenges that writing presents. Surely, to subject oneself to the trials and tribulations of a writing career, one would have to find it amusing on some level. The myriad challenges are illustrated in or can be inferred from Chapters 3 through 7 in the context of the interviewees' commentary on various aspects of their writing processes. Passages in which the interviewees *explicitly discuss* the challenges of writing are addressed later in this chapter, while the next section will explore an emergent pattern more closely related to reasons for writing.

Role of Art, Including Writing

The emergent pattern treated in this section broaches interviewees' opinions about the wide-reaching contributions of their art and, in many cases, of art in general. Of course, the desire to leave a mark on the world through literature might be a reason for writing and, thus, data presented in this section might be construed as a subset of data presented in the previous section. Nevertheless, though lines between interview passages assigned to these subcategories may seem thin at times, these data can be distinguished by consideration of the author's focus. To be more precise, data discussed in the previous section stress how the author is served by the act of writing. The data informing this section focus more broadly on how literature and art in general serve society.

Perhaps the most obvious manifestation of this outward gaze is a sense of moral imperative to improve the human condition, to elevate or edify people in some way. Robert Stone articulates this purpose while clarifying his intense concentration on the relationship between meaning and style, asserting that literature should strive to "crowd the reader out of his own space and occupy it with [the writer's] in a good cause."[19] Several interviewees would agree although their ideas of "good causes" may differ. John Gardner is the most prolific commentator on this matter, arguing that writers should portray "positive ways of surviving, of living," that art should rest on the premise that "life is better than death" and should raise and respond to all the

---

18. Grossman, *The Paris Review Interviews*, 412.
19. Robert Stone, interview by William Crawford Woods, in *The Paris Review Interviews*, vol. 1, ed. Philip Gourevitch (New York: Picador, 2006), 309.

questions relevant to a work's subject matter that would impress that message on readers.[20] Celebrating life may be a worthy goal, but Joyce Carol Oates and John Cheever seemingly wish to inhabit even loftier ground stating, respectively, that literature ought to help people "rise out of limited, parochial states of mind,"[21] that it ought to "enlarge" them and "give them their divinity."[22]

Also representative of this theme is Ted Hughes who compares the act of experiencing art to taking medicine. While noting the healing effect that art can have on the creator (as discussed in the previous section), he emphasizes its healing effect on consumers, which explains their intense desire for it.[23] Though invoking a different metaphor, E. B. White presumably would agree with Hughes about the restorative capacity of art. White explains his role in helping readers discover this capacity as delivering "the warming rays of the sun" in language, ideally providing "inspiration, guidance and challenge" along the way.[24] As a check on all these expressions of positive intention, a couple of authors remind readers that the objective of affirming life is not necessarily packaged in flowery paper and bright, shiny bows; rather, some of the most life-affirming literature is that which portrays the seamy, cruel, violent sides of existence as points of reference for advocating and supporting more optimistic and supportive ways of living.[25]

Continuing with the theme of moral imperatives, several authors believe the primary purpose of literature is to relay truth. Setting aside the question of whether or not there exists some sort of transcendental truth, the data relevant to this theme line up with a statement of literary purpose uttered by Robert Stone: "There's only one subject for fiction or poetry [...]–*how it is*. In all the arts, the payoff is always the same—recognition. If it works, you say that's real, that's truth, that's life, that's the way things are."[26] Despite the philosophical complexities the term "truth" raises, a significant majority of interviewees who share Stone's view are not shy about invoking it in some form when naming the ultimate accomplishment of their vocation. Only a few in the large camp

---

20. John Gardner, interview by Paul F. Ferguson, John R. Maier, Frank McConnell and Sara Matthiessen, in *The Paris Review Interviews*, vol. 2, ed. Philip Gourevitch (New York: Picador, 2007), 151–53.
21. Oates, *The Paris Review Interviews*, 173.
22. Cheever, *The Paris Review Interviews*, 166.
23. Ted Hughes, interview by Drue Heinz, in *The Paris Review Interviews*, vol. 3, ed. Philip Gourevitch (New York: Picador, 2008), 294.
24. E. B. White, interview by George Plimpton and Frank H. Crowther, in *The Paris Review Interviews*, vol. 4, ed. Philip Gourevitch (New York: Picador, 2009), 149.
25. Gardner, *The Paris Review Interviews*, 170; Peter Carey, interview by Radhika Jones, in *The Paris Review Interviews*, vol. 2, ed. Philip Gourevitch (New York: Picador, 2007), 458.
26. Stone, *The Paris Review Interviews*, 310.

of authors speaking to this theme employ alternate phrasing, explaining that the artist's responsibility is to avoid "lying,"[27] to deliver "reality,"[28] or "to create believable people in credible moving situations."[29] Regardless, it bears acknowledging that communicating truth does not require fiction and poetry to depict realistic scenarios, a fact that John Gardner stresses in his declarations about the role of literature. Employing the example of Dostoyevsky's protagonist in *Crime and Punishment*, Gardner insists: "Obviously Raskolnikov could have been a giant saurian, as long as his character is consistent and convincing, tuned to what we know about actual feeling. The point is realism of imagination, convincingness of imagination."[30] Whatever the degree of verisimilitude to the world readers are living in, the notion of writing as "truth-telling" is preeminent in the minds of numerous authors whose interviews were analyzed for this study, with some pronouncing that the title "great author" belongs to those whose works do the best job of embodying realities of human existence.[31]

Related to the endeavor of communicating truth is the attempt to help readers see beauty and detail in the world around them, to preserve in words the results of a writer's acutely honed skills of observation, with the goal of shining light on phenomena that are easily missed by the more casual observer. Several of the interviewees who remark on the role of literature cite their responsibility to share the rewards of this skill through their art. For Philip Larkin, the role of art is to capture and keep alive what the artist observes or feels through apt expression that will resonate with others.[32] Marilynne Robinson eloquently reinforces Larkin's view in the following statement: "Cultures cherish artists because they are people who can say, Look at that. And it's not Versailles. It's a brick wall with a ray of sunlight falling on it."[33] Stephen King would appreciate Robinson's emphasis on noticing and celebrating the ordinary when communicating through art, advocating that authors should always opt for the most specific detail available when representing the world around them: "It's a Pepsi [...] not a soda," he exclaims in his interview, charging that authors must "Say what

---

27. Baldwin, *The Paris Review Interviews*, 256.
28. Norman Mailer, interview by Andrew O'Hagan, in *The Paris Review Interviews*, vol. 3, ed. Philip Gourevitch (New York: Picador, 2008), 402.
29. William Faulkner, interview by Jean Stein, in *The Paris Review Interviews*, vol. 2, ed. Philip Gourevitch (New York: Picador, 2007), 48.
30. Gardner, *The Paris Review Interviews*, 152–53.
31. Ibid., 173–74; Maya Angelou, interview by George Plimpton, in *The Paris Review Interviews*, vol. 4, ed. Philip Gourevitch (New York: Picador, 2009), 247–48.
32. Philip Larkin, interview by Robert Phillips, in *The Paris Review Interviews*, vol. 2, ed. Philip Gourevitch (New York: Picador, 2007), 225, 211.
33. Robinson, *The Paris Review Interviews*, 447.

[they] mean. Say what [they] see. Make a photograph" for readers.[34] Haruki Murakami also embraces the role of careful spectator of the world and its people, but he adds a qualification, namely that the artist should refrain from judging or tendering conclusions about the objects of that careful gaze.[35] Other authors in the interview corpus speak about the contributions of art in helping people notice what they might otherwise miss or in helping them absorb it more fully by activating their senses. While the additional passages coded to this theme do help solidify its status as such, they are comparatively generic, doing little more than echoing the claim that the purpose of literature and other arts is to preserve the world through the artist's intense and sensitive vision.

Yet another responsibility of art and the artist points to literature's entertainment value. Just as many authors acknowledge that they write for their own amusement, nearly as many believe that literature, first and foremost, should provide a fulfilling form of recreation for readers. Jorge Luis Borges, for instance, believes that the quality of literature should be measured by the enjoyment it brings to others,[36] and Kurt Vonnegut underscores this notion when insisting that it should fill readers' leisure time productively, leaving the impression that their time is valued.[37] For Isaac Bashevis Singer, this involves building tension in a narrative, thereby enticing readers to stick around because they must know how the story resolves.[38] John Cheever agrees, declaring that "The first principle of aesthetics is either interest or suspense."[39] John Ashbery extends this revelation by suggesting that the feeling of building suspense created in a literary work should be capped with "a pleasant surprise," which he identifies as the most prized human emotion.[40] Along these lines, other interviewees speak of "possessing" readers[41] or involving them in the literary work so deeply that they barely recognize that they're reading.[42]

---

34. Stephen King, interview by Christopher Lehmann-Haupt and Nathaniel Rich, in *The Paris Review Interviews*, vol. 2, ed. Philip Gourevitch (New York: Picador, 2007), 486.
35. Haruki Murakami, interview by John Wray, in *The Paris Review Interviews*, vol. 4, ed. Philip Gourevitch (New York: Picador, 2009), 347.
36. Jorge Luis Borges, interview by Ronald Christ, in *The Paris Review Interviews*, vol. 1, ed. Philip Gourevitch (New York: Picador, 2006), 131.
37. Vonnegut, *The Paris Review Interviews*, 195.
38. Isaac Bashevis Singer, interview by Harold Flender, in *The Paris Review Interviews*, vol. 2, ed. Philip Gourevitch (New York: Picador, 2007), 100.
39. Cheever, *The Paris Review Interviews*, 160.
40. John Ashbery, interview by Peter Stitt, in *The Paris Review Interviews*, vol. 4, ed. Philip Gourevitch (New York: Picador, 2009), 188–89.
41. Roth, *The Paris Review Interviews*, 235.
42. Angelou, *The Paris Review Interviews*, 250.

While several additional passages from the interview transcripts emphasize the entertainment value of literature, they are rather general statements about the goal of amusing the audience. In the end, whether to affirm life, communicate truth, expand or intensify readers' vision and/or entertain them, the goals of writing pose weighty obligations that help elucidate some of its challenges. The degree and nature of consternation that these challenges present are clarified in the following sections.

Difficulty of Writing

In the two thousand plus pages of *PR* interview transcripts reviewed for this study, readers would be hard pressed to find an author who hasn't suffered for art. The only such author discovered in the context of this study is Kurt Vonnegut, who boldly states, "I've always found it easy to write."[43] The closest any others come to Vonnegut's sentiment is to hinge their enjoyment of the profession on the fact that it is challenging and that they value the intensive stimulation.[44] Beyond these few authors, the overwhelming majority of interviewees are united in assessing their craft as mentally and/or physically exacting, and some of them do so in disparaging terms.

Commenting specifically on the mental anguish associated with writing, John Cheever describes the psychological shock and dark, cold emptiness that overcomes him after purging his imagination of a story, a process typically accompanied in his experience by intermittent "bouts of frustration and inertia and depression."[45] Norman Mailer calls the act of writing a novel "an extremely dangerous psychological journey […] that uses you profoundly."[46] Philip Roth feels "harshly" used when writing, which he considers a "very trying spiritual exercise."[47] He elaborates this observation by explaining that having to confront moral dilemmas in their fiction and poetry, as all creative writers do, causes them to feel like sword-swallowers (as opposed to ventriloquists or impersonators, an analogy implied in the notion that authors don covers or disguises in asserting their convictions through characters or symbols).

---

43. Vonnegut, *The Paris Review Interviews*, 179.
44. William Gaddis, interview by Zoltan Abadi Nagy, in *The Paris Review Interviews*, vol. 2, ed. Philip Gourevitch (New York: Picador, 2007), 298; Morrison, *The Paris Review Interviews*, 366; Robinson, *The Paris Review Interviews*, 456; Chinua Achebe, interview by Jerome Brooks, in *The Paris Review Interviews*, vol. 3, ed. Philip Gourevitch (New York: Picador, 2008), 258.
45. Cheever, *The Paris Review Interviews*, 146, 164, 174.
46. Mailer, *The Paris Review Interviews*, 403–4.
47. Roth, *The Paris Review Interviews*, 212.

Complementing these representative accounts of mental wounds inflicted by writing is considerable testimony about its physical toll. Rebecca West, for instance, feels nauseous when writing,[48] while too many to name focus on the energy it requires and the resulting fatigue. Carrying the standard for this latter group are V. S. Naipaul and Haruki Murakami. Naipaul lists numerous physical ramifications of writing a book: "At the end of it I am so tired. Something is wrong with my eyes; I feel I'm going blind. My fingers are so sore that I wrap them in tape." Sadly, he continues by lamenting the cumulative effects of this sort of physical strain on the aged writer: "I've given so much to this career for so long. I spend so much time trying to feel well. One becomes worn out by living, by writing, by thinking."[49] Murakami comments on the physical impact of maintaining a rigid writing schedule, comparing it to the aftermath of having gone through survival training and asserting that physical strength is as essential to writing (or to writing novels, at least) as is artistic sensibility.[50]

In the long run, the mental and physical stress caused by writing leads some authors to rather shocking revelations. Georges Simenon refers to it as a "vocation of unhappiness" and would encourage all aspiring authors to choose a different career.[51] James Baldwin attests that the energy and courage that writing requires render it "a terrible way to make a living."[52] Although Chinua Achebe is one of the few mentioned above who find writing to be exciting despite the strain, he ultimately compares it, after acknowledging how physically draining it is, to a term of imprisonment.[53] Given how difficult composing can be, it is no wonder that some authors struggle from time to time with confidence, the next emergent pattern to be explored.

Confidence, or Lack Thereof

The overview of the first emergent pattern addressed in this chapter, reasons for writing, reveals that many acclaimed writers believe that they have valuable insights to share with the world and that they are uniquely prepared to articulate those insights. To be sure, the lore surrounding famous creators across disciplines tends to support an image of artists and scientists as supremely

---

48. Rebecca West, interview by Marina Warner, in *The Paris Review Interviews*, vol. 1, ed. Philip Gourevitch (New York: Picador, 2006), 257.
49. Naipaul, *The Paris Review Interviews*, 306–7.
50. Murakami, *The Paris Review Interviews*, 350.
51. Georges Simenon, interview by Carvel Collins, in *The Paris Review Interviews*, vol. 3, ed. Philip Gourevitch (New York: Picador, 2008), 21–22.
52. Baldwin, *The Paris Review Interviews*, 251.
53. Achebe, *The Paris Review Interviews*, 258.

self-assured, if not somewhat arrogant. Although the data informing this study do not necessarily undermine that image, they do qualify it, indicating that some authors harbor deep misgivings regarding their powers to achieve their literary ideals. Martin Amis pinpoints the dispositions that many authors embody relevant to confidence, explaining that they will shift between frames of mind depending on time and circumstance:

> Novelists have two ways of talking about themselves. One in which they do a very good job of pretending to be reasonably modest individuals with fairly realistic opinions of their own powers and not atrociously ungenerous in their assessments of their contemporaries. The second train of thought is that of the inner egomaniac; your immediate contemporaries are just blind worms in a ditch, slithering pointlessly around, getting nowhere. Basically they're just stinking up the place. You open the book pages and you can't understand why it isn't all about you. Or, indeed, why the whole *paper* isn't all about you. [...] There's also the flip side, of course—terrific vulnerability, crying jags, the seeking of the fetal position after a bad review and all that kind of stuff.[54]—Copyright © by *The Paris Review*, used by permission of The Wylie Agency LLC.

Fortunately, a number of the interviewees who confess such doubts felt them subsiding or becoming increasingly benign with age and experience, often in the wake of positive feedback from critics and other readers.

As for their early timidity, it seems rooted largely in reverence for great poets and fiction writers who preceded them and a reluctance to count themselves among the literary elite. Joan Didion felt this way as a student at Berkeley, where she claims that she and her peers were constantly inundated with the message "that everybody else had done it already and better."[55] Alice Munro recalls such feelings when she began working on her second novel; having retreated for privacy to her book store on a Sunday when it was closed for business, she scanned the shelves of great literature before her and thought, "You fool! What are you doing here?"[56] Remarking more generally on the initial concern that some writers experience over their potential, Jorge Luis

---

54. Martin Amis, interview by Francesca Riviere, in *The Paris Review Interviews*, vol. 3, ed. Philip Gourevitch (New York: Picador, 2008), 356.
55. Joan Didion, interview by Hilton Als, in *The Paris Review Interviews*, vol. 1, ed. Philip Gourevitch (New York: Picador, 2006), 482.
56. Alice Munro, interview by Jeanne McCulloch and Mona Simpson, in *The Paris Review Interviews*, vol. 2, ed. Philip Gourevitch (New York: Picador, 2007), 405.

Borges blames it on the fear that their ideas are trivial or ordinary (an impression that causes them, inadvisably he claims, to suffocate their subject matter in ornamentation).[57]

Despite Luis Borges' take on the psyche of young writers, it seems he never fully escaped the bounds of insecurity, disclosing that he refuses to reread his own work out of concern he'll be ashamed of it.[58] Certainly, Luis Borges isn't the only interviewee for whom a lack of confidence remained a constant. Prompted by his interviewer to comment on the most literary of his tales, Stephen King names *It* and *Lisey's Story* as the most Dickensian but then quickly demurs: "I'm shy talking about this, because I'm afraid people will laugh and say, Look at that barbarian trying to pretend he belongs in the palace." Later in the interview, he expands on this notion: "As a writer, I've always been extremely conscious of my place. I've never tried to be highfalutin or to put myself on a level with my betters. I'm serious about what I do, but I never wanted to indicate to anybody that I was better than what I was."[59] Salman Rushdie demonstrates similar humility while reflecting on his first three novels, describing them in exceptionally harsh terms. During this part of his career, before finishing *Midnight's Children*, he felt constantly agitated, believing that he had made no headway as a serious author in contrast to others in his generation who were surpassing him. Speaking, then, about the latter part of his career, having enjoyed substantial fame, he shares that writing never gets any easier: "Most of the time you feel dumb. I always think you start at the stupid end of the book, and if you're lucky you finish at the smart end. When you start out, you feel inadequate to the task. You don't even understand the task."[60]

These words from Rushdie, along with the sentiments of others cited in this section, establish that confidence is a tenuous disposition in writers, in some cases becoming strengthened as their reputations solidify, in other cases, not so much. The significant majority of data constituting this pattern establishes that renowned authors, while they aspire to standards different from those of inexperienced writers, suffer in similar ways over the products of their effort. Because the labor is so hard and the emotions so draining, many authors resort to elaborate means in creating circumstances for their daily lives and work environments that are as conducive to composing as possible. Means by which they might do so are addressed in the following section.

---

57. Luis Borges, *The Paris Review Interviews*, 144.
58. Ibid., 147.
59. King, *The Paris Review Interviews*, 483, 499.
60. Salman Rushdie, interview by Jack Livings, in *The Paris Review Interviews*, vol. 3, ed. Philip Gourevitch (New York: Picador, 2008), 375, 379.

Conditions for Writing

Strikingly, each of the conditions discussed in this section carries enough data to be considered an emergent pattern in and of itself. However, the obvious nature of the unifying thread between them—that is, the heavy emphasis on external phenomena that the authors identify as being critical for launching or maintaining their careers—warrants viewing them together in the interest of efficiently illuminating how they might interact with each other. The manner in which the data converge around certain themes reveals significant agreement regarding favorable conditions for writing, and yet the idiosyncratic nature of composing practices demonstrated in previous chapters of this book would predict some divergence, as well. In sorting these findings, this section designates five conditions favorable to writing: financial security, time, solitude, writing schedule and resolve in the face of constraint. In addition to illustrating the authors' shared needs relevant to these conditions, the following discussion will clarify where certain authors distinguish themselves from others.

Numerous passages in the interview transcripts combine in establishing the threat of financial instability. Many of these passages speak generally to economic concerns that divided or diluted the writers' attentions to the detriment of their authorial careers, at least until they scored their first big contract. While a fortunate few enjoyed the assistance of grants that financed at least a short reprieve during otherwise hard times, most of the interviewees were forced to accept what they viewed as unsatisfying jobs that offered little solace in return for the hours and energy they stole.

A common choice among this group was contributing to journalistic venues, as well as to the television and film industries.[61] James Cain, for example, earned money by contributing to *The New Yorker*, which, as it prioritized light entertainment, drained him of any sense of pride or fulfillment[62]; Georges Simenon engaged in similar work but didn't regard it as writing per se.[63] Sounding a similar note, after boosting her cash reserves with regular contributions to the *Saturday Evening Post*, Joan Didion fixed her sights on screenplays—work that can teach some fictional technique but that really doesn't count as writing in her estimation.[64] John Cheever also tapped the film industry, moving to and

---

61. Another common choice was teaching, and it garnered both positive and negative commentary as a "side career." It is not discussed as a theme in this section of the chapter because attitudes about creative writing courses from a student's and a teacher's perspective earned standing as a separate emergent pattern.
62. James M. Cain, interview by David L. Zinsser, in *The Paris Review Interviews*, vol. 1, ed. Philip Gourevitch (New York: Picador, 2006), 214.
63. Simenon, *The Paris Review Interviews*, 25.
64. Didion, *The Paris Review Interviews*, 484–85.

remaining for awhile in Hollywood to earn some money despite the fact that he hated his existence there.[65] In the end, as far removed as this sort of writing might have seemed from the high art these interviewees aspired to, they arguably were exercising abilities and honing skills relevant to their ultimate goals.

In contrast, several other interviewees resorted to work that appeared unrelated to their literary goals, at least on the surface. Representative of this group, William Faulkner paid for his basic needs (food, shelter, liquor) by taking on a variety of odd jobs, which included house painting, boat running and piloting small aircraft.[66] Also a man of multiple talents, Jack Kerouac spent time as a sailor, a secretary and a brakeman for freight trains.[67] Adding to the mix, Philip Larkin made ends meet as administrator for a small community library, James Baldwin waited tables, Peter Carey worked for an advertising firm and Raymond Carver labored for three years as a hospital janitor. Particularly noteworthy about interviewees who worked in areas unrelated to composing fiction and poetry, several of them make a point of expressing their appreciation for the writing time that those jobs afforded them.[68] Aside from food and shelter, time registers as their most precious commodity and reigns as another essential condition for writing represented in the data at large.

For some of the interviewees, the obsession with time reflects the weight of aging, the sense that the days are slipping away and that they will never be able to finish all the work they had imagined. James Thurber attests that aging is a pronounced fear of American writers, citing conversations with William Faulkner, John O'Hara and Earnest Hemingway on the subject.[69] Reinforcing this notion, Stephen King reflects on writers who become distracted by criticism and other pastimes and admonishes: "Get busy. You have a short life span. [...] God gave you some talent, but he also gave you a certain number of years."[70] Jack Gilbert shares King's frustration charging that certain poets are satisfied with too little output: "I don't understand why they're not greedy for what's inside them. The heart has the ability to experience so much—and we don't have much time."[71] Of course, Americans aren't the only ones who allude to the

---

65. Cheever, *The Paris Review Interviews*, 150.
66. Faulkner, *The Paris Review Interviews*, 49–50.
67. Jack Kerouac, interview by Ted Berrigan, in *The Paris Review Interviews*, vol. 4, ed. Philip Gourevitch (New York: Picador, 2009), 123.
68. Larkin, *The Paris Review Interviews*, 216; Baldwin, *The Paris Review Interviews*, 242; Carey, *The Paris Review Interviews*, 448; Carver, *The Paris Review Interviews*, 221.
69. James Thurber, interview by George Plimpton and Max Steele, in *The Paris Review Interviews*, vol. 2, ed. Philip Gourevitch (New York: Picador, 2007), 32–33.
70. King, *The Paris Review Interviews*, 484.
71. Jack Gilbert, interview by Sarah Fay, in *The Paris Review Interviews*, vol. 1, ed. Philip Gourevitch (New York: Picador, 2006), 455.

encroachment of death on their writing plans, but they do seem to be the most preoccupied with it, or at least the most specific in articulating their fear of it. Hemingway voices the depth of his fear while lamenting waning relationships with old friends. As one gets older, he explains, "you are more alone because that is how you must work and the time to work is shorter all the time and if you waste it you feel you have committed a sin for which there is no forgiveness."[72] Across the passages coded as relevant to limited time for writing, the authors identify a variety of causes, including certain jobs, romantic relationships, child rearing and duty to the profession in the form of mentoring. Ironically, fame itself also proved to be a culprit, the very goal many strove for becoming a drain on the life that remained.

While some authors contemplate the big picture when speaking about time with their interviewers, others' comments are rooted in the more immediate, focusing on the amount of time it took to compose a given work or bemoaning the difficulty of securing a few uninterrupted hours. During the early part of his career, Robert Lowell could manage only two or three poems per year that he was willing to submit for publication.[73] E. B. White spent two years sporadically drafting *Charlotte's Web* and another year revising it (evidence that children's books don't necessarily take less out of an author).[74] This time frame would make sense to Toni Morrison, who requires three years to write a single novel, while Ralph Ellison needed four to complete *Invisible Man*.[75] These authors are just a few of the interviewees who attest to the immense amount of time a single work of literature might consume, with several suggesting that preparation and incubation in support of their plans claim just as many hours as converting their ideas to manuscript form. In the final analysis, time, while necessary, was not in and of itself sufficient to realizing their authorial objectives. On the contrary, the majority who comment on favorable conditions for writing note that solitude was equally vital to their success.

The interviewees who express a need for solitude tend to focus on why they need it and on how they generate and guard it. James Baldwin does both, explaining that intentionally isolating himself paved the way for accepting himself and his purpose. Because, as his reputation was rising, he was always in a home filled with children, he wrote primarily at night, after the rest of

---

72. Earnest Hemingway, interview by George Plimpton, in *The Paris Review Interviews*, vol. 1, ed. Philip Gourevitch (New York: Picador, 2006), 45.
73. Robert Lowell, interview by Frederick Seidel, in *The Paris Review Interviews*, vol. 2, ed. Philip Gourevitch (New York: Picador, 2007), 64.
74. White, *The Paris Review Interviews*, 139.
75. Morrison, *The Paris Review Interviews*, 394; Ralph Ellison, interview by Alfred Chester and Vilma Howard, in *The Paris Review Interviews*, vol. 3, ed. Philip Gourevitch (New York: Picador, 2008), 12.

the family had gone to bed. Even with his own children grown and his reputation secured, he continued to write at night because that was when he could depend on being alone.[76] Raymond Carver relates similar experiences, sharing that, when his children were still at home, he would retreat to his car and compose while balancing a tablet on his knee. This quest for solitude was apparently ongoing, as he indicates at the time of his interview: "It's important to me to have my own place. Lots of days go by when we just unplug the telephone and put out our 'NO VISITORS' sign."[77] Going a step further than Carver, some authors are so adamant about protecting their solitude that they rent small apartments or offices that serve no other purpose than to provide a distraction-free sanctuary for engaging in their art.

Actively shutting out others and escaping to isolated spaces to write are recognized as part and parcel of the profession according to several passages in the interview transcripts. On this point, Norman Mailer specifically and matter-of-factly observes:

> Being a novelist means you have to be ready to live a monastic life. When you're really working on a novel there can be ten days in a row when you're just out there working and offering nothing to your mate and nothing to anyone else. You don't want to be bothered, you don't want to answer the phone, you don't want even to talk a great deal to your kids— you want to be left alone while you're working.[78] —Copyright © by *The Paris Review*, used by permission of The Wylie Agency LLC. Copyright © Andrew O'Hagan. Reproduced by permission of the author c/o Rogers, Coleridge & White Ltd., 20 Powis Mews, London W11 1JN.

For some, though, the need to sequester themselves as such is as much an offshoot of personality as it is an ideal working condition.

Like Mailer, Joyce Carol Oates invokes religious metaphor to describe the ideal writing lifestyle but observes that she would tend toward a "claustral" existence regardless, given her deeply introverted nature.[79] Similarly, Jack Gilbert's aversion to small talk causes him to limit interactions with others,[80] and Marilynne Robinson admits that she actually relishes alone time. With the most effusive statement of this desire, Robinson expands on her confession as such:

---

76. Baldwin, *The Paris Review Interviews*, 244, 255.
77. Carver, *The Paris Review Interviews*, 223, 241.
78. Mailer, *The Paris Review Interviews*, 422.
79. Oates, *The Paris Review Interviews*, 176.
80. Gilbert, *The Paris Review Interviews*, 459–60.

> I go days without hearing another human voice and never notice it. I never fear it. […] It's a predisposition in my family. […] I grew up with the confidence that the greatest privilege was to be alone and have all the time you wanted. That was the cream of existence. I owe everything that I have done to the fact that I am very much at ease being alone. It's a good predisposition in a writer.[81]—Copyright © by *The Paris Review*, used by permission of The Wylie Agency LLC and with permission of Sarah Fay.

Predisposition or not, the overriding tenor of the data coded to the theme of solitude is that authors must have lots of it. Nevertheless, a few of the authors do outwardly complain or imply that they suffer an inevitable sense of loneliness despite their realization that long periods of isolation are essential to their success.

Also essential to their success is establishing a schedule or structuring their days so as to most effectively support their mental and physical energies. Although the data supporting this theme make clear that authors' preferences cover the gamut from wee morning to late evening hours, most indicate that they are at their best in the morning. For Toni Morrison, the optimal time to begin writing is immediately following the transition to dawn:

> I always get up and make a cup of coffee while it is still dark—it must be dark—and then I drink the coffee and watch the light come. […] for me this ritual comprises my preparation to enter a space that I can only call nonsecular. […] Writers all devise ways to approach that place where they expect to make the contact, where they become the conduit, or where they engage in this mysterious process. For me, light is the signal in the transition. It's not being *in* the light, it's being there *before it arrives*. It enables me in some sense.[82]—Copyright © by *The Paris Review*, used by permission of The Wylie Agency LLC and with permission of Claudia Brodsky.

Less mystical than Morrison but just as compulsive, Alice Munro is more concerned with the number of words produced per morning than with the symbolic significance of those early hours. Typically, she writes from eight a.m. until eleven a.m., Monday through Sunday, and, if she realizes she cannot reach her word quota on a given morning because of other commitments, she will work ahead to make certain she hits the predesignated number for that would-be sitting.[83] While not obsessed with word count, Salman Rushdie is as

---

81. Robinson, *The Paris Review Interviews*, 464–65.
82. Morrison, *The Paris Review Interviews*, 358.
83. Munro, *The Paris Review Interviews*, 428.

rigid as Munro in his own way, unrelenting in devoting "the first energy of the day" to his writing: "Before I read the newspaper, before I open the mail, before I phone anyone, often before I have a shower, I sit in my pajamas at the desk. I do not let myself get up until I have done something that I think qualifies as working."[84]

Several of the interviewees who reserve the mornings for their art, as well as a few who prefer working in the afternoon or evenings, reveal that writing consumes only a portion of most days. Some are pulled away from their primary occupation by family and other professional responsibilities; others leave it for the purpose of efficiency, having discovered that, if they sit too long at the desk, their mental and physical acuity begins to wane and they will need to redo much of what they've composed after a few hours. Further demanding attention, the toll on the body of a sedentary lifestyle (broached in the above section on the difficulty of writing) seems to have prompted several of the authors to integrate physical activity into their daily routines. Jack Gilbert, John Ashbery, David Grossman and Alice Munro enjoy walking, while Haruki Murakami opts for running and swimming. Evidently not a fan of exercise, Georges Simenon combats the physical toll in a different way. Simenon forces himself to compose a chapter each day once he begins a novel, writing straight through without stopping. He writes for eleven days in a row, but his body will hold out no longer (that's why, he says, all his novels are so brief). To prepare for this marathon, he clears his calendar for those eleven days and then meets with his doctor for blood pressure and other tests to make certain his body is up to the strain.[85]

Of course, physicality limits what writers can accomplish and the manner in which they'd like to do so. In addition, writers must navigate a host of externally imposed constraints, and their relationship to those constraints—their resolve in the face of them—is the final theme to be explored relevant to conditions for writing. The external source of constraint receiving by far the most attention in the interview transcripts is literary form, but treatment of this data deserves qualification in light of data addressed in early chapters of this study. As discussed in Chapter 3 on first insight as conceived in the creative process model, form can be generative since it provides "constructive constraints"[86] that suggest ways of encapsulating one's ideas. As emphasized in Chapter 4 on experimentation in the context of preparation, it can also be generative if deemed insufficient to the author's purpose. At that point, breaking free of form by adjusting it or replacing it with structure better suited to the immediate goal can propel creative processes and facilitate solutions to

---

84. Rushdie, *The Paris Review Interviews*, 386–87.
85. Simenon, *The Paris Review Interviews*, 28–29.
86. Margaret Boden, "What Is Creativity?," in *Dimensions of Creativity*, ed. Margaret Boden Cambridge, MA: MIT Press, 1996), 79.

creative problems. The paragraphs to follow elaborate those earlier treatments of form through more general or holistic application to the larger act of composing, as opposed to one of its elements. For purposes of exploring its pervasive influence as perceived by many of the interviewees, the term "form" will refer to macro- and micro-level textual matters.

Saul Bellow's relationship with form evolved over time, and he credits his ever-growing willingness to abandon formal restraints with an increasing comfort level regarding the novels he took to print:

> My first two books are well made. I wrote the first quickly but took great pains with it. I labored with the second and tried to make it letter-perfect. In writing *The Victim* I accepted a Flaubertian standard. Not a bad standard, to be sure, but one which, in the end, I found repressive. […] I could not, with such an instrument as I developed in the first two books, express a variety of things I knew intimately. Those books, though useful, did not give me a form in which I felt comfortable. A writer should be able to express himself easily, naturally, copiously in a form that frees his mind, his energies. Why should he hobble himself with formalities? With a borrowed sensibility? With the desire to be "correct"? Why should I force myself to write like an Englishman or a contributor to *The New Yorker?* [87]—Copyright © by *The Paris Review*, used by permission of The Wylie Agency LLC.

With these words, Bellow suggests that writers may benefit from burying what teachers or other literary works have taught them about the means of giving structure to their thoughts. Though perhaps a bit more generous, Robert Lowell would likely agree with Bellow's sentiments but with an eye toward poetic genres and their building blocks. Lowell and his interviewer converse at length on this topic, but, in particular, a few lines on his grapplings with various types of poetry indicate his affinity with those who rail against a sort of blind submission to form: "I felt that the meter plastered difficulties and mannerisms on what I was trying to say to such an extent that it terribly hampered me."[88] Joining the chorus, Paul Auster implies a love/hate relationship with form through his tale of transformation from "written out" poet to successful novelist. Commenting on his recovery from a long bout of writer's block, he explains: "[The block ended] when I stopped caring about making

---

87. Saul Bellow, interview by Gordon Lloyd Harper, in *The Paris Review Interviews*, vol. 1, ed. Philip Gourevitch (New York: Picador, 2006), 93–94.
88. Lowell, *The Paris Review Interviews*, 70.

'Literature.' [...] [F]rom that point on, writing became a different kind of experience for me. [...] The only thing that mattered was saying the thing that needed to be said. Without regard to preestablished conventions, without worrying about what it sounded like."[89]

The authors referenced directly above speak for the many interviewees who resist formal constraint. Clearly, (as previewed in Chapter 4) the relaxation or abandonment of constraints energizes them and leaves them reveling in a newfound sense of possibility. Others, however (as previewed in Chapter 3), voice appreciation for the guidance provided by formal expectations or, at least, they perceive them as more malleable than others do. Lowell has moments of fitting into this category of writers, especially when he is expounding on the flexibility of the couplet.[90] In like fashion, David Grossman celebrates and details the extensive pliability of Hebrew, which, he lauds, invites linguistic play.[91] John Gardner also prioritizes the freedom associated with given formal constraints when remarking on processes involved in reimagining myths (as he does in *Grendel*) with the goal of comprehending "the modern world in light of the history of human consciousness." Specifically, he notes: "You've got to end [your version] the way the story ends—traditionally, but you can get to do it in your own way."[92]

These writers, as well as those who resist constraints imposed by literary form, are joined by several other interviewees in commenting on the constraints and potential of tools in their creative domain. Coupled with data pertinent to this issue presented in Chapters 3 and 4, the tension between freedom and constraint relevant to form seems especially profound. A few interviewees do mention other sources of constraint affecting their art, including fame and social mores, but the numbers of passages coded to these phenomena are considerably fewer. With regard to these additional categories of constraint, the authors recall feeling stressed and fettered—stressed relevant to expectations for behavior and the quality of subsequent work and fettered relevant to subject matter and the question of whether or not they (especially women) should pursue writing as a career. One takeaway from this discussion of conditions for writing, combined with the remaining subcategory of data to be addressed in this chapter, is that the challenges associated with becoming a writer and sustaining a writing career might be eased and productively informed through associations or apprenticeships with other writers.

---

89. Paul Auster, interview by Michael Woods, in *The Paris Review Interviews*, vol. 4, ed. Philip Gourevitch (New York: Picador, 2009), 316–17.
90. Lowell, *The Paris Review Interviews*, 67–68.
91. Grossman, *The Paris Review Interviews*, 428–29.
92. Gardner, *The Paris Review Interviews*, 148.

Attitudes toward Creative Writing Courses

The interviews sampled for this study contain extensive conversation about the efficacy of teaching creative writing as financial support for those who are working to establish careers as poets or fiction writers and as a means of preparation or proper schooling for aspiring authors. Opinions are decidedly mixed on both counts, with some interviewees ascribing specific benefits to creative writing courses and less official forms of mentoring for both instructors and students and others viewing such enterprises as wasted time. This divide mirrors ongoing debates in the academy about the worth of undergraduate and graduate creative writing degrees. While these degrees remain popular at many institutions, administrators, teachers and especially parents worry about the earning potential of graduates when considering the elite few who actually turn those degrees into the careers they hope for. Many end up working in demanding community college writing programs or in editing, and many others end up working in areas completely unrelated to their course of study—all of which detract in time and energy from the dreams that caused them to earn the degree in the first place. Looking more closely at this debate, this section proceeds by synthesizing the arguments of those who present a pessimistic outlook on the possibility of teaching and learning how to write creatively and will then review the appraisals of those who regard these pursuits more optimistically.

Those who question the validity of creative writing courses believe formal instruction is of no aid to art, a conviction that leads James M. Cain to declare: "[Creative writing] has to be learned, but it can't be taught. This bunkum and stinkum of college creative writing courses! The academics don't know that the only thing you can do for someone who wants to write is to buy him a typewriter."[93] Several interviewees in agreement with Cain offer justifications for this conviction. Some, like Richard Price, view the forces that drive creative writing as too difficult or elusive to fathom and convey to others, as is the case for talent in most any area of achievement.[94] Although Jack Gilbert believes basic technique can be taught, he sides with Price on the issue at large while citing feeling as the difficult and elusive element of writing[95]; for Robert Lowell, that element is the deep and intense impulse that spawns all creative acts.[96] Taking a slightly different tack, T. S. Eliot, who does advocate for sharing detailed feedback on individual works, argues that the problem of any sort of generalizing approach to instruction, such as inevitably occurs

---

93. Cain, *The Paris Review Interviews*, 215.
94. Richard Price, interview by James Linville, in *The Paris Review Interviews*, vol. 1, ed. Philip Gourevitch (New York: Picador, 2006), 394.
95. Gilbert, *The Paris Review Interviews*, 455.
96. Lowell, *The Paris Review Interviews*, 61.

in creative writing courses, lies in a lack of commonality in the way writers operate, in the processes by which they beget inspiration and produce viable text.[97] These writers' belief that the very nature of composing precludes its being passed along in ways that suffice for other disciplines or knowledge domains carries obvious implications for students. Perhaps not quite as obvious are potentially deleterious effects on the teachers' attitudes and, by extension, the state of literature at large.

Alluding to paper-grading burnout that threatens all writing teachers, Philip Larkin predicts that too much time fretting about the work of others would prove mind-numbing and, over time, would turn teachers against the whole business of literature.[98] Living Larkin's fears to some degree, Elizabeth Bishop, who never wanted to teach but did so to earn some money, reports losing all judgment of quality in light of the heavy barrage of poems she was expected to assess.[99] Alice Munro, who also turned to teaching because she needed money, apparently didn't feel overburdened by the paper load, but she did resent feeling mired in cliché as she responded to her students' work and slipping into an adversarial position toward them as she strove to help them improve.[100] Robert Lowell, who is cited earlier as doubting the value of formal creative writing instruction for students, also ponders its effects on teachers, allowing that immersion in a classroom culture might encourage them to be more adventurous when they return to their own writing[101]—an advantage beyond the fact that it helps writers maintain some financial security as they are clawing their way toward publication and literary standing.

In fact, quite a few interviewees do mention financial stability as a primary appeal of teaching, but that is by no means the only positive outcome to be acknowledged. Both Ted Hughes and John Ashbery contend that writing teachers can learn much while teaching others to write, with Ashbery offering specific insight on the matter:

> You are forced to bring a critical attention into play when you are reading students' work that you would not use otherwise, and that can help when you return to your own writing. And being immersed

---

97. T. S. Eliot, interview by Donald Hall, in *The Paris Review Interviews*, vol. 1, ed. Philip Gourevitch (New York: Picador, 2006), 80.
98. Larkin, *The Paris Review Interviews*, 214.
99. Elizabeth Bishop, interview by Elizabeth Spires, in *The Paris Review Interviews*, vol. 1, ed. Philip Gourevitch (New York: Picador, 2006), 286.
100. Munro, *The Paris Review Interviews*, 416.
101. Lowell, *The Paris Review Interviews*, 61.

in a group of young unproven writers who are fiercely serious about what they are doing can have a chastening effect sometimes on us blasé oldsters.[102]—Copyright © by *The Paris Review*, used by permission of The Wylie Agency LLC. "John Ashbery" in *The Paris Review Interviews*, Vol. IV. Copyright © 2009 by John Ashbery. Reprinted by permission of Georges Borchardt, Inc., on behalf of the author's Estate.

Similarly appreciative of the opportunity to head a classroom of literary-minded individuals, John Gardner talks at length about how teaching both literature and creative writing has edified him. As for teaching creative writing courses in particular, he credits them with sharpening his own sense of successful fiction while pondering the greatness he found in many of his students' work.[103] (Alice Munro, in her overridingly critical view of teaching, begrudgingly admits the same benefit though she attaches it more to her own preparation and reaction to students.[104]) Gardner also appreciates the stimulation of inventing possible plots as part of the classroom collective, which has led to solidifying ideas for his own stories.[105]

Completing the scope of analysis promised near the beginning of this section, all that's left is to tout purported benefits of creative writing classes on students as portrayed in the interview transcripts. Of course, students sign up for creative writing degrees in hopes of practicing their craft under the tutelage of expert writers and other aspiring authors with the intention of starting, honing and polishing publishable work. Robert Stone affirms that these programs do provide an environment conducive to helping some students achieve this goal,[106] and John Gardner supports this observation, claiming that he's found it to be "fairly easy to transform an eager, intelligent student to a publishing creative writer."[107] Richard Price apparently was such a student, as he traces the genesis of his novel *The Wanderers*, to assignments completed in the creative writing program at Columbia.[108]

A number of authors whose memories of their time as teachers and students inhabit this study comment on specific benefits of creative writing courses, or at least the good ones. Continuing with the reflections of Richard Price, it seems one benefit of such courses is exposure to models of the profession—to

---

102. Ashbery, *The Paris Review Interviews*, 202.
103. Gardner, *The Paris Review Interviews*, 168.
104. Munro, *The Paris Review Interviews*, 416.
105. Gardner, *The Paris Review Interviews*, 168.
106. Stone, *The Paris Review Interviews*, 323.
107. Gardner, *The Paris Review Interviews*, 165.
108. Price, *The Paris Review Interviews*, 394.

living, breathing, famous authors—as he implies in the following anecdote from his years at Cornell:

> It was the first time I sat in a room with a teacher who wasn't as old as my father. Here was a guy wearing a vest over a T-shirt. He had boots on, and his hair was longer than mine. A novelist! I couldn't take my eyes off him. I felt, Ah, to be a writer! I could be like this teacher and have that long, gray hair [...] boots up on the table and cursing in class! It made me dizzy just to look at the guy. I don't remember a thing he said to me, except that he usually made encouraging noises: You're good. You're okay, keep writing, blah, blah.[109]—Copyright © by *The Paris Review*, used by permission of The Wylie Agency LLC and with permission of James Linville.

Making the dream more tangible must be of substantial consequence to young authors given the constant negativity surrounding their choice of career, not only the statistical improbability of landing their work in print but also the skepticism of family and friends about the value of a creative writing degree when it comes to making a living. To this point, William Styron and John Ashbery also voice appreciation for the motivating, confidence-building impact of creative writing teachers.[110]

While attitudes diverge among the interviewees regarding the possibility of instruction with respect to technique, Marilynne Robinson is adamant about the teacher's ability to help students find the strength in early versions of their projects, "an image or a moment that is strong enough to center" it.[111] Price appears to agree when he observes that a large part of a teacher's contribution is helping writers "find their story," a mission of "lining up the archer with the target.[112] But it seems teachers aren't the only source of morale and productive feedback: as Ted Hughes discovered during his stint as a creative writing instructor, the students learned much from each other, and the influence of a single gifted student could magnify the abilities of the entire group.[113] In other words, the more linguistically gifted people there are in a room reading and reacting to each other's writing, the more exposure to effective poetry and fiction there is, which can heighten the critical acumen of students in support of drafting and revision skills.

---

109. Ibid., 382.
110. Styron, *The Paris Review Interviews*, 3; Ashbery, *The Paris Review Interviews*, 180.
111. Robinson, *The Paris Review Interviews*, 454.
112. Price, *The Paris Review Interviews*, 402.
113. Hughes, *The Paris Review Interviews*, 295.

A Couple of Emergent Observations about Emergent Patterns

Hughes's hopeful revelation seems a fitting place to close discussion of this study's emerging patterns—for that matter, all the data-based findings in this discourse analysis of sample *PR* interviews as it underscores the symbiotic nature of language skills in the production and enjoyment of literature, activities that likely drew readers to this study. It is also a fitting place to close this chapter because the question of whether or not formal creative writing instruction effectively serves aspiring authors in achieving their goals provides a suitable transition to the final chapter of this book. That chapter draws conclusions from trends in the data as demonstrated in Chapters 3 through 8 (for a succinct reminder, see Appendix C) that promise to productively inform expository writing pedagogy.

Chapter 9

IMPLICATIONS FOR WRITING INSTRUCTION

The select anecdotes and observations woven into the preceding chapters merely hint at the hours of entertainment *The Paris Review* (*PR*) interviews will afford those who are intrigued by famous authors and the circumstances that shaped their careers. For readers looking to grow as writers, the interviews yield countless lessons in composing, and, as Chapter 1 demonstrates, more than a few aspiring authors have cherry-picked the interviews for that purpose. Adopting a more comprehensive and systematic approach to mining this rich repository of composing advice, the study detailed in this book analyzes a large sample of the interviews for patterns in author experience and practice, with the ultimate goal of entertaining their relevance for individualized and large-scale expository writing pedagogy.[1] Of course, the findings reported near the end of Chapter 8 combine for a mixed review of formal creative writing instruction, as several interviewees contend that gains produced by writing courses are negligible, while others attribute such courses with a variety of benefits. Despite these authors' attitudes about creative writing classes, they are staples in the contemporary university, as are required courses in expository composition, and teachers are always searching for strategies that can assist them in educating their students.

As for the expository composition classroom (the focus of this chapter), pedagogical theories have waxed and waned across the last several decades, resulting in fluctuating emphases. Interest in composing processes flourished during the late 1970s and 1980s, soon inviting important and ongoing qualifications and elaborations regarding the extracognitive, social aspects of

---

1. Given that the researcher's expertise is in the field of rhetoric and composition, teaching applications will be discussed from that perspective. Nevertheless, based on the crossover between expository and creative writing addressed in Chapter 2, creative writing instructors are encouraged to assess the recommended strategies for application within their curricula.

writing (see Chapter 1 for more on such concerns).[2] Of course, the discipline's evolution in this respect is by no means a sorry development; on the contrary, alternate theories have illuminated important aspects of writing that overzealous and undernuanced process instruction largely ignores. The fear, though, is that in the presence of alternate theories, process instruction may become too vague, too limited and too inconsistent to realize its promise. Reassuringly, the recent onslaught of research on metacognition, knowledge transfer and neurobiology (again, see Chapter 1) demonstrates a revived interest in the nature of composing processes and how best to nurture them.

It is the assumption of this study that expository writing instruction should not excessively revere or degrade any theoretical contribution widely confirmed as having advanced the profession in understanding how to guide inexperienced writers. And yet, judging from conference programs and publication trends in rhetoric and composition, it seems the discipline periodically becomes so taken with what is in vogue at the moment that it is more bent on displacing already substantiated domain knowledge than on working to figure out and demonstrate how new ideas and discoveries effectively enlarge the existing mosaic of writing pedagogy. That composition studies on the whole should treat its theory and research more systematically (ideally producing more empirical scholarship) to advance knowledge about writing and writing instruction is not a new argument.[3] Neither is the argument that writing pedagogy should help students view each act of composing as a complex of interweaving phenomena.

The purpose of this chapter is to build on these arguments through the findings of the empirical research completed for this study as viewed through the lenses of creativity and composition scholarship. Some of the instructional applications to be discussed are based on direct statements from the interview subjects, while others are inferred from the subjects' reflections as recorded in the interview transcripts. Whatever the case, all applications heed the caveat laid out in the book's introduction that there can be no "one size fits all"

---

2. For a concise historical review of the downturn in emphasis on process, see Paul K. Matsuda, "Process and Post Process: A Discursive History," *Journal of Second Language Writing* 12 (2003): 65–83. For a larger historical perspective on process in the discipline, see James Berlin, *Rhetoric and Reality: Writing Instruction in American Colleges, 1900–1985*, 1st edition (Carbondale: Southern Illinois University Press, 1987).
3. See, for example, Christina Haas, Pamela Takayoshi and Brandon Car, "Analytic Strategies, Competent Inquiries, and Methodological Tensions in the Study of Writing," in *Writing Studies Research in Practice: Methods and Methodologies*, ed. Lee Nickoson and Mary P. Sheridan (Carbondale: Southern Illinois University Press, 2012), 51. See also in the same volume Richard Haswell, "Quantitative Methods in Composition Studies: An Introduction to Their Functionality," 185.

approach to writing instruction, especially when it comes to managing composing processes. The suggestions rooted in this study's data, then, should be regarded not as edicts but as possibilities for expanding one's instructional repertoire in the interest of reinforcing best practices in the discipline and suggesting fresh strategies that students might experiment with as they work to build on and improve their composing knowledge and abilities.

Application of Findings

Setting the stage for exploring and managing composing processes at large

The possibilities for orchestrating process pedagogy are endless[4]; after all, pedagogy, in general, and writing process pedagogy, in particular, are creative acts in and of themselves. When layering initiatives identified with various theoretical perspectives on composing, the prospect of developing a writing curriculum may seem daunting, especially one that can accomplish all it needs to within the confines of a quarter, a semester or even a two-course sequence. The pages to follow are not intended to present a comprehensive composition course. Rather, they will forward principles for sustaining attention to composing processes in the context of multifaceted curricula that capitalize on best practices as established by the discipline.[5] Sustaining attention is achieved by emphasizing recursivity, and it should be kept in mind while reading this discussion that, just as writing processes themselves inevitably and productively circle back on each other, so should pedagogical strategies as a means of facilitating the cyclical flow of the act they're designed to support.

With learning and teaching mirroring each other as such, any writing pedagogy committed to sustained attention to composing processes must provide students with the concepts and language appropriate to understanding them and, therefore, becoming better prepared to promote and coordinate them.[6]

---

4. This chapter forwards instructional principles and, occasionally, a general strategy for executing a principle. Nevertheless, limited space prevents more detailed illustration of pedagogical advice suggested by the research findings. For those interested in a more specific treatment of many ideas addressed in this chapter, see my textbook *Invention and Craft: Exercising Creativity in College Writing and Research*, Second Edition (Anthem Press, 2024).
5. For a list of current best practices recognized by the discipline at large, refer to the Council of Writing Program Administrators' Outcomes Statement for First-Year Composition, http://wpacouncil.org/aws/CWPA/pt/sd/news_article/243055/_PARENT/layout_details/false.
6. I have made this argument elsewhere, most fully in my monograph, *Preludes to Insight: Creativity, Incubation, and Expository Writing* (Cresskill, NJ: Hampton Press, 2006). Further, I enacted the approach in my composition textbook mentioned in note 4.

Defining for students the constructs constituting the creative and composing process models presented in Chapter 2 of this book is a good place to begin. Metaphor can be effectively invoked to help concretize the more nebulous constructs from the creative and composing process models (e.g., incubation, insight). These definitions and metaphors may then come to life through illustrations from select *PR* interviews such as those culled for this study and through the vast array of retrospective essays and professional memoirs published by renowned authors. In fact, without such illustration, some of the concepts may prove challenging to grasp in ways that will aid implementation; moreover, students may default to the perspective that the definitions are merely academic and that real writers don't actually experience such phenomena or engage in such behaviors and practices. Besides, as mentioned above, such illustrations are also entertaining, especially when attached to names or works that students may recognize from high school English classes or pleasure reading. Such personal identification can forge investment in the pedagogy from the outset.

Instituting this sort of foundation at the very beginning of a writing course serves another purpose: it foregrounds the pedagogical assumption undergirding the discussion to come that—before students can master finer points of rhetoric, genre analysis, style, etc.—they must feel some measure of control over their individual writing processes. Many of the study's findings collectively stress this notion while emphasizing the manner in which affect can impact process. The discipline of rhetoric and composition at large is well aware of the importance of actively encouraging positive affect, and it has produced considerable pedagogical scholarship focused on that goal. That goal can be elusive, however, in the face of the many responsibilities composition teachers must juggle and the low self-esteem many students bear with regard to their writing ability. Nevertheless, data from this study imply that it is a goal worth prioritizing, and they reinforce recommendations for doing so as already recognized by professionals in the field.

The PR interviews sampled for this study are filled with reflections on the difficulty of writing as associated with cognitive challenges, research demands, time commitments, isolation, the sting of critique and even the physical tolls. Further, conversations focused on that difficulty reveal the negative impact it can render on the attitudes and overall writing confidence of even accomplished writers. Granted, their projects tend to be more complex than those encountered by college composition students, and established authors' pressures to succeed may feel more profound (e.g., supporting a family as opposed to passing a class). However, keeping in mind developmental level and experience, it is not much of a stretch to conclude that students of writing suffer from the same manifestations of difficulty listed above, though perhaps to varying degrees (as is true of the interviewees themselves). While those manifestations may be constant, the findings of the discourse analysis suggest that teachers should work diligently to address the emotional tensions and confidence-undermining fallout many students grapple with as they transition to college-level writing courses and confront increasingly sophisticated rhetorical scenarios as presented by their degree requirements. Certainly, this is no searing revelation for the field of composition studies. However, these findings remind teachers of the severity and extent of the anxiety some students may experience and reinforce the import of directly and persistently broaching such issues.

Compounding the challenges inherent to writing is the common belief that it comes easily for accomplished writers or, put another way, that such individuals become accomplished because writing comes easily for them. Many students carry this conviction into the composition classroom and, further, assume that writing comes easily for many of their peers. Teachers need to dispel this notion and replace it with evidence that all writers struggle at times and that most struggle often, over long periods of time relevant to many composing tasks. This is a specific point in writing curricula where excerpts from *The PR* interviews and other such resources might prove helpful, as will tales from teachers' own composing experiences. On this latter point, in the fashion of genuine mentorship so highly valued by the interview subjects, teachers should be forthcoming and deliberate in sharing their own struggles and the behaviors and practices they invoke to overcome them. Doing so requires abandoning detached, authoritarian attitudes toward craft in hopes of offering immediate and tangible examples of the truisms that writing is demanding by nature and that there exists an array of strategies to work around myriad sources of writer's block. As follows, writers should be encouraged to test various strategies across diverse writing projects in search of workable combinations fitting the individual and the rhetorical situation at hand.

Surely it is hard to sell the writing strategies and skills students need to learn when they believe their struggles with composing are unique to them. Accurately identifying, purposefully confronting and productively managing the difficulties associated with writing require deep self-awareness, as is evidenced in the interview transcripts. The specificity with which so many of the interviewees articulate the genesis of their ideas, their bouts with writer's block and the nature and evolution of their drafting and revision processes demonstrates that they have profited from serious reflection on their craft, reinforcing yet another well-validated practice in the discipline of composition studies.[7] While, in recursive fashion, reflection should be cultivated throughout

---

7. See especially Kathleen Blake Yancey, *Reflection in the Writing Classroom* (Logan: Utah State University Press, 1998) and L. Lennie Irvin, *Reflection between the Drafts* (New York: Peter Lang, 2020).

a course pertinent to all creative and composing subprocesses, instructors will want to test the efficacy of this strategy relevant to affect, in particular, since reflection activities provide students informal and safe venues to forge a writer's identity marked by both trials and victories. Productive reflection might search out sources of negative and positive feelings students harbor toward writing and cause them to interrogate the negatives in the interest of better understanding their deleterious impact. Further, in the quest to boost positive affect, appropriately guided reflection can help students explore motivations for writing whether personal or connected with career plans. It can also lead them to explore how passions that they don't necessarily associate with writing might benefit from improving their writing abilities (e.g., the avid computer gamer who suddenly grasps the significance of applying rhetorical concepts when interpreting and designing applications). By arranging opportunities for group-shares of responses to reflective exercises, teachers can shore up the sense of community in their classrooms through students' recognition of mutual feelings about and experiences with writing.

In light of interview data that convey the intimidation writers feel at the beginning of a project and that clarify the level of subject matter immersion required to produce insightful writing, validating students' interests and passions as viable sites for inquiry seems crucial. While it may be healthy to engage students with assignments that move them out of their comfort zones, this practice does not preclude enabling them to write about what genuinely motivates them. Even in the context of directed assignments, teachers should strive for at least some flexibility, helping students to stretch their notion of what counts as appropriate academic subject matter so as to find ways of marrying assignment requirements to issues they honestly care about. This seems especially vital when realizing that students ordinarily are more apprehensive about the blank page than experienced authors are and when considering that students often assume that the parameters for school-based assignments are more narrow than teachers intend.[8] The further teachers can go in connecting their instructional objectives to students' passions and interests, the more likely the latter will be (as is the case with accomplished

---

8. This observation calls to mind a sophomore in one of my undergraduate academic writing courses whose motivation levels soared upon realizing that his hobby, paint ball, might yield a host of topics suitable for scholarly inquiry through lenses from economics, the social sciences or even the hard sciences. His familiarity with the sport lent him an air of authority that translated to a more authentic voice and other improvements in his writing, as contrasted with assignments completed before he identified paint ball as the focus for his major course project.

writers) to remain invested and enjoy feelings of success that come with generating work that garners positive feedback.

A somewhat surprising finding to arise from the data relevant to the composing act at large is the degree to which the authors comment on the physicality of writing. Readers will recall that numerous poets and fiction writers depend on felt sense as a harbinger of first insight. In addition, several mention *feeling* when a manuscript in progress is finally doing what they want it to do, and much is made across the collection of transcripts about the toll writing takes on the body. Helping students tune into the sensations associated with invention certainly would involve reflection and group-shares about how various writers listen to their bodies when searching for topics or struggling to make a draft respond to their intentions. Exercises and activities intended to highlight the rhythm of language and the sensations that accompany the phenomenon of words, sentences and paragraphs in perfect cooperation with each other should also prove illuminating. Writing while listening to music can assist students in experiencing that sort of rhythm, as can recitation and analysis of writing that excels in this manner. On a more practical note regarding the physicality of writing, demands on the body should be acknowledged with attention to their impact on affect, and strategies for coping with them should be discussed. Teachers inclined to allow for movement within their classrooms feed the strengths of kinesthetic learners in particular,[9] but, ultimately, movement is crucial for all serious writers, whether in the manner of periodically changing writing positions or building exercise routines into one's writing schedule.

The mention of a writing schedule raises another skill touted by the interview subjects—that is, time management. So many of the authors lament the amount of time that good writing requires, the quickness with which that time passes and the unpleasant effects of the excessive time commitment on other areas of their lives. Although most students are not in the midst of professional writing careers, the fact is that, relative to where they are in their own lives, they view writing as drawing too much time away from their other responsibilities and pastimes. Between class loads, jobs, family obligations (and, yes, some downtime, which they need and deserve), finding the hours essential to adequately completing college-level writing assignments for multiple courses may seem impossible. Obviously, one way of helping them cope is to discuss time-management strategies specifically relevant to composing, at least more specifically relevant than those encountered in general study skills seminars aimed at incoming freshmen (e.g., have them think about what their personal

---

9. Howard Gardner, *Frames of Mind: The Theory of Multiple Intelligences*, 3rd edition (New York: Basic Books, 2011).

writing needs and preferences suggest about pursuing other commitments, undermine the pull of the all-night drafting marathon). Again, *The PR* interviews and other retrospective accounts of writing processes serve as rich resources of time management advice, as do teachers' own practices. They should remind students that effective time management need not be limited to carving out more time for writing but can include strategies for using whatever time is available more efficiently—for example, through taking breaks (or incubating) when warranted.

Allowing for movement in the classroom, changing writing positions and taking breaks point to interactions with the writing environment, namely how to maneuver within it and when to leave it for a while. These and other issues pertinent to environment pervade the interviewees' commentary, with many of them noting that their processes are enabled by deliberate decisions they've made in establishing an optimum writing space. As is the case with several of the study's findings about composing processes at large, discussions of writing environment can be aided by studying other writers and experimenting with the different possibilities they present until arriving at a comfortable and inspiring combination. Indeed, it is pointless to assert axioms about environment other than to note that it may be one of the most idiosyncratic aspects of composing. Sure, most writers need quiet, but not all. Some need a piece of furniture fit for reclining, while others prefer leaning forward on a desk surrounded by research notes and outlines. Some seek a venue separate from their home, while others respond more positively to familiar surroundings.

Perhaps what most students need in this regard is to hear that there is no single right or wrong way of proceeding and that the search for a workable approach may continue for some time. They may also benefit from seeing their teachers experimenting with the classroom or university environment in ways that cater to specific needs (e.g., conducting invention activities in asynchronous online environments to ensure more equitable discussion, moving to another space on campus to enable certain research activities or spark insights by switching up visual stimuli). In the end, with respect to all such writing preferences—those relevant to environment, as well as to time requirements and physical necessities—teachers should focus ample attention on conditions for writing in the interest of heightening students' consciousness about what does or doesn't work for them and on advocating experimentation.

Just as many recollections from the interviews encourage experimenting with time and environment, many encourage experimenting with content and form, which includes interrogating conventions, breaking boundaries and viewing writing as bendable to one's purposes. Certainly, this is in line with creativity scholarship's emphasis on wonderment and play as essential to avoiding ruts in thinking and spawning insights. That being established, it is also widely accepted wisdom that it is impossible to interrogate conventions and break boundaries until one knows exactly what they are. As follows, while instruction must accept responsibility for familiarizing students with the parameters of knowledge domains within which they are working, it must also entice students to question such strictures and take risks in response to them. Types of activities for doing so might include asking students to analyze and imitate varied examples of a given genre, including some that are especially innovative in their treatment of formal conventions and acceptable subject matter in the context of particular rhetorical situations. Such exercises would seem especially important when teaching academic writing since students' understanding of compositions fitting this category tends to be exceedingly narrow. Moreover, finding ways of rewarding students for taking risks, as well as devising assignments and modes of assessment that require them to do so, can go a long way in fomenting the kind of experimental spirit exhibited by the interviewees and associated with creativity in all fields of inquiry.

Ample opportunity for experimentation exists in the call to cross-disciplinary inquiry or, as it is classified in the findings of this study, a type of "cross-pollination." Cross-pollination breeds unique connections that spur innovation and is applicable to most every element of the creative and composing process models as evidenced across the interview transcripts sampled for this study. Whether in pursuit of insights at the very beginning of a project or while researching or drafting, the convergence of stimuli from different fields or schools of thought focuses fresh lenses on familiar subjects and challenges writers beyond their usual ways of processing information. Many of the authors featured in this study share experiences that exemplify this principle, a good number having been raised in homes that exposed them to diverse arts and pastimes that later influenced their composing endeavors. And several of the interviewees actively sought opportunity to practice other arts alongside or in between writing projects for the stimulation they represented relevant to content or style.

To pave the way for cross-pollination in composition courses, teachers might share stories about cross-disciplinary innovation across history, and they can devise activities that ask students to consider how their various interests and hobbies inform or clarify each other. In addition, they can punctuate instruction geared toward invention by tapping various art forms and inspire students to apply those modes of expression in formulating and clarifying their ideas. In the case of academic discourse in particular, teachers might reinforce the call to cross-disciplinary inquiry by representing scholarship from multiple fields when discussing issues for writing, thus encouraging students to continue to do so as they develop their resulting projects. More subtle manifestations of cross-pollination can occur during incubation when students leave a text in progress (ordinarily in the face of writer's block) and engage in an unrelated activity. Even if the eventual polished text isn't overtly derivative of that unconscious meshing of diverse stimuli, engagement in a different activity and the fresh exposure it implies can supply a missing piece of the mental equation essential to achieving insight.

As stated near the beginning of this section, students need to be made aware of how incubation, insight and all other components of the creative process model function and how they can be productively managed. Instruction should include not only teacher-led activities and exercises that compel students to become aware of and experience these phenomena but also plenty of scaffolding aimed at helping them enact these creative subprocesses on their own. The section to follow takes up each of the creative process model's components individually and offers advice for addressing each of the subprocesses in line with the goals just stated. Further, as was a matter of course in this section, the next section will consider how affect can influence and is influenced by the nature of each of these subprocesses.

First insight

Findings reported in Chapter 3 on first insight establish that the anticipation of it is a time typically marked by anxiety and frustration. Whether caught in an overwhelming chaos of possibility for kickstarting their next project or a gaping void of ideas for proceeding, some interviewees awaiting first insight began doubting their capacity for further contributing to the literary world. In certain cases, an excruciatingly long period of time passed before they were able to find a way forward, but ultimately their patience paid off. As these literary giants report, the route to first insight was ordinarily fraught with cognitive dissonance, and, though some experienced inspiration as a sudden jolt, most realized that their progression was fueled by exposure to all varieties of experience and serious, ongoing reflection about matters they deemed significant.

An important pedagogical principle to arise from the data relevant to this element of the creative process model is that students need to hear a dismantling of the spontaneous generation myth or the idea that valid inspirations come to their creators out of the blue and fully formed. In place of the myth, teachers can foreground specific examples of the reality that good writing (in fact, performance in any field) grows from questions and incongruities along with ample opportunity to explore them. Further, they can stress that the scope of good writing is defined by hard thinking about an ultimate contribution for the target audience or discipline at large. The latter lesson can be concretized by discussing the concepts of constructive constraints and domain knowledge as clarified in Chapter 2—a lesson that will continue to guide students during preparation and verification processes. Whatever examples of cognitive dissonance and resulting innovation are utilized,[10] they should prepare students to embrace initial mental and emotional discomfort as signs that they are engaged in meaningful inquiry and should alleviate their fears about delaying decisions regarding topic choices or theses.

Along these lines, significant emphasis should be placed up front on defining a problem worthy of pursuing in light of the rhetorical situation (and on projecting a rhetorical situation if one is not posited). Doing so implies a shift in what appears to be a long-standing tendency in writing pedagogy: rushing to closure relevant to topics and theses, in effect launching drafting efforts after only a brief nod to invention. A simple invention exercise or two will not suffice. All writers need time to formulate worthwhile projects, and a premature plunge into drafting may undermine the potential of students to perform well, or at least make their drafting efforts more laborious and circuitous than they need to be. Considering all the lower- and higher-order concerns they are juggling while drafting, it makes good sense to spend time early on helping them identify legitimate topics for writing and establishing adequate focus (inexperienced writers are likely to set themselves up for covering too much ground in a single piece of writing). In pursuit of these objectives, teachers should consider employing diverse media during the introduction to a unit and invention activities so as to capitalize on the stimulating effects of imagery and form relevant to first insight as reported by multiple authors cited in earlier chapters. All the better would be to use media that collectively strive for disciplinary cross-pollination.

Preparation

As the interview data suggest, cross-pollination is highly facilitative in generating, refining and researching ideas for writing en route to insight. This realization points to the advantages of having students view issues they are writing about through different lenses from various fields of study. With this goal in sight, teachers can compel cross-disciplinary inquiry and can work to condition students to view such inquiry as a matter of course whenever considering what to write about, how to narrow the scope of a piece and how to conduct research. Of course, interdisciplinary studies are not the only source of cross-pollination. Many of the authors whose transcripts were sampled for this project point to the cathartic aspects of writing, approaching it as a method of

---

10. With a nod to recursivity, teachers should note that all dissonance won't automatically disappear upon achieving first insight—research questions continue to evolve during preparation.

interpreting and surmounting complex or troubling experiences. To be sure, a simple search in any database on writing and healing calls forth plenty of scholarship touting the therapeutic benefits of writing. Nevertheless, especially when writing for academic venues, students tend to extract their emotions and steer clear of personal experience. Indeed, they seem captive to the notion that the only acceptable disposition in academic discourse is a positivistic or "objective" one, yet scholars commonly integrate emotional anecdotes and personal experiences to captivate readers and/or to contextualize or illustrate issues they are confronting. Enabling students to view academic writing more broadly than they are accustomed to by exploring genres that not only allow for emotion but even require it—autoethnography, for example—can assist in breaking down artificial barriers that exist in some students' minds between the blending of affect and cognition in scholarly forums. For genres that are defined by a positivistic stance, affect can be tapped in preliminary reading and writing as a means of becoming invested in the subject matter. (Imagine, for instance, an assignment intended to have students explore some aspect of the climate crisis for a scientific publication that begins with journal writing about the manner in which the crisis impacted the student's or a relative's home town or a place they may have visited or hope to visit.)

Thinking further about autoethnography, in particular, brings to mind another key finding from the interview transcripts—that is, famous literary figures not only spend considerable time and effort formally researching their novels, shorts stories and poems but they also engage in a variety of research strategies. Clearly, keen observation was essential to many of their works, and many employed other social science methods such as interviews, immersion in a culture, etc. In the midst of such research methods, the majority emphasized the importance of careful note-taking. Obviously, these findings point to the need for introducing students to diverse research strategies and exploring how they complement each other. In practice, however, traditional research-based writing pedagogy seems too willing to settle for citing documents written by others as backing for students' assertions in contrast to having them practice empirical research methods as a way of broadening their information-gathering repertoire. In fact, teaching the basics of empirical research methods yields a number of additional benefits relevant to creativity. For example, it causes students to think critically about the importance of marrying purpose with the most illuminating and convincing data possible in response to a given question; it reinforces cross-disciplinarity, as certain research methods are commonly associated with certain fields; and it enables them to tap other, or even their best, intelligences, allowing for observation and conversation with others as data-gathering methodologies in contrast to reading or textual analysis alone.

Of course, reading is not to be discounted or even downplayed. The idea is to expand possible tools for research, not to displace those that are already valued, and the findings of this study reveal, not at all surprisingly, that the interviewees read voraciously. The contention that reading is vital to writing breeds little controversy. Perhaps more controversial is the contention that reading skills should be directly addressed in a college-level composition classroom. While basic reading skills might be assumed outside developmental writing courses, instructors working with students of all ability levels serve their charges well by emphasizing the many ways in which reading informs writing beyond providing facts or quotes to bolster one's arguments. More specifically, instruction might stress that reading presents models of particular genres or rhetorical moves; broadens exposure to ideas, experiences and perspectives (many of which provide springboards for counterargument); and offers opportunity for immersing oneself in a subject matter. All of these potentialities are crucial to effective preparation—even that involving empirical research, which demands contextualization with regard to previous scholarship. Teachers who leave students on their own to discover the dividends of reading (and also effective strategies for taking notes on that reading, as alluded to previously) will have to return to such matters for direct instruction upon recognizing that these skills don't occur by osmosis. Also requiring direct instruction is the role of student voice in conversation with the authors whose work they are referencing. Many students at the beginning of their academic careers will lose themselves in their sources, regurgitating or parroting what they've read as opposed to critically engaging it and perhaps taking issue with it pertinent to their intentions. The importance of finding one's voice relevant to creative performance can't be overstated if the words of the interviewees informing this study are any indication.

To repeat an earlier observation, all of these matters take time and deserve it in the interest of creating the conditions essential to insightful writing. But in a quarter- or semester-long composition course, preparation time for every assignment is inevitably constrained. In the face of this pedagogical challenge, teachers should consider employing thematic assignment sequences, which pose several different writing tasks on the same subject matter as opposed to the more conventional approach to course design, which challenges students to write several different papers on various topics. Thematic pedagogies have been detailed and advocated in published composition scholarship,[11] one

---

11. Ronda Leathers Dively, "Incubating the Expert Persona: Theory and Practice for Enhancing Academic Literacy," *Writing on the Edge* 10, no. 1 (1998/99); David Bartholomae and Anthony Petrosky, *Facts, Artifacts, and Counterfacts: Theory and Method for a Reading and Writing Course* (Portsmouth: Heinemann, 1986).

of their primary advantages being that they allow students to dive increasingly deeper into a particular area of inquiry instead of starting anew with each major assignment. Of course, this approach privileges conditions for immersion so essential to preparation capable of producing insight. In the context of academic writing courses, this approach more accurately emulates scholarly enterprise. Moreover, if all students are writing in the same area of inquiry, it forges a sense of scholarly community wherein conversations and peer response to drafts in progress are cognizant of research in the same knowledge domain and thus become more specific to the tasks at hand than they would be in the context of a more conventional course design. Beyond these benefits for critical thinking and creativity, circling back to the issue of limited time that spawned this overview of thematic assignment sequences, it is obviously less onerous from a research perspective to engage in a deep dive that can support numerous projects than it is to launch multiple, vastly different research agendas.

Incubation

Incubation on the results of preparation also implies the need for time—opportunity to enjoy some distance from a project so that the mechanisms of incubation explained in Chapters 2 and 5 can fulfill their promise in facilitating insight. This study's findings on incubation support those of previous scholarship on the construct, illustrating its perceived facilitation of insight in the face of writer's block, as well as its ephemeral nature. Since incubative processes are largely intangible and explanations for their productivity largely theoretical, it is crucial for teachers to define the construct both conceptually and operationally, reinforcing these depictions with examples from the experiences of famous creators and with recollections from the students' own experiences relevant to writing or other problem-solving activities. Of course, along with insight, writer's block is central to defining incubation, and it would make good sense to share how prevalent writer's block is, even for famous authors, and to summarize findings of scholarship on the causes of writer's block so as to help students better understand and more successfully sidestep issues that can trigger it.[12] Given its more tangible nature, creative worrying as a manifestation of incubation should also be covered in these definitional efforts, and

---

12. For example, see Mike Rose's foundational study, *Writer's Block: The Cognitive Dimension* (Urbana: NCTE, 1984). For a more recent perspective, see Muhammet Bastug, Ihsan Ertem and Hasan Kagan Keskin, "A Phenomenological Research Study on Writer's Block: Causes, Processes, and Results," *Education + Training* 59, no. 6 (2017): 605–18.

both constructs should be distinguished from procrastination so as to heighten students' awareness of the difference between taking reasonable breaks from focused attention on a project and simply avoiding work or wasting time.

As findings of this study relevant to incubation illustrate in concert with other published scholarship on the phenomenon, loosely focused mentation and dream states are its hallmarks; therefore, students should be primed to tune in to these states of mind, ready to act on their contributions. For example, teachers might emphasize the wisdom of trusting gifts of the unconscious—even if their relevance isn't immediately apparent—and might encourage students to take notes in response to dreams and sudden wakeful glimpses of ways to proceed with a writing task. Often, nebulous or incomplete flashes of potential solutions to problems evolve and clarify as more time passes and conscious work proceeds. To reinforce the value of partial flashes of insight that incubation produces, teachers can build breaks into students' engagement with given projects, having them focus on related informal writing activities or even begin preliminary work on another major project. Furthermore, instruction should encourage students to emulate these practices in their time outside of the writing classroom as they are working more independently. Teachers and students might also want to experiment with meditation or relaxation techniques as a way of loosening the strictures of a conscious mind locked into unproductive trains of thought that prevent insight, the subject of the following section.

Insight

While defining constructs is crucial to all the pedagogical strategies suggested by the findings of this study, the inevitable recursivity of composing demands that definitions of certain terms be reiterated. One such term is "insight," as that is the ultimate goal of any creative endeavor, and having this goal in mind at the earliest stages of a project can help reinforce purpose and channel inquiry. With regard to insight, it is crucial to stress again the notion of knowledge domains and to explore what counts as an influential addition to a given domain. Such notions become more concrete for students by means of specific examples, not merely through tales of important historical breakthroughs or discoveries but also through detailed analysis of the contexts that defined them as valid contributions.

Students are likely to recognize the value of contributions upon grasping the status of knowledge in the field when they were made, the manner in which they brought previous understanding into question and the degree to which they advanced understanding. Especially instructive are contrasting examples that demonstrate an insight need not be completely original or transformative of the discipline to be considered valuable. This is an important message to convey in the interest of building positive affect since inexperienced writers tend to doubt the worth of their ideas, especially when writing for academic forums. As for examples addressed in the interview transcripts, few of the authors' insights radically redefined their genre of choice. Rather, they tweaked it by broaching unchartered subject matter, experimenting with certain aspects of form, effecting a fresh narrative style and so on, and students need to know this so that they can appreciate the potential of their own ideas and experiences, which they may assume are obvious or mundane. Sharing instances from *The PR* interviews (as well as other publications on creative processes) to illustrate the range of what qualifies as an insight would be instructive in this respect.

Once insight is conceptualized, students would benefit from understanding how they can recognize when they are experiencing it. As the interview transcripts illustrate, insight prompts flow: the sensation of unfettered expression, words spilling rapidly from keyboard (or pen) to screen (or page), accompanied by the impression that they are perfectly fitting for the rhetorical situation. Because flow occurs in the context of all creative acts, teachers can help students identify it by connecting it to other activities or hobbies they've pursued. By having them reflect on the manner in which flow operates relevant to other areas of their lives, teachers can reinforce lessons about fostering conditions essential to it and recognizing when and why a presumed flow state might have been a false alarm. The purposes of such lessons reify the overriding purpose of this chapter, which is to raise awareness about the subprocesses of composing so that students can recognize and more effectively manage them.

Yet another strategy suggested by the interview findings for familiarizing students with the concept of insight is to stress the importance of connection-making—more specifically, the reality that insights often arise from intersections of unlikely entities. Retrospective accounts of such moments abound in scholarship on creativity, so instructors wouldn't need to depend solely on the findings of this study to illustrate the phenomenon. The odds of forging fruitful connections increase with a commitment to interdisciplinarity in reading assignments, as well as in coverage of research techniques and rhetorical situations established in composing challenges that teachers set for their students. Connection-making can also be facilitated through invention exercises such as mind mapping or clustering. Both call for concise visual representations of composing plans that provide for at-a-glance comprehension of the many thoughts students may be juggling, and they enable easy addition of elements that can be represented as connecting with already existent elements. Regardless of the countless activities teachers might draw on in prompting productive connections, they, like all other insights, must be tested for viability. The next section addresses instructional principals germane to that objective.

Verification

Another key to successful writing careers and courses is assessment, both self-assessment and that by potential readers. *The PR* interviews sampled for this study overflow with commentary on the impact of assessment from these vantage points, and they demonstrate the emotional trauma that even famous authors may suffer in the wake of harsh judgment. These expressions of pain (which echo sentiments widely addressed in the composition scholarship on response and grading) underscore the importance of creating a classroom culture in which students and teachers are viewed, respectively, as already capable writers and more experienced collaborators or mentors—this in contrast to potential culprits/offenders and lawmakers/judges. The value of the former approach has long been established as the more enlightened and humane, yet students still enter new writing classes laden with horror stories about harshly critical instructors and toxic peer feedback sessions.

The authors cited in earlier chapters are exceptionally forthcoming about the frustrations caused by critique from editors, professional critics and even the public. Simultaneously, though, many of them acknowledge the advantages of a healthy author-editor relationship, one founded on honesty and mutual respect, as well as a spirit of give and take toward manuscripts in question. These data suggest that teachers should not only offer plenty of feedback but also interrogate their own response practices in a quest to make them less controlling, foregoing a judgmental or directive tone in exchange for one that elicits conversation and negotiation relevant to teacher and student purposes. Furthermore, they must constantly guard against falling into weakness- or error-finding mode in contrast to an approach that begins with identifying successes in the text.

As follows, preparing the class for peer review exercises that imitate this type of feedback becomes crucial, a feat that takes considerable time and repetition. Guidance in the form of teacher-generated peer response questions will help stimulate positive feedback and specificity in all commentary, which become symbiotically crucial for honing both writers' and responders' critical sensibilities. The interview data additionally support the notion that students should reach beyond the classroom for mentors and more generally prepared readers to react to their works, as many of the authors consulted numerous and diverse sources of feedback to their benefit. On a related point, teachers may also want to find ways of submitting student work to living, breathing members of audiences they establish for certain assignments.

Delving more deeply into the nature of composing processes associated with verification, namely revision and editing, teachers should take care in distinguishing between the two and in emphasizing the willingness to engage in large-scale revision, as inexperienced writers in particular are prone to resisting major overhauls to drafts that have progressed to several pages in length. Illustrating through retrospective accounts or actual snapshots of manuscripts in progress the extent to which famous authors revise may assist teachers in impressing upon students the good that can come to a project when they remain open to the possibility of changes. Breaks in flow serve as signs that such action may be warranted, and students should be alerted to that fact. Moreover, students should be reminded that composing is a recursive act and, accordingly, breaks in flow may come at multiple points while drafting. In other words, students should be flexible, revising when the need arises since problems ignored in the moment may be compounded as drafting continues. As they are coming closer to the point where they believe a draft is ready for submission, they may find it helpful, as several of the authors cited in this study did, to enact revision strategies that cause them to slow their reading processes and concentrate more fully on small-scale revision or editing.

After those texts are finally submitted and teacher assessment has been proffered, stressing all that is good in a batch of papers provides yet another opportunity for elevating affect, and the data for this study reveal that many of the interviewees craved positive commentary not only from their editors but also from their audiences. Most assuredly, publicly celebrating composing successes feeds a supportive, affirming classroom environment whether through small-group or whole-class sharing, creating classroom awards for various writing strengths (every student gets one) and publishing class anthologies of each student's best work(s). Such acknowledgment assures students of their writing strengths and brings a satisfying sense of closure to a given creative act.

Some Final Remarks

In bringing some sense of closure to this chapter and the study at large, it's presumably clear that pedagogical possibilities tied to writing courses founded on principles derived from this discourse analysis of select *PR* interviews are virtually endless. The discipline of composition studies is undergirded by a body of scholarship, including textbooks and instructional anthologies, addressing the application of best practices in a variety of writing classrooms. The teaching strategies suggested by the findings of this study reinforce the wisdom driving those best practices and build on them by means of wider and additional lenses—those offered by the discipline of creativity studies at large and systematic analysis of specific creative practices as reported by some of the world's most renowned fiction writers and poets. They build in ways that should help writing teachers capitalize on the familiarity and joy that students may more readily associate with other creative processes, helping to ease understanding of certain concepts and skills and to provide openings for positively influencing affect. Indeed, the latter is one of the great surprises of this project as one would likely expect to learn about writing technique when reading a collection of *PR* interviews but wouldn't necessarily anticipate so much insight into the way famous authors feel about the act of writing. Their willingness to share their feelings is of no small consequence, as reflecting on them—and applying suggestions based on them—will help teachers more productively address a perennial and daunting problem in the writing classroom.

Beyond the writing classroom, *The PR* interviews offer fascinating glimpses of the creative processes and behaviors involved in some of the most celebrated literary works ever written. The patterns in the interviews sampled for this study are not absolutely consistent across authors and composing experiences, but they do reveal trends in dispositions, preparations and practices relevant to writing. Moreover, the creation stories contained in the interviews lay bare the intense dedication, sacrifice, effort, self-doubt and ongoing struggle these literary giants endured to bring their ideas to larger audiences, whether to entertain, inform, persuade and/or incite. These stories also highlight the call to authorship, as well as the joys, triumphs and sense of satisfaction associated with writing success. Whether illuminating with regard to process, affect or the profession at large, the patterns discovered within these stories help reinforce and add texture to current understanding of literary production, composing processes and creativity in all disciplines.

Appendix A

CODING TABLE

First insight	Preparation	Incubation
Felt sense: (I) 224, 402 (II) 95, 206 (III) 31, 33, 60, 140, 292, 296, 297, 335, 336, 394; (IV) 4, 138, 194, 328 **[Total: 18]**	**Mentorship**: (I) 21–22, 23, 43, 176, 177, 190, 191, 225, 312, 313, 321, 380, 409–410 (II) 63, 79, 83, 98, 124, 130, 160, 161, 162, 183–184, 246, 260, 364, 398, 413–414, 436, 438, 465 (III) 3, 46, 54, 55, 66, 88,122, 147, 148, 152–153, 186, 202, 218, 219, 221, 247, 248, 272–273, 335, 338, 340, 341, 367, 370, 371, 372, 373, 391, (IV) 3, 22, 23–24, 59, 60, 136, 176, 184–185, 216, 261, 263, 264–265, 286, 290, 301, 316, 369, 404, 408, 411, 441, 442, 463 **[Total: 81]**	**Nature of incubation**: • *Unconscious/subconscious*: (I) 22, 27, 73, 95, 138, 218, 224, 295, 419, 452, 462, 465 (II) 7, 8, 9, 36, 44, 73, 95, 131, 156–157, 170, 197, 210, 248, 291, 401, 409 (III) 110, 137, 161, 184, 262, 280, 297, 304, 321, 345–346, 396, 414 (IV) 4, 86, 78, 192, 194, 196, 206, 296, 311, 329, 341, 349, 350, 365, 376, 378 **[Total: 56]** • *Creative worrying*: (I) 31, 494 (II) 31, 123, 169, 246, 407, 408, 411, 413, 444, 449, 458, 459 (III) 26, 69, 71, 120, 121, 293, 321 (IV) 86, 109, 139, 155, 224, 297, 325, 326, 329, 385, 458 **[Total: 32]**
Cognitive dissonance: (II) 130, 256, 277, 296, 364, 382, 458, 468 (III) 30, 57, 62, 75, 153, 180, 201, 293, 310, 378, 396, 404 (IV) 51, 161, 197, 206, 226, 231, 268, 283, 444, 448, 452, 458, 459 **[Total: 33]**	**Distinctive personal experience**: (I) 31, 55, 149, 172, 293, 315, 381, 388, 394, 410, 419, 447, 459, 477, 482 (II) 57, 72, 94, 108–109, 123, 124, 129, 131, 135, 136, 159, 162, 163, 185–186, 190, 192, 193, 249, 254, 255, 262–263, 375, 398–399, 403, 405, 412, 419, 420, 436, 454, 467–468, 474, 475, 489 (III) 26, 67, 120, 121, 135, 178, 179, 206, 214, 219, 228, 259, 263, 309, 315, 320, 361, 376; (IV) 11, 26, 93, 110, 139, 159, 186, 214, 215, 222–223, 227, 242, 243, 244, 246, 284, 289, 296, 319, 322–323, 323–324, 325, 325–326, 328, 351, 369, 388, 392, 393 **[Total: 96]**	**Precursors of incubation**: • *Blocks*: (I) 71, 333, 384, 396, 397, 455, 482, 492, 494 (II) 64, 70, 187, 188, 210, 217, 225, 230, 244, 251, 407, 419, 422, 424 (III) 11, 108, 140, 165, 284, 335, 353 (IV) 9, 29, 36, 74, 100, 162, 195, 208, 209, 225, 316, 332, 378–379, 415 **[Total: 44]** • *Breaks*: (I) 30–31, 59, 75, 96, 128, 307, 308, 384, 417 (II) 110, 145, 210, 236, 239, 365, 381, 407, 417, 475, 480, 481, 490 (III) 12, 83, 173, 199, 230, 231, 232, 237, 292, 284, 389, 387, 395 (IV) 11, 36, 113, 138, 139, 156, 195, 207, 225, 241, 332, 414, 421, 458 **[Total: 49]**

(continued)

APPENDIX A

First insight	Preparation	Incubation
Preference for certain literary elements: (I) 70, 72, 77, 82 (II) 8, 196, 197, 253, 276, 287, 379, 442, 445 (III) 9, 12, 26, 27, 31, 34, 55, 93, 160, 184, 228, 257, 304, 310, 320, 321, 361, 377, 415 (IV) 10, 30, 197, 205, 244, 247, 271, 325, 352, 356, 358, 359, 387, 388, 413, 443, 446, 453 **[Total: 50]**	**Formal research**: (I) 11, 26, 57, 95, 116, 215–216, 249, 273, 279, 292, 333, 391, 392, 396, 401, 406, 445, 446, 447, 482, 487–488, 490, 491, 493, 494–495, 496 (II) 47, 130, 146, 186, 192, 200, 225, 243, 248, 287, 374, 393, 413, 450, 451, 497 (III) 39, 51, 54, 68, 95–96, 175, 178, 202, 322, 324, 325, 328, 361, 365, 393, 395, 400, 421 (IV) 77, 197, 257, 285, 301, 346, 347, 351, 386, 415, 454, 463 **[Total: 72]**	
Specific images: (I) 13 (II) 44, 48, 95, 169, 194, 384, 385, 386, 413, 444, 445, 465, 467, 471 (III) 74, 129, 163, 293 (IV) 242, 274, 342, 361, 413 **[Total: 24]**	**Study of others' literary works**: (I) 46, 64, 65, 84, 126, 135, 218, 240, 254, 314, 320, 381, 383, 442, 478, 479, 480, 481 (II) 7, 8, 15, 27, 64, 71, 81, 82, 85, 88, 89, 90, 119, 154, 155, 164, 166, 184, 185, 187, 219, 224, 243, 247, 262, 263, 278, 423, 440–441, 445, 449–450, 468, 488, 489, (III) 3, 4, 12, 39, 58, 59, 71, 90–91, 109–110, 161, 182, 184, 185, 211, 228, 250–251, 272, 273, 274, 286, 289, 343, 346, 384, 387, 402 (IV) 1, 3, 8, 30, 31, 32, 57, 84, 104, 180, 238, 239, 240, 243, 274, 275, 314, 315, 344, 347, 348, 358, 359, 360, 368, 375, 382, 386, 397, 404, 417–418, 419, 443 **[Total: 106]**	
	Prewriting strategies: (I) 44, 82, 119, 217, 219, 248, 279, 292, 419, 449, 476, 477, 489 (II) 22, 44, 108, 121, 122, 130, 135, 166, 407, 424, 444, 478, 491 (III) 68, 110, 115, 157, 171, 172, 174, 177, 180, 187, 200, 254, 282, 286, 375, 400 (IV) 29, 36, 48, 55, 63, 110, 149, 155–156, 197, 200, 206, 222–223, 225, 272, 274, 292, 304, 311, 351, 352, 378, 382, 384, 385, 386, 387, 398, 411, 453 **[Total: 71]**	

APPENDIX A

First insight	Preparation	Incubation
	Cross-pollination between disciplines: (I) 27, 47, 188, 252, 284, 397, 450, 476, 479 (II) 47, 63, 75, 138, 187, 217, 241, 243, 380, 383, 384, 465, 468, 490 (III) 17, 34, 38, 56, 60, 119, 122, 124, 150, 180, 185, 260, 297, 298–299, 323, 345, 348, 367, 389, 390, 391, 419–420 (IV) 22, 23–24, 48, 53, 58, 65, 100, 103, 104, 142, 178, 199–200, 273, 274, 316, 327, 366, 387, 458 **[Total: 64]**	

Insight	Verification
Effortless drafting/flow: (I) 31, 397 (II) 95, 185, 188, 196, 225, 359, 400, 405, 407, 408, 483, 485, 496 (III) 83, 165, 230, 279, 376, 395 (IV) 9, 34, 83, 84, 156, 196, 209, 257, 258, 291, 293, 382, 413–414, 456 **[Total: 35]**	**Self-evaluation:** • *Author's identity as a writer*: (I) 19–20, 41, 119, 208, 381–382 (II) 186, 241, 242, 265, 366, 367, 402, 440 (III) 209, 219, 247–248, 251–253, 273–274, 375 (IV) 119, 132, 163, 176, 245, 287, 290–291, 292, 342–343, 380, 381 **[Total: 30]** • *Revision practices*: (I) 28, 30–31, 39, 74, 95–96, 128, 142, 144, 189, 256, 307, 325, 384–385, 386, 416, 462, 476, 492; (II) 12, 22, 60, 67, 68, 86, 102, 122, 132, 139, 156–157, 228, 255, 257, 361, 365, 399–400, 407, 424, 443, 481 (III) 21, 130, 163, 171, 173, 174, 177, 231–232, 233–234, 325, 335, 347–348, 349, 386, 387 (IV) 16, 76, 84, 139, 140, 143, 157, 196, 198, 199, 206, 208, 228, 241, 257, 296, 310, 313, 329, 334, 345, 349, 350, 379, 416, 420, 457 **[Total: 81]** • *Author's sense of rightness*: (I) 21, 224, 452, 493 (II) 42, 43, 53, 74, 120, 121, 133, 173, 217, 252, 254, 276, 362, 405, 409, 440 (III) 33, 84, 86, 110, 111, 120, 129, 130, 145, 163, 165, 166, 210, 251, 279, 346, 347, 392 (IV) 13, 33, 52, 76, 139, 140, 143, 158, 167, 187, 206, 208, 240, 241, 276, 293, 330, 415, 457 **[Total: 57]**

APPENDIX A

Insight	Verification
Autonomous literary elements: (I) 131, 320, 324, 391, 452 (II) 43, 108, 120, 122, 136, 140, 157, 168, 234, 247, 253, 254, 376–377, 480, 482, 497, 498 (III) 16, 55, 60, 128, 129, 130, 183, 257, 259, 280, 292, 335, 337, 352, 362, 363, 376, 377, 396 (IV) 35, 328, 329, 341, 348, 413, 420 **[Total: 48]**	**Evaluation by others**: • *Audience*: (I) 49, 77, 98, 134, 144, 145, 147, 179, 190, 195, 222, 223, 322, 380, 421, 424, 464, 477, 489, 498 (II) 31, 43, 72, 76, 87, 120, 167, 183, 187, 211, 227, 241, 258, 296, 297, 300, 361, 365, 368, 440, 451, 469, 477, 478 (III) 6, 10, 11, 22, 23, 24, 25, 35, 38, 48, 49, 52, 82, 84, 100, 112, 119, 120, 136, 137, 139, 152, 158, 160, 183, 233, 240, 261, 262, 281, 301, 337, 346, 360, 361, 362 (IV) 13, 147, 179, 188, 190, 191–192, 201, 208, 234, 242, 244, 245, 256, 267, 269, 277, 284, 285, 293, 331, 341, 397, 411, 416, 428 **[Total: 105]** • *Literary establishment*: (I) 23, 31, 32, 46, 66, 67, 68, 73, 79, 98, 137, 142, 152, 186, 187, 198, 209, 226, 283, 288, 385, 394, 463, 487 (II) 25, 53, 64, 75, 83, 87, 92, 109, 127, 134, 198, 201, 212, 233, 258, 268, 269, 299, 301, 362, 363, 387, 390, 400, 418, 422, 426, 439, 446, 447, 451, 456, 475, 482, 493, 498 (III) 3, 11, 21, 36, 37, 41, 47, 49, 102, 125, 136, 139, 145, 146, 147, 151, 154, 155, 159, 166, 170, 171, 176, 180, 188, 189, 202, 210, 222, 237, 239, 251, 253, 262, 280, 281, 283, 289, 309, 337, 338, 339, 340, 350, 356, 379, 383, 384, 391, 393, 404, 419, 429 (IV) 6, 12, 14, 28, 37, 41, 45, 58, 62, 70, 82, 83, 119, 132, 155, 160, 164, 170, 171, 177, 179, 187, 189, 190, 201, 240, 241, 243, 256, 261, 267, 268, 285, 291, 292, 293, 300, 330, 331, 345, 375, 379, 394, 430, 442, 444, 455, 462 **[Total: 161]**
Discovery writing: (II) 47, 95, 135, 147, 157, 211, 242, 276, 405, 406, 442 (III) 27, 47, 68, 74, 126, 130, 251, 313, 375, 377, 489 (IV) 209, 224, 228, 231, 248, 270, 329, 332, 349, 385, 414, 415, 420 **[Total: 35]**	
Sudden connections: (I) 73–74, 419 (II) 234, 411, 466–467 (III) 62, 257, 293, 361 (IV) 35–36, 39, 124, 257, 291, 342, 387, 398, 413–414 **[Total: 18]**	

APPENDIX A

Emergent patterns

Reasons for writing: (I) 54, 191, 248, 260, 322, 396–397, 408, 449, 464, 465, 500 (II) 10, 23, 33, 36, 37, 43, 165–166, 167, 211, 224, 225, 236, 242, 250, 256, 260, 298, 364, 366, 367, 387, 388, 393, 429, 430, 442, 454, 460–461, 495, 496 (III) 22, 47, 51–52, 149, 167, 173, 193, 199, 200, 201, 219, 230, 232, 233, 237, 238, 242, 254, 280–281, 287, 294, 304, 335, 354, 394, 404, 406, 425 (IV) 3, 5, 6, 17, 25, 173, 176, 210, 212, 244, 248, 255, 285, 287, 290, 291, 292, 297, 304, 306, 314, 340, 369, 370, 377, 384, 396, 410, 411, 412, 417, 426, 430, 436, 456, 458, 459, 464 **[Total: 107]**

Role of art, including writing: (I) 9, 58, 61, 103, 109, 123, 131, 144, 195, 263, 309, 310, 327, 328, 448, 451, 453, 454, 465 (II) 37, 48, 54, 95, 100, 113, 127, 134, 136, 147, 148, 151, 152–153, 170, 171, 173, 174, 182, 211, 225, 240, 243, 253, 256, 257, 263, 271, 366, 382, 458, 469, 474, 481, 483, 486, 499 (III) 5, 6, 9, 10, 17–18, 23, 24, 25, 35, 36, 38, 75, 144, 160, 163, 166, 173, 194, 213, 233, 242, 247–248, 256, 260, 294, 301–302, 344, 345, 351, 357, 361, 362, 366, 381, 382, 402, 412, 419 (IV) 7, 8, 47, 55, 56, 68, 71, 84, 147, 148–149, 188, 210, 212, 230, 234, 235, 242, 245, 247–248, 250, 253, 277, 284, 290, 298, 300–301, 302, 319, 331, 342, 347, 351, 362, 364–365, 377, 378, 391, 392, 420, 421, 427, 429, 432, 436, 447 **[Total: 138]**

Difficulty of writing: (I) 56, 95, 179, 257, 307, 325, 461, 475–476, 492 (II) 43, 75, 107, 190, 194, 195, 251, 257, 266, 298, 366, 408, 410 (III) 12, 16, 22, 28, 29, 41, 71, 145, 146, 164, 165, 174, 178, 180, 189, 201, 258, 285, 349, 379, 381, 402, 403, 404, 420, 422 (IV) 4, 29, 54, 110, 139, 151, 156, 212, 240, 258, 266, 306, 307, 350, 378, 421, 452, 456 **[Total: 66]**

Confidence: (I) 15, 93, 119, 144, 147, 298, 393, 401, 482, (II) 405, 424, 425, 438, 456, 483, 499 (III) 125, 155, 171, 238, 353, 356, 375, 378, 379, 381, 393, 401, 435 (IV) 75, 132, 187, 288, 303, 378 **[Total: 35]**

Conditions for writing:
- *Financial security*: (I) 3, 13–14, 41, 197, 214, 258, 286, 306, 315, 484–485 (II) 37, 38, 49, 102, 181, 213, 215, 216, 242, 245, 255, 276, 434–435, 437, 448, 474, 489, 492 (III) 25, 36, 47, 67, 150, 153–154, 219–220, 221, 223, 254, 275, 373, 420 (IV) 16, 60, 109, 123, 135, 163, 164, 177, 181, 194, 407, 409, 433, 434 **[Total: 56]**
- *Time*: (I) 45, 81, 197, 253, 257, 273, 279, 280–281, 308, 333, 402, 411, 455, 461, 468, 500 (II) 7, 32–33, 64, 138, 203, 210, 216, 236, 264, 357, 358, 359, 394, 403, 404, 405, 407, 421, 425, 428, 429, 448, 484, 499; (III) 12, 69, 139, 221, 223, 234, 258, 266, 275, 279, 324, 326, 349, 353–354, 376, 381, 386 (IV) 36, 113–114, 138, 139, 156, 181, 194, 207, 209, 270, 290, 327, 341, 393, 420, 430, 455, 464, 465, 467 **[Total: 77]**
- *Solitude*: (I) 45, 383, 386, 459, 460, 500 (II) 138, 193, 244, 255, 408, 420, 447, 478 (III) 28, 92, 176, 209, 221, 223, 241, 272, 276, 324, 326, 355, 379, 386, 422 (IV) 5, 104, 114, 172, 239, 321, 346, 376, 395–396, 398, 410, 419–420, 456, 464–465 **[Total: 43]**

Emergent patterns

- *Solitude*: (I) 45, 383, 386, 459, 460, 500 (II) 138, 193, 244, 255, 408, 420, 447, 478 (III) 28, 92, 176, 209, 221, 223, 241, 272, 276, 324, 326, 355, 379, 386, 422 (IV) 5, 104, 114, 172, 239, 321, 346, 376, 395–396, 398, 410, 419–420, 456, 464–465 **[Total: 43]**
- *Writing schedule*: (I) 28, 30–31, 38, 74–75, 384, 465, 467 (II) 12, 139, 196, 210, 255, 357, 358, 359, 428, 448, 479 (III) 28, 29, 69, 172, 230, 349, 353, 386–387 (IV) 156, 195, 207, 241, 349, 350, 419, 420, 456 **[Total: 35]**
- *Resolve in the face of constraints*: (I) 75, 93, 94, 96–97, 395 (II) 67–68, 69, 70, 72, 148, 149, 204, 225, 243, 244, 367, 369, 370, 372, 446, 460 (III) 25–26, 35, 84, 90, 92, 93, 110, 115, 139, 140, 192, 254, 281, 303, 304, 343, 351, 401, 406, 431 (IV) 38, 39, 87, 104, 206, 221–223, 229, 271, 317, 318, 429, 448 **[Total: 53]**

Attitudes toward creative writing courses: (I) 50, 79–80, 215, 286, 287, 323, 331, 380, 382, 394, 402, 403, 455 (II) 43, 60–61, 109, 165, 166, 167, 168, 169, 214, 230, 248, 252, 265, 274, 416, 447 (III) 249, 254, 266, 295, 296 (IV) 3, 4, 180, 202, 441, 442, 454 **[Total: 41]**

Appendix B
LIST OF CITED *PARIS REVIEW* INTERVIEWEES

Copyright © by *The Paris Review*, used by permission of The Wylie Agency LLC.

Chinua Achebe
Martin Amis
Maya Angelou
John Ashbery ("John Ashbery" in *The Paris Review Interviews,* Vol. IV. Copyright © 2009 by John Ashbery. Reprinted by permission of Georges Borchardt, Inc., on behalf of the author's Estate)
Paul Auster
James Baldwin
Saul Bellow
Elizabeth Bishop
Jorge Luis Borges
James M. Cain
Truman Capote
Peter Carey (Copyright © Peter Carey. Reproduced by permission of the author c/o Rogers, Coleridge & White Ltd., 20 Powis Mews, London W11 1JN; and with permission of Radhika Jones)
Raymond Carver
John Cheever
Joan Didion
Isak Dinesen
T. S. Eliot
Ralph Ellison
William Faulkner ("William Faulkner, The Art of Fiction #12" Copyright © 1956 by Jean Stein. All rights not specifically granted herein are hereby reserved to the Licensor)
William Gaddis (and with permission of Zoltan Abadi-Nagy)
Gabriel Garcia Marquez
John Gardner (and with permission of the Brockport Writers Forum)
Jack Gilbert
Graham Greene

David Grossman (and with permission of Jonathan Shainin)
Earnest Hemingway
Ted Hughes
Jack Kerouac
Stephen King (Excerpts from *The Paris Review Interviews* by Stephen King. Copyright © 2006 by Stephen King. All rights reserved. Used courtesy of Darhansoff & Verrill Literary Agents; and with permission of the estate of Christopher Lehmann-Haupt)
Philip Larkin
Robert Lowell
Norman Mailer (Copyright © Andrew O'Hagan. Reproduced by permission of the author c/o Rogers, Coleridge & White Ltd., 20 Powis Mews, London W11 1JN)
Marianne Moore
Jan Morris
Toni Morrison (and with permission of Claudia Brodsky)
Alice Munro
Haruki Murakami
V. S. Naipaul
Joyce Carol Oates
Orhan Pamuk
Dorothy Parker
Harold Pinter
Richard Price (and with permission of James Linville)
Jean Rhys
Marilynne Robinson (and with permission of Sarah Fay)
Philip Roth
Salman Rushdie (and with permission of Jack Livings)
Georges Simenon
Isaac Bashevis Singer
Stephen Sondheim (and with permission of the estate of James Lipton)
Robert Stone
William Styron
James Thurber
Kurt Vonnegut
Evelyn Waugh
Eudora Welty
Rebecca West
E. B. White
Billy Wilder
William Carlos Williams
P. G. Wodehouse

Appendix C

DIAGRAM OF ANALYTICAL CATEGORIES, SUBCATEGORIES AND THEMES

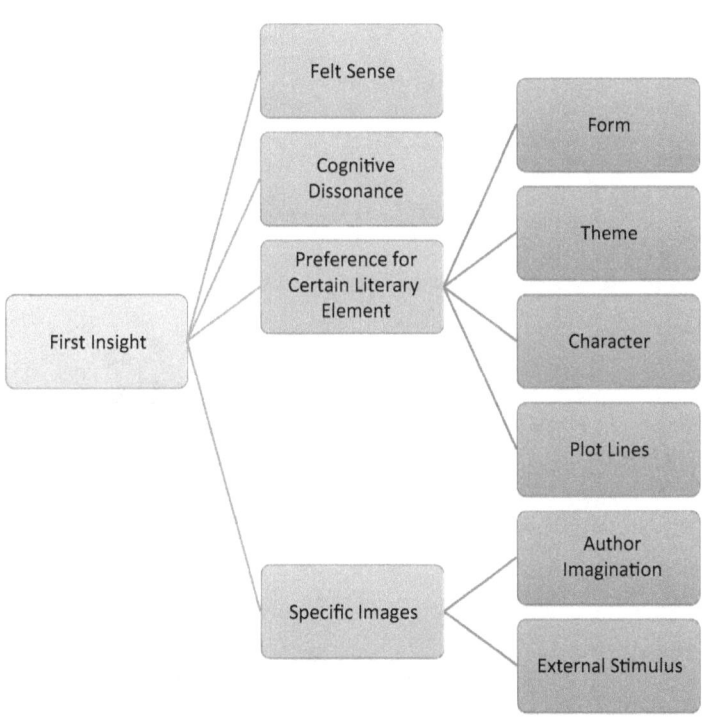

APPENDIX C

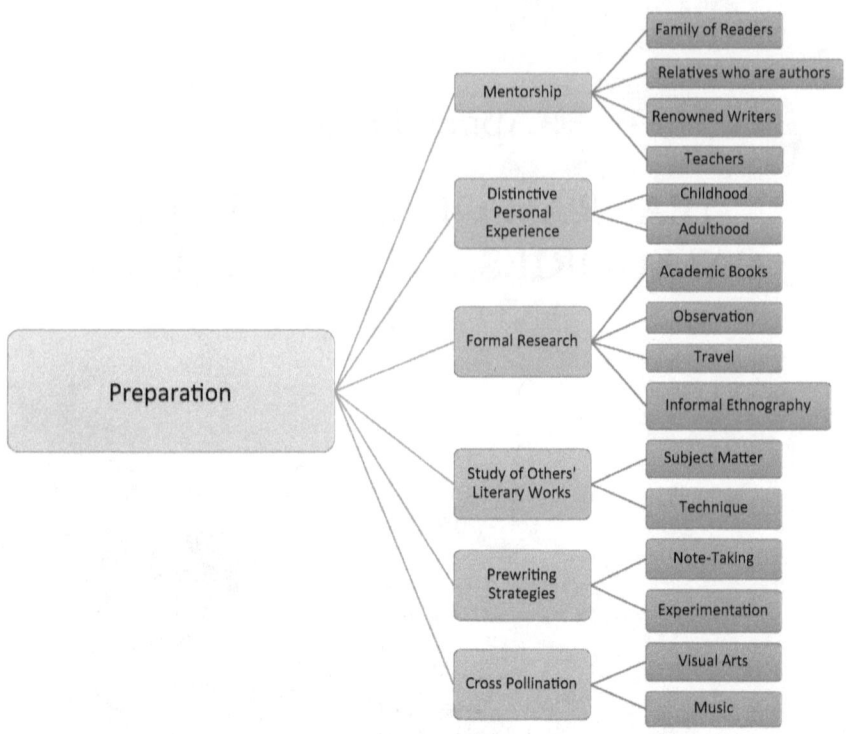

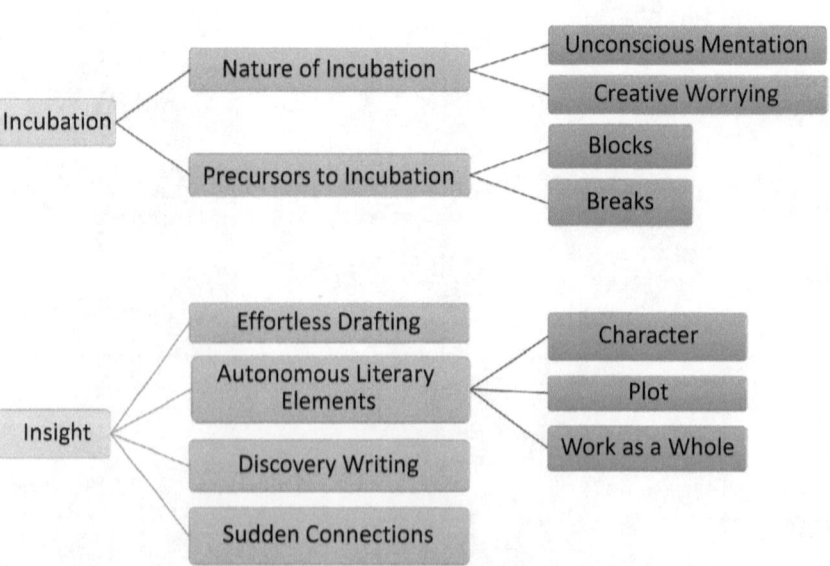

APPENDIX C

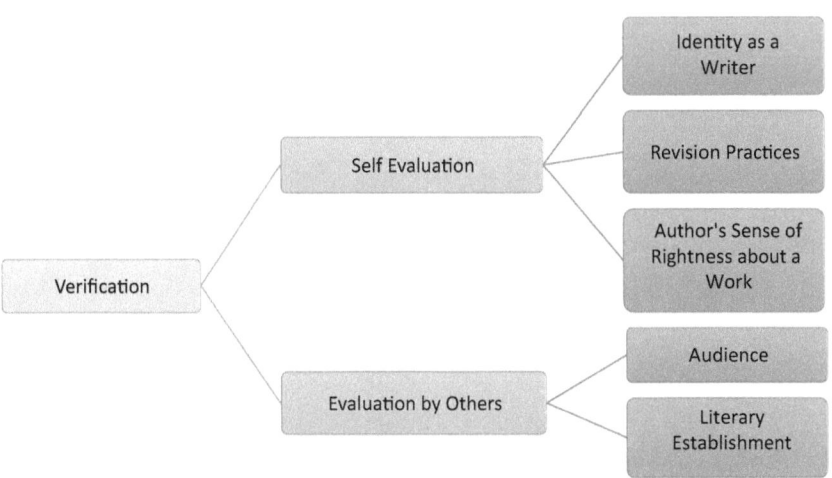

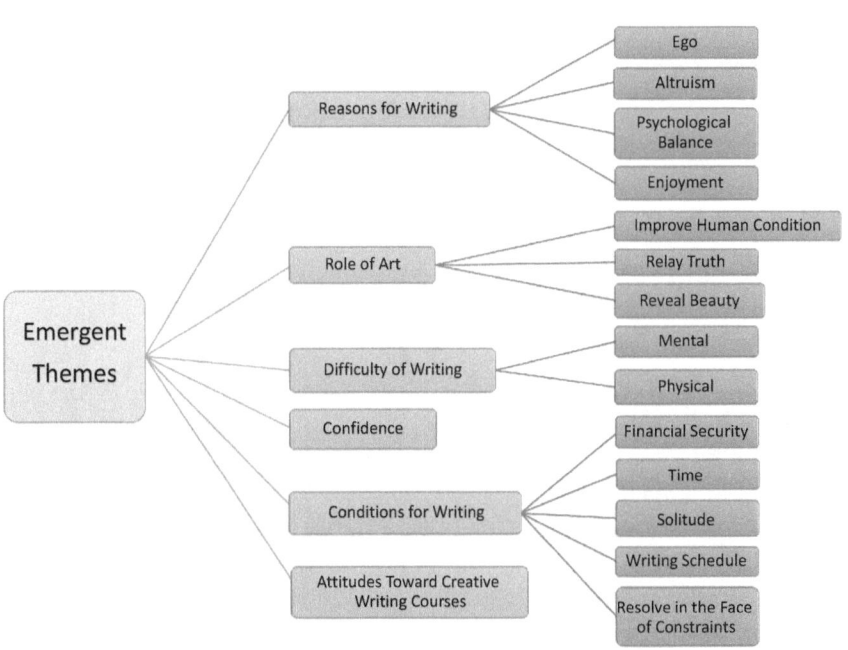

REFERENCES

Abdulla, Ahmed M., Sue Hyeon Paek, Bonnie Cramond and Mark A. Runco. "Problem Finding and Creativity: A Meta-Analytic Review." *Psychology of Aesthetics, Creativity, and the Arts* 14, no. 1 (2020): 3–14.
Achebe, Chinua. Interview by Jerome Brooks. In *The Paris Review Interviews*, vol. 3, edited by Philip Gourevitch, 246–69. New York: Picador, 2008.
Aldous, Carol R. "Modelling the Creative Process and Cycles of Feedback." *Creative Education* 8 (2017): 1860–77.
American Psychological Association Dictionary of Psychology. "Cognitive Dissonance." Accessed April, 9, 2020. https://dictionary.apa.org/cognitive-dissonance.
Amis, Martin. Interview by Francesca Riviere. In *The Paris Review Interviews*, vol. 3, edited by Philip Gourevitch, 334–59. New York: Picador, 2008.
Angelou, Maya. Interview by George Plimpton. In *The Paris Review Interviews*, vol. 4, edited by Philip Gourevitch, 236–58. New York: Picador, 2009.
Ashbery, John. Interview by Peter Stitt. In *The Paris Review Interviews*, vol. 4, edited by Philip Gourevitch, 174–202. New York: Picador, 2009.
Auster, Paul. Interview by Michael Wood. In *The Paris Review Interviews*, vol. 4, edited by Philip Gourevitch, 308–34. New York: Picador, 2009.
Bains, Christopher. "Critics Abroad: The Early Years of *The Paris Review* (1953–65)." In *The Oxford Critical and Cultural History of Modernist Magazines*, edited by Peter Brooker and Andrew Thacker, 759–76. Oxford: Oxford University Press, 2012.
Baldwin, James. Interview by Jordan Elgrably. In *The Paris Review Interviews*, vol. 2, edited by Philip Gourevitch, 237–71. New York: Picador, 2007.
Barron, Frank, Alfonso Montouri and Anthea Barron, eds. *Creators on Creating: Awakening and Cultivating the Imaginative Mind*. New York: Jeremy P. Tarcher/Putnam, 1997.
Bartholomae, David, and Anthony Petrosky. *Facts, Artifacts, and Counterfacts: Theory and Method for a Reading and Writing Course*. Portsmouth: Heinemann, 1986.
Bastug, Muhammet, Ihsan Ertem and Hasan Kagan Keskin, "A Phenomenological Research Study on Writer's Block: Causes, Processes, and Results." *Education + Training* 59, no. 6 (2017): 605–18.
Bellow, Saul. Interview by Gordon Lloyd Harper. In *The Paris Review Interviews*, vol. 1, edited by Philip Gourevitch, 86–110. New York: Picador, 2006.
Berlin, James. *Rhetoric and Reality: Writing Instruction in American Colleges, 1900–1985*. Carbondale: Southern Illinois University Press, 1987.
Bishop, Elizabeth. Interview by Elizabeth Spires. In *The Paris Review Interviews*, vol. 1, edited by Philip Gourevitch, 275–302. New York: Picador, 2006.
Bishop, Wendy. "Crossing the Lines: On Creative Composition and Composing Creative Writing." *Writing on the Edge* 4, no. 2 (1993): 117–33.

REFERENCES

Blakeslee, Ann, and Cathy Fleischer. *Becoming a Writing Researcher*. Mahwah, NJ: Lawrence Erlbaum, 2007.

Boden, Margaret. "What Is Creativity?," In *Dimensions of Creativity*, edited by Margaret Boden, 75–118. Cambridge, MA: MIT Press, 1996.

Britton, James, Tony Burgess, Nancy Martin, Alex McLeod and Harold Rosen. *The Development of Writing Ability* (11–18). London: Macmillan Education, 1975.

Burke, Kenneth. *A Grammar of Motives*. New York: Prentice-Hall, 1952.

Cain, James M. Interview by David L. Zinsser. In *The Paris Review Interviews*, vol. 1, edited by Philip Gourevitch, 206–27. New York: Picador, 2006.

Calcutt, Andrew. "Reconstructing the Public Sphere: From *The Paris Review* to Intelligent Life." *Reconstruction: Studies in Contemporary Culture* 8, no. 1 (2008): 42 paragraphs. http://reconstruction.eserver.org/Issues/081/calcutt.shtml.

Capote, Truman. Interview by Pati Hill. In *The Paris Review Interviews*, vol. 1, edited by Philip Gourevitch, 17–33. New York: Picador, 2006.

Carey, Peter. Interview by Radhika Jones. In *The Paris Review Interviews*, vol. 2, edited by Philip Gourevitch, 432–61. New York: Picador, 2007.

Carlson, Peter. "Post-Plimpton *Paris Review* Is Thriving." *Chicago Tribune*, October 19, 2006. https://www.chicagotribune.com/news/ct-xpm-2006-10-19-0610190010-story.html.

Carver, Raymond. Interview by Mona Simpson and Lewis Buzbee. In *The Paris Review Interviews*, vol. 3, edited by Philip Gourevitch, 216–45. New York: Picador, 2008.

Cheever, John. Interview by Annette Grant. In *The Paris Review Interviews*, vol. 3, edited by Philip Gourevitch, 143–68. New York: Picador, 2008.

Coleridge, Samuel Taylor. "Preface to 'Kubla Khan.'" In *English Romantic Poetry and Prose*, edited by Russell Noyes, 391. New York: Oxford University Press, 1956.

Council of Writing Program Administrators. "Outcomes Statement for First-Year Composition." July 18, 2019. http://wpacouncil.org/aws/CWPA/pt/sd/news_article/243055/_PARENT/layout_details/false.

Cowley, Malcolm. "Introduction: How Writers Write." In *The Paris Review Interviews Writers at Work*, edited by Malcolm Cowley, 3–21. New York: Penguin, 1977.

Csikszentmihalyi, Mihaly. *Creativity: Flow and the Psychology of Discovery and Invention*. New York: HarperCollins, 1996.

Csikszentmihalyi, Mihaly. *Flow: The Psychology of Optimal Experience*. New York: HarperCollins, 1990.

"Declarations of Genius." *The Scotsman*, December 14, 2007. http://www.scotsman.com/lifestyle/declarations-of-genius-1703847#ixzz3z7f87zmt.

Didion, Joan. Interview by Hilton Als. In *The Paris Review Interviews*, vol. 1, edited by Philip Gourevitch, 473–500. New York: Picador, 2006.

Dinesen, Isak. Interview by Eugene Walter. In *The Paris Review Interviews*, vol. 3, edited by Philip Gourevitch, 42–62. New York: Picador, 2008.

Dively, Ronda Leathers. "Incubating the Expert Persona: Theory and Practice for Enhancing Academic Literacy." *Writing on the Edge* 10, no. 1 (1999): 85–100.

———. *Invention and Craft: A Guide to College Writing*. New York: McGraw-Hill, 2016.

———. *Preludes to Insight: Creativity, Incubation and Expository Writing*. Cresskill, NJ: Hampton Press, 2006.

Donadio, Rachel. "*The Paris Review* Faces Its Future, Finds New Editor." *The New York Observer*, January 5, 2004. https://observer.com/2004/01/the-paris-review-faces-its-future-finds-new-editor/.

Eder, Richard. "Pursuing Writers, but Letting Them Lead the Chase." *The New York Times*, January 6, 2007. http://www.nytimes.com/2007/01/06eder.html?emc=etal&_r=0.

Eliot, T. S. Interview by Donald Hall. In *The Paris Review Interviews*, vol. 1, edited by Philip Gourevitch, 62–85. New York: Picador, 2006.

Ellison, Ralph. Interview by Alfred Chester and Vilma Howard. In *The Paris Review Interviews*, vol. 3, edited by Philip Gourevitch, 1–18. New York: Picador, 2008.

Epel, Naomi, ed. *Writers Dreaming: Twenty-Six Writers Talk about Their Dreams and the Creative Process*. New York: Vintage, 1993.

Fassler, Joe, ed. *Light the Dark: Writers on Creativity, Inspiration, and the Artistic Process*. New York: Penguin, 2017.

Faulkner, William. Interview by Jean Stein. In *The Paris Review Interviews*, vol. 2, edited by Philip Gourevitch, 34–57. New York: Picador, 2007.

Flower, Linda, and Linda J. Carey. *Foundations for Creativity in the Writing Process: Rhetorical Representations of Ill-Defined Problems*. Washington, DC: Office for Educational Research and Improvement, June, 1989.

Flower, Linda, and John Hayes. "The Cognition of Discovery: Defining a Rhetorical Problem." *College Composition and Communication* 31, no. 1 (February 1980): 21–32.

———. "Problem-Solving Strategies and the Writing Process." *College English* 39, no. 4 (December 1977): 449–61.

Gaddis, William. Interview by Zoltan Abadi-Nagy. In *The Paris Review Interviews*, vol. 2, edited by Philip Gourevitch, 272–75. New York: Picador, 2007.

Garcia Marquez, Gabriel. Interview by Peter H. Stone. In *The Paris Review Interviews*, vol. 2, edited by Philip Gourevitch, 178–206. New York: Picador, 2007.

Gardner, Howard. *Creating Minds: An Anatomy of Creativity as Seen through the Lives of Freud, Einstein, Picasso, Stravinsky, Eliot, Graham and Gandhi*. New York: Basic Books, 1993.

———. *Frames of Mind: The Theory of Multiple Intelligences*, 3rd ed. New York: Basic Books, 2011.

Gardner, John. Interview by Paul F. Ferguson, John R. Maier, Frank McConnell and Sara Matthiessen. In *The Paris Review Interviews*, vol. 2, edited by Philip Gourevitch, 142–77. New York: Picador, 2007.

Gates, Rosemary L. "Applying Martin Greenman's Concept of Insight to Composition Theory." *Journal of Advanced Composition* 9, no. 1–2 (1989): 59–68.

Gendlin, Eugene. *Focusing*. New York: Everest House, 1978.

Ghiselin, Brewster, ed. *The Creative Process: Reflection on Invention in the Arts and Sciences*. Berkeley: University of California Press, 1985.

Gilbert, Jack. Interview by Sarah Fay. In *The Paris Review Interviews*, vol. 1, edited by Philip Gourevitch, 436–72. New York: Picador, 2006.

Gourevitch, Philip. "Introduction." In *The Paris Review Interviews*, vol. 1, edited by Philip Gourevitch, vii–xi. New York: Picador, 2006.

Greene, Graham. Interview by Shuttleworth and Simon Raven. In *The Paris Review Interviews*, vol. 2, edited by Philip Gourevitch, 1–17. New York: Picador, 2007.

Greene, Stuart, and Lorraine Higgins. "'Once upon a Time': The Use of Retrospective Accounts in Building Theory in Composition." In *Speaking about Writing: Reflections on Research Methodology*, edited by Peter Smagorinsky, 115–40. Thousand Oaks, CA: Sage, 1994.

Grossman, David. Interview by Jonathan Shainin. In *The Paris Review Interviews*, vol. 4, edited by Philip Gourevitch, 400–37. New York: Picador, 2009.

Haas, Christina, Pamela Takayoshi and Brandon Car. "Analytic Strategies, Competent Inquiries, and Methodological Tensions in the Study of Writing." In *Writing Studies Research in Practice: Methods and Methodologies*, edited by Lee Nickoson and Mary P. Sheridan, 51–62. Carbondale: Southern Illinois University Press, 2012.

Harris, Muriel. "Composing Behaviors of One- and Multi-Draft Writers." *College English* 51, no. 2 (1989): 174–91.

Haswell, Richard. "Quantitative Methods in Composition Studies: An Introduction to Their Functionality." In *Writing Studies Research in Practice: Methods and Methodologies*, edited by Lee Nickoson and Mary P. Sheridan, 185–96. Carbondale: Southern Illinois University Press, 2012.

Hazlin, Mark. "*Paris Review* Digs into Literary History." *USA Today*, November 10, 2004. http://usatoday30.usatoday.com/life/books/news/2004-11-10-paris-review_x.htm.

Hemingway, Earnest. *Hemingway on Writing*. Edited by Larry W. Phillips. New York: Scribner, 1984.

———. Interview by George Plimpton. In *The Paris Review Interviews*, vol. 1, edited by Philip Gourevitch, 34–61. New York: Picador, 2006.

Hertzel, Laurie. "Great Writers Make Their Work an Open Book for *Paris Review*." *Star Tribune*, December 5, 2009. http://www.startribune.com/great-writers-make-their-work-an-open-book-for-paris-review/78475222/.

Hesse, Douglas. "The Place of Creative Writing in Composition Studies." *College Composition and Communication* 62, no. 1 (2010): 31–52.

Hughes, Ted. Interview by Drue Heinz. In *The Paris Review Interviews*, vol. 3, edited by Philip Gourevitch, 270–306. New York: Picador, 2008.

Irvin, Lennie L. *Reflection between the Drafts*. New York: Peter Lang, 2020.

Joy, David. "10 Tips from *The Paris Review*'s Art of Fiction." *The Strand*, March 10, 2017. https://strandmag.com/10-tips-from-the-paris-reviews-art-of-fiction/.

Karnezis, George T. "Reclaiming Creativity for Composition." In *Teaching Writing Creatively*, edited by David Starkey, 29–42. Portsmouth: Boynton/Cook, 1998.

Kent, Thomas, ed. *Post-Process Theory: Beyond the Writing-Process Paradigm*. Carbondale: Southern Illinois University Press, 1999.

Kerouac, Jack. Interview by Ted Berrigan. In *The Paris Review Interviews*, vol. 4, edited by Philip Gourevitch, 79–127. New York: Picador, 2009.

King, Stephen. Interview by Christopher Lehmann-Haupt and Nathaniel Rich. In *The Paris Review Interviews*, vol. 2, edited by Philip Gourevitch, 462–500. New York: Picador, 2007.

———. *On Writing: A Memoir of the Craft*. New York: Scribner, 2000.

Kneller, George R. *The Art and Science of Creativity*. New York: Holt, Rinehart and Winston, 1965.

Koestler, Arthur. *The Act of Creation*. London: Penguin Books, 1664.

Larkin, Philip. Interview by Robert Phillips. In *The Paris Review Interviews*, vol. 2, edited by Philip Gourevitch, 207–37. New York: Picador, 2007.

Lauer, Janice. "Writing as Inquiry: Some Questions for Teachers." *College Composition and Communication* 33, no. 1 (1982): 89–93.

Lewis, Kelley Penfield. "Interviews at Work: Reading *The Paris Review* Interviews 1953–1978." PhD diss., Dalhousie University, 2009.

Linville, James, Jeanne McCulloch and George Plimpton. "*The Paris Review* at Forty." *Publishing Research Quarterly* (Winter 1993–94): 53–65.

Lowell, Robert. Interview by Frederick Seidel. In *The Paris Review Interviews*, vol. 2, edited by Philip Gourevitch, 58–95. New York: Picador, 2007.

Luis Borges, Jorge. Interview by Ronald Christ. In *The Paris Review Interviews*, vol. 1, edited by Philip Gourevitch, 111–59. New York: Picador, 2006.

Mailer, Norman. Interview by Andrew O'Hagan. In *The Paris Review Interviews*, vol. 3, edited by Philip Gourevitch, 399–436. New York: Picador, 2008.

Manning, Margaret. "Writers Talk about Writing and Other Writers." *Boston Globe*, August 26, 1984. https://search-proquest-com.proxy.lib.siu.edu/docview/294200496?accountid=13864.

Maran, Meredith, ed. *Why We Write*. New York: Plume, 2013.

Matsuda, Paul K. "Process and Post Process: A Discursive History." *Journal of Second Language Writing* 12 (2003): 65–83.

Moore, Marianne. Interview by Donald Hall. In *The Paris Review Interviews*, vol. 4, edited by Philip Gourevitch, 19–48. New York: Picador, 2009.

Morris, Jan. Interview by Leo Lerman. In *The Paris Review Interviews*, vol. 3, edited by Philip Gourevitch, 307–33. New York: Picador, 2008.

Morrison, Toni. Interview by Elissa Schappell and Claudia Brodsky Lacour. In *The Paris Review Interviews*, vol. 2, edited by Philip Gourevitch, 355–94. New York: Picador, 2007.

Munro, Alice. Interview by Jeanne McCulloch and Mona Simpson. In *The Paris Review Interviews*, vol. 2, edited by Philip Gourevitch, 395–431. New York: Picador, 2007.

Murray, Donald. "The Essential Delay." In *When a Writer Can't Write*, edited by Mike Rose, 219–26. New York: Guilford, 1985.

Murray, Mary M. *Artwork of the Mind: An Interdisciplinary Description of Insight and the Search for It in Student Writing*. Cresskill, NJ: Hampton Press, 1995.

Murakami, Haruki. Interview by John Wray. In *The Paris Review Interviews*, vol. 4, edited by Philip Gourevitch, 335–70. New York: Picador, 2009.

Naipaul, V. S. Interview by Tarun Tejpal and Jonathan Rosen. In *The Paris Review Interviews*, vol. 4, edited by Philip Gourevitch, 279–307. New York: Picador, 2009.

Oates, Joyce Carol. Interview by Robert Phillips. In *The Paris Review Interviews*, vol. 3, edited By Philip Gourevitch, 169–95. New York: Picador, 2008.

———. "Introduction." In *Writers at Work: The Paris Review Interviews*, edited by George Plimpton, xi–xviii. New York: Penguin, 1988.

Olton, Robert M. "Experimental Studies of Incubation: Searching for the Elusive." *Journal of Creative Behavior* 13, no. 1 (1979): 9–22.

Pamuk, Orhan. "Driven by Demons." *The Guardian*, October 26, 2007. https://www.theguardian.com/books/2007/oct/27/fiction.orhanpamuk.

———. Interview by Angel Gurria-Quintana. In *The Paris Review Interviews*, vol. 4, edited by Philip Gourevitch, 371–99. New York: Picador, 2009.

"*The Paris Review* Reviewed." *The University Times*, January 20, 2010. http://www.universitytimes.ie/2010/01/the-paris-review-reviewed/.

Parker, Dorothy. Interview by Marion Capron. In *The Paris Review Interviews*, vol. 1, edited by Philip Gourevitch, 1–16. New York: Picador, 2006.

Perl, Sondra. *Felt Sense: Writing with the Body*. New York: Heinemann, 2004.

———. "Understanding Composing." *College Composition and Communication* 31 (December 1980): 363–69.

Perry, Susan K. *Writing in Flow: Keys to Enhanced Creativity*. Cincinnati: Writers Digest Books, 1999.

Phelan, Stephen. "Unravelling the DNA of Literature." *Sunday Herald*, January 21, 2007. https://search-proquest-com.proxy.lib.siu.edu/docview/331277165?accountid=13864.

Pinter, Harold. Interview by Lawrence M. Bensky. In *The Paris Review Interviews*, vol. 3, edited by Philip Gourevitch, 117–42. New York: Picador, 2008.

Portanova, Patricia, Michael Rifenburg and Duane Roen, eds. *Contemporary Perspectives on Cognition and Writing*. Boulder: University Press of Colorado, 2017.

Price, Richard. Interview by James Linville. In *The Paris Review Interviews*, vol. 1, edited by Philip Gourevitch, 376–411. New York: Picador, 2006.

Rhys, Jean. Interview by Elizabeth Vreeland. In *The Paris Review Interviews*, vol. 3, edited by Philip Gourevitch, 196–215. New York: Picador, 2008.

Robinson, Marilynne. Interview by Sarah Fay. In *The Paris Review Interviews*, vol. 4, edited by Philip Gourevitch, 438–68. New York: Picador, 2009.

Rose, Mike. *Writer's Block: The Cognitive Dimension*. Urbana, IL: National Council of Teachers of English, 1984.

Roth, Philip. Interview by Hermione Lee. In *The Paris Review Interviews*, vol. 4, edited by Philip Gourevitch, 203–35. New York: Picador, 2009.

Rushdie, Salman. Interview by Jack Livings. In *The Paris Review Interviews*, vol. 3, edited by Philip Gourevitch, 360–98. New York: Picador, 2008.

Sawyer, R. Keith. *Explaining Creativity*, 2nd ed. Oxford: Oxford University Press, 2012.

Schubert, Daniel S. "Is Incubation the Silent Rehearsal of Mundane Responses?," *Journal of Creative Behavior* 13, no. 1 (1979): 36–38.

Seifert, Colleen, David E. Meyer, Natalie Davidson, Andrea L. Patalano and Yaniv Ilan. "Demystification of Cognitive Insight: Opportunistic Assimilation and the Prepared-Mind Perspective." In *The Nature of Insight*, edited by Robert J. Sternberg and Janet E. Davidson, 65–124. Cambridge, MA: MIT Press, 1995.

Sharp, Laurie A. "Acts of Writing: A Compilation of Six Models That Define the Processes of Writing." *International Journal of Instruction* 9, no. 2 (July 2016): 77–90.

Sherman, Scott. "Talking on against Time." *The Nation*, June 7, 2010. 41–44.

Simenon, Georges. Interview by Carvel Collins. In *The Paris Review Interviews*, vol. 3, edited by Philip Gourevitch, 19–41. New York: Picador, 2008.

Singer, Isaac Bashevis. Interview by Harold Flender. In *The Paris Review Interviews*, vol. 2, edited by Philip Gourevitch, 96–116. New York: Picador, 2007.

Smith, Steven M. "Fixation, Incubation, and Insight in Memory and Creative Thinking." In *The Creative Cognition Approach*, edited by Steven M. Smith, Thomas B. Ward and Ronald S. Finke, 135–56. Cambridge, MA: MIT Press, 1995.

Sondheim, Stephen. Interview by James Lipton. In *The Paris Review Interviews*, vol. 4, edited by Philip Gourevitch, 259–78. New York: Picador, 2009.

Stevenson, Robert Louis, "A Chapter on Dreams." In *Across the Plains*. New York: Charles Scribner's Sons, 1892. https://etc.usf.edu/lit2go/110/selected-essays-of-robert-louis-stevenson/5111/a-chapter-on-dreams/.

Stone, Robert. Interview by William Crawford Woods. In *The Paris Review Interviews*, vol. 1, edited by Philip Gourevitch, 303–35. New York: Picador, 2006.

Strauss, Robert. "Still in the Game; At Times It Was a Struggle but George Plimpton's *Paris Review* Has Made It to Its 50th Anniversary." *Los Angeles Times*, June 14, 2003. https://www.latimes.com/archives/la-xpm-2003-jun-14-et-strauss14-story.html.

Styron, William. Interview by George Plimpton and Peter Matthiessen. In *The Paris Review Interviews*, vol. 4, edited by Philip Gourevitch, 1–18. New York: Picador, 2009.

———. "Letter to an Editor." *The Paris Review*, Spring 1953. https://www.theparisreview.org/letters-essays/5220/letter-to-an-editor-william-styron.

Sullivan, Patrick. "The UnEssay: Making Room for Creativity in the Composition Class." *College Composition and Communication* 67, no. 1 (2015): 6–34.
Thurber, James. Interview by George Plimpton and Max Steele. In *The Paris Review Interviews*, vol. 2, edited by Philip Gourevitch, 18–33. New York: Picador, 2007.
Vonnegut, Kurt. Interview by David Hayman, David Michaelis, George Plimpton and Richard L. Rhodes. In *The Paris Review Interviews*, vol. 1, edited by Philip Gourevitch, 160–205. New York: Picador, 2006.
Wallas, Graham. *The Art of Thought*. New York: Harcourt Brace, 1926.
Waugh, Evelyn. Interview by Julian Jebb. In *The Paris Review Interviews*, vol. 3, edited by Philip Gourevitch, 63–77. New York: Picador, 2008.
Welty, Eudora. Interview by Linda Kuehl. In *The Paris Review Interviews*, vol. 2, edited by Philip Gourevitch, 117–41. New York: Picador, 2007.
West, Rebecca. Interview by Marina Warner. In *The Paris Review Interviews*, vol. 1, edited by Philip Gourevitch, 228–74. New York: Picador, 2006.
White, E. B. Interview by George Plimpton and Frank H. Crowther. In *The Paris Review Interviews*, vol. 4, edited by Philip Gourevitch, 128–51. New York: Picador, 2009.
Wilbers, Usha. "The Author Resurrected: *The Paris Review*'s Answer to the Age of Criticism." *American Periodicals* 18, no. 2 (2008): 192–212.
———. "Enterprise in the Service of Art: A Critical History of *The Paris Review*, 1953–1973." PhD diss., Radboud University, 2006.
Wilder, Billy. Interview by James Linville. In *The Paris Review Interviews*, vol. 1, edited by Philip Gourevitch, 412–35. New York: Picador, 2006.
Williams, William Carlos. Interview by Stanley Koehler. In *The Paris Review Interviews*, vol. 3, edited by Philip Gourevitch, 78–116. New York: Picador, 2008.
Winterowd, Ross W. "Creativity and the Comp Class." *Freshman English News* 7, no. 2 (1978): 1–16.
Wodehouse, P. G. Interview by Gerald Clarke. In *The Paris Review Interviews*, vol. 4, edited by Philip Gourevitch, 152–73. New York: Picador, 2009.
Wordsworth, William. "Preface to the Lyrical Ballads." In *English Romantic Poetry and Prose*, edited by Russell Noyes, 357–67. New York: Oxford University Press, 1956.
Yancey, Kathleen Blake. *Reflection in the Writing Classroom*. Logan: Utah State University Press, 1998.
Young, Richard, Alton Becker and Kenneth Pike. *Rhetoric, Discovery and Change*. New York: Harcourt, Brace and World, 1970.

INDEX

Note: The page preferences with letter n denotes note numbers.

academic writing 23–24, 154, 154n8, 157, 160, 162, 164
Achebe, Chinua 44, 105–6, 133
affect 27, 28n25, 152, 154, 155, 158, 160, 164, 166, 167
aging 40–41, 78, 137–38
altruism 124–25, 179
Amis, Martin 53–54, 92–93, 94, 95, 110, 134
Angelou, Maya 44, 61, 65, 85, 91, 108, 109, 112
Ashbery, John 104, 107, 111, 115, 131, 141, 145–47
assessment 19, 29, 83, 103, 111, 113, 134, 157, 165, 166. *See also* verification
audience 20, 27, 78, 83, 102, 103, 113–15, 119, 120, 121, 129, 130–32, 134, 158, 165, 166, 167
Auster, Paul 37–38, 63–64, 65, 82, 87, 91, 110, 113, 142–43
authorial identity 104–6, 124, 154

Baldwin, James 60, 64–65, 78, 78n20, 82, 104, 106, 111–12, 120, 125, 133, 137, 138–39
Bellow, Saul 77, 84, 142
Bishop, Elizabeth 69, 145
blocks 8, 23, 27, 29, 31, 35, 66n47, 74–5, 79, 81–86, 88, 89, 91, 94, 102, 142, 153, 158, 162
Borges, Jorge Luis 68, 77, 85, 115, 131, 135
breaks 11, 23, 24, 28, 84–88, 156, 157, 163, 166

Cain, James M. 104, 112, 113–14, 136, 144

Capote, Truman 56, 85, 104, 108, 109, 112–13, 120
Carey, Peter 60, 67, 97–98, 104, 109, 118, 137
Carver, Raymond 7, 104, 107, 108, 124, 126, 137, 139
Cheever, John 45, 56, 76, 82, 92, 101, 111, 113, 118, 119, 124, 129, 131, 132, 136
childhood 46, 51, 52, 56–57, 59, 64–65, 66, 100, 104, 105
coding 10–13, 11n29, 17, 36, 36n4, 45, 49, 51, 66, 80, 84, 90, 92, 116
cognitive dissonance 29, 36, 38–43, 45, 158, 159, 159n10
composing process model 11, 24, 25–28, 30, 31, 32n34, 33, 35n2, 103, 106, 152, 157
conceptual space 40
confidence 83, 83n31, 133–35, 152, 158, 167
connection-making 29, 41n19, 71, 74, 86, 88, 89, 100–102, 100n39, 157, 164–65
constraints 40, 79, 136, 141–43, 158
creative process model 10–12, 17, 24–26, 28–33, 35, 35n1, 36n4, 37, 42, 50, 51, 57, 69, 73, 76, 83n31, 89, 90, 103, 106, 121, 123, 141, 158. *See also* Chapters 3–7
creative worrying 29n26, 74, 79–81, 87, 162
creative writing 2, 9n22, 11, 16, 19–23, 25, 30, 33, 55, 64, 66, 86, 123, 136n61, 144–47, 149, 149n1
critics 6, 94, 103, 113, 116, 118–21, 134, 165
cross-pollination 52, 69–71, 86–88, 157–58, 159. *See also* interdisciplinarity

Didion, Joan 58, 62, 109, 117, 134, 136
Dinesen, Isak 53, 62, 69–70
discourse analysis 2, 10–13, 10n23, 11n26, 49, 49n44, 69, 116, 148, 153, 166
discovery writing 89, 96–99, 127
drafting 11, 12, 22n16, 24, 26–27, 31, 32, 35n2, 54, 63, 66n47, 67–69, 71, 76n9, 77, 80, 84–86, 88, 89, 90–92, 94, 96–99, 101, 102, 103, 107, 107n11, 109, 110, 127, 138, 147, 153, 156, 157, 159, 166
dreaming 28, 74–75, 77, 78, 163

editing 6, 11, 24, 26, 27, 31, 32, 84, 103, 107, 107n11, 110, 117, 121, 144, 166
editors 8, 67n48, 113, 116–18, 121, 165, 166
Eliot, T. S. 43, 44, 76, 81, 82, 85, 102, 110, 114, 117, 144–45
Ellison, Ralph 58–59, 82, 114, 138
environment 3n4, 16, 19n2, 28, 28n25, 57, 59, 74, 86, 88, 91, 123, 135, 146, 156, 166
ethnography 59, 61–62, 160
experimentation 2, 8, 9, 16, 42, 43, 48, 56, 68, 71, 141, 151, 156, 157, 163, 164
expository writing 1, 2, 8–9, 11, 17, 19, 19n2, 20, 23–26, 30–33, 81, 149, 149n1, 150. *See also* nonfiction

fame 56, 121, 124, 135, 138, 143
family 4, 39, 52, 53, 58, 63, 67n48, 103, 106, 138, 140, 141, 147, 152, 155
Faulkner, William 46–47, 54, 55, 58, 60, 93, 111, 112, 119, 137
feedback 67n48, 91–92, 106, 114, 116, 117, 118, 119–20, 121, 134, 137, 144, 147, 152, 154, 155, 162, 165
felt sense 36–39, 36n6, 45, 111, 155
film 48, 70n61, 115, 136–37
financial status 65, 75, 105, 121n87, 136, 144, 145
first insight 11, 17, 28–31, 35–50, 35n2, 36n4, 51, 66, 66n47, 68–69, 71, 73, 76n9, 88, 90, 91, 100, 111, 122, 141, 155, 158–59, 159n10. *See also* inspiration
flow 31–32, 38, 50n49, 89, 89n1, 90–92, 95–96, 102, 103, 107, 164, 166. *See also* incubation effect and insight

Gaddis, William 42, 43, 97, 98
Gardner, John 47, 52–53, 56, 58, 60, 87, 93, 95, 107, 112, 128–29, 130, 143, 146
Gilbert, Jack 62, 95, 113, 137, 139, 141, 144
Greene, Graham 78
Grossman, David 61–62, 94, 96, 99, 101, 108, 115, 126, 127–28, 141, 143

habit 8, 71, 85, 109
Hemingway, Earnest 4n7, 57, 58–59, 60, 108, 109, 137–38
heuristics 26, 26n23, 66. *See also* prewriting
Hughes, Ted 38, 43, 46, 47, 56–57, 59, 104, 129, 145, 147, 148

imagery 23, 36, 37, 45–48, 49, 75, 100, 100n39, 147, 159
imagination 8, 46, 47, 60, 63, 113, 130, 132
immersion 23, 24, 53, 56, 61–62, 63, 69, 124, 145, 154, 160, 162
incubation 11, 17, 23, 24, 28n26, 28–30, 31, 42, 49n44, 72, 73–88, 91, 109, 122, 138, 152, 157, 158, 162–63
incubation effect 74–75, 88, 89. *See also* flow and insight
insight 11, 17, 24, 28n24, 29, 29n28, 30, 31, 35, 35n1, 35n2, 36, 36n4, 38, 41n19, 49n44, 51, 66n47, 69, 72, 73, 74, 75, 76, 76n9, 77, 79, 81, 84, 86, 88, 89–102, 103, 122, 127, 133, 145, 152, 156, 157, 158, 159, 162, 163–65, 167. *See also* flow and incubation effect
inspiration 28, 37, 39, 43, 48, 49, 50, 57, 72, 76, 102, 121, 129, 145, 157, 158. *See also* first insight
interdisciplinarity 3n4, 22–23, 159, 164. *See also* cross-pollination
interviewing 14–16, 26, 59
invention 11, 24, 26, 27, 28, 31, 35n2, 39, 43, 49, 77, 84, 155–57, 159, 164

journaling 26, 68, 69, 160

Kerouac, Jack 68, 80, 101, 118, 137
King, Stephen 4, 41–42, 49, 56–57, 61, 63, 67, 86, 87, 96, 100, 109, 114, 120, 130–31, 135, 137

INDEX

knowledge domain 21, 40, 55, 56, 59, 71, 143, 145, 150, 157, 158, 162, 163

Larkin, Philip 82, 91, 98, 110, 130, 137, 145
Lowell, Robert 46, 47, 55, 78, 83, 111, 114, 117, 138, 142, 143, 144, 145

Mailer, Norman 67–68, 120, 130, 132, 139
Marquez, Gabriel Garcia 43–44, 45, 47–48, 56–57, 83, 90, 91, 104, 115
meditation 77, 163. *See also* rumination
mentorship 9, 52–56, 67n48, 138, 143, 144, 153, 165
Moore, Marianne 100, 102
Morris, Jan 2n3, 44, 65, 76
Morrison, Toni 40–41, 42, 70–71, 86, 92, 93, 94, 95, 105, 106, 108, 116–17, 125, 138, 140
motivation 23, 38, 99, 106, 119, 124, 125, 154, 154n8
Munro, Alice 57–58, 60, 78, 80–81, 104, 111–12, 117, 120, 134, 140–41, 145, 146
Murakami, Haruki 43, 58, 69, 71, 78, 104–5, 108, 131, 133, 141
Muses 28, 28n24, 91
music 38, 48, 59, 70–71, 113, 155

Naipaul, V. S. 53–54, 64–65, 78, 91–92, 104, 106, 126, 133
nonfiction 2, 5, 26, 62. *See also* expository writing
note-taking 67–68, 69, 160, 161, 163

Oates, Joyce Carol 16, 56, 58, 60, 69, 87, 93, 108, 120, 126, 129, 139
observation 20, 26n23, 42, 59, 60–61, 130, 160, 161

painting 19, 48, 60, 70, 137
Pamuk, Orhan 8, 44, 65, 100, 101, 104, 114, 127
Parker, Dorothy 56
personal experience 3, 14, 28, 46, 47, 49, 51, 52, 59, 60, 61, 63–66, 83, 84, 101, 106, 160, 164
physicality 36, 37, 39, 50, 51, 82, 89, 127, 132, 133, 140, 141, 152, 155, 156

Pinter, Harold 83, 111, 112, 120
post-process theory 1, 1n1, 2n2, 11n26, 25
preparation 11, 17, 23, 24, 28–31, 28n4, 29n8, 35n2, 42, 50, 51–72, 73, 76n9, 77, 86, 87, 90, 99, 102, 122, 133, 138, 141, 144, 151, 159–62
prewriting 23, 26, 26n23, 28, 52, 66–69, 99. *See also* heuristics and warm-up writing
Price, Richard 57, 61, 64, 83, 85, 94, 95, 104, 105, 108, 113, 117–18, 124, 144, 146–47
problem-solving 30, 30n29, 42, 74n3, 78, 79, 81, 88, 102, 112, 162
procrastination 23, 73, 73n1, 163
psychological distress 38, 39, 51, 82, 125–26, 132–33, 159
publishing 103, 113, 117, 119, 145, 146, 166

qualitative research 10, 11, 11n28, 12, 13n31, 74, 123

reading 8, 9, 23, 26, 52, 53, 55, 56, 57, 58, 59, 60, 69, 74, 85, 100, 101, 105, 110, 111, 160, 161, 164
recursivity 11n26, 22n16, 26, 27, 32, 35n2, 36, 50, 51, 66, 73, 76n9, 84, 96, 106, 107, 151, 153, 159n10, 163, 166
reflection 1, 2, 2n3, 3, 4, 6, 7, 8–9, 11n29, 14, 15–16, 23, 24, 28, 36, 37, 41, 45, 50, 51, 64, 67, 103, 110, 111, 152–55, 158, 164
religion 4, 39, 40, 55, 76, 139
research 11, 14, 24, 26, 28, 31, 50, 73, 84, 90, 152, 156, 157, 159–62, 164. *See also* Chapter 4
revision 11, 15, 22n16, 24, 26, 27, 31, 32, 67n48, 84, 85, 103, 106–13, 107n11, 116, 118, 121, 127, 138, 147, 153, 166
Rhys, Jean 58, 84, 125–26
Robinson, Marilynne 39, 40, 59, 90, 119, 130, 139–40, 147
Roth, Philip 65–66, 85, 99, 126, 127, 132
rumination 31, 44, 84. *See also* meditation
Rushdie, Salman 91, 94, 96–97, 98, 115, 135, 140–41

Simenon, Georges 44, 70, 112, 133, 136, 141
Singer, Isaac Bashevis 131
solitude 136, 138–40
Sondheim, Stephen 48, 99
spontaneous generation 49–50, 77, 158
Stone, Robert 85, 100–101, 108, 128, 129, 146
Styron, William 5, 84, 112, 126, 147

The Paris Review (PR) 3, 7, 19, 36, 39, 41, 51, 75, 89, 103, 149
Thurber, James 80, 108, 137
time 23, 24, 31, 32, 35, 43, 52, 54, 55, 61, 62, 63, 71, 73, 79, 80, 81, 82, 83, 84, 85, 86, 87, 90, 91, 92, 96, 107, 108, 110, 111, 116, 118, 133, 136, 137–38, 140, 142, 144, 145, 152, 153, 155, 156, 158, 159, 160, 161–63
travel 2n3, 62
truth-telling 14, 20, 112, 129–30, 132

unconscious 28, 29n26, 38, 44, 74–81, 76n9, 84, 88, 158, 163

verification 103–22. *See also* assessment
voice 37, 60, 78, 91, 93, 97, 106, 154n8, 161
Vonnegut, Kurt 115, 119, 124, 125, 131, 132

warm-up writing 69. *See also* prewriting
Waugh, Evelyn 56, 65–66
Welty, Eudora 49, 57–58, 68, 78, 94–95, 108, 109, 110, 112
West, Rebecca 69, 133
White, E. B. 49, 86, 104–5, 111, 112, 129, 138
Wilder, Billy 114–15
Williams, William Carlos 112
Wodeouse, P. G. 49, 68, 104, 120

www.ingramcontent.com/pod-product-compliance
Lightning Source LLC
Chambersburg PA
CBHW021142230426
43667CB00005B/218